MARY TUDOR

Judith M. Richards

Routledge
Taylor & Francis Group

LONDON AND NEW YORK

First published 2008
by Routledge
2 Park Square, Milton Park, Abingdon, Oxon, OX14 4RN

Simultaneously published in the USA and Canada
by Routledge
270 Madison Ave, New York, NY 10016

Routledge is an imprint of the Taylor & Francis Group, an informa business

© 2008 Judith M. Richards

Typeset in Garamond by Saxon Graphics Ltd, Derby
Printed and bound in Great Britain by TJ International Ltd, Padstow, Cornwall

British Library Cataloguing in Publication Data
A catalogue record for this book is available from the British Library

Library of Congress Cataloging in Publication Data
    Richards, Judith M., 1938-
    Mary Tudor / Judith M. Richards.
    p. cm. -- (Routledge historical biographies)
    Includes bibliographical references and index.
    1. Mary I, Queen of England, 1516-1558. 2. Great Britain--History--Mary I,
    1553-1558. 3. Queens--Great Britain--Biography. I. Title.
    DA347.R46 2008
    942.05'4'092--dc22

ISBN10: 0-415-32720-2 (hbk)
ISBN10: 0-415-32721-0 (pbk)

ISBN13: 978-0-415-32720-6 (hbk)
ISBN13: 978-0-415-32721-3 (pbk)

MARY TUDOR

'This highly readable book supplies an important reassessment of a much maligned figure in English history. In place of the narrow-minded bigot and "hysterical" woman of familiar tradition, Judith Richards offers us a rounded portrait of a poised Renaissance ruler, struggling – at times, skilfully – to perform the daunting role of a 'female king' in a patriarchal age.'

Peter Marshall, *Warwick University*

Mary Tudor is often written off as a hopeless, twisted queen who tried desperately to pull England back to the Catholic Church that was so dear to her mother, and sent many to burn at the stake in the process. This timely new study is a radical re-evaluation of the first 'real' English queen regnant, in which Judith M. Richards challenges her reputation as 'Bloody Mary' of popular historical infamy. Richards carefully locates Mary within the wider cultural, religious and political context of her times, contending that she was closer to the more innovative, humanist side of the Catholic Church.

Richards argues persuasively that Mary, neither boring nor basically bloody, was a much more hard-working, 'hands-on' and decisive queen than is commonly recognized. Had she not died in her early forties and failed to establish a Catholic succession, the course of history could have been very different, England might have remained Catholic and Mary herself might even have been treated more kindly by history.

This illustrated and accessible biography is essential reading for all those with an interest in one of England's most misrepresented monarchs.

Judith M. Richards was previously senior lecturer in History at La Trobe University, and is now a research associate. She has published a number of studies of topics in early modern history, and has more recently focussed on English and British monarchy from 1553–1642.

ROUTLEDGE HISTORICAL BIOGRAPHIES

SERIES EDITOR: ROBERT PEARCE

Routledge Historical Biographies provide engaging, readable and academically credible biographies written from an explicitly historical perspective. These concise and accessible accounts will bring important historical figures to life for students and general readers alike.

In the same series:

Bismarck by Edgar Feuchtwanger
Emmeline Pankhurst by Paula Bartley
Gladstone by Michael Partridge
Henry VII by Sean Cunningham
Hitler by Martyn Housden
Lenin by Christopher Read
Louis XIV by Richard Wilkinson
Mao by Michael Lynch
Martin Luther by Michael Mullet
Martin Luther King Jr by Peter J. Ling
Mary Queen of Scots by Retha M. Warnicke
Mussolini by Peter Neville
Nehru by Ben Zachariah
Oliver Cromwell by Martyn Bennett
Trotsky by Ian Thatcher

Forthcoming:

Edward IV by Hannes Kleineke
Henry VIII by Lucy Wooding
Neville Chamberlain by Nick Smart

To the memory of E. M. K. M.

Contents

LIST OF PLATES AND FIGURES   ix
ACKNOWLEDGEMENTS   xi
A NOTE ON SPELLING   xv
ABBREVIATIONS   xvii

Introduction: the reputation of Mary Tudor   1

1   Establishing the Tudor regime   12

2   The early years of Mary Tudor   27

3   The education of a princess: learning life and politics, 1525–1536   45

4   The restoration of Lady Mary, 1536–1547   63

5   Mary in the reign of Edward VI, 1547–1553   82

6   Edward and Mary: the final struggles   102

7   Establishing England's first female monarch   121

8   Problems for a marrying queen regnant   142

9   The prosperous year of Philip and Mary, July 1554 to August 1555?   162

10   Religious trials and other tribulations   182

11   The road to war and the loss of Calais   203

12   The end of the regime of Mary Tudor   223

NOTES   243
FURTHER READING BY CHAPTER   253
INDEX   261

LIST OF PLATES AND FIGURES

PLATES (BETWEEN PAGES 110 AND 111)

1 Henry VIII, *c.*1535, attributed to Joos van Cleve
2 Katherine of Aragon, attributed to Lucas Horenbout (or Hornebolte)
3 Title-page to 1539 'Great Bible'
4 Mary Tudor, *c.* 1544, by Master John
5 Elizabeth Tudor, *c.* 1546
6 Edward VI when Prince of Wales, *c.* 1546, attributed to William Scrots
7 Framlingham Castle
8 Mary I as queen regnant, 1553
9 Great Seal of England, 1554, showing Philip and Mary
10 Mary I exercising the royal touch

FIGURES

1 Tudor (and Lancastrian) Line
2 House of York descendants from Edward III (selectively)

ACKNOWLEDGEMENTS

My thanks go first to my colleagues at La Trobe, who listened critically and constructively to my early efforts to reassess Mary's life and reign. Above all, as ever, I must acknowledge Lotte Mulligan, to whom I am indebted for support and encouragement over more years than I now care to calculate.

As I moved beyond Australia with this study I met many new obligations. Tom Freeman has saved me from many misrepresentations of Mary's nemesis, John Foxe, and he has generously shared information on many other matters. Sue Doran, Bill Wizeman and Jeri McIntosh have also helped and encouraged this study in many ways. My thanks go to them and the others too numerous to list, whose comments at conferences and seminars have spurred me on.

Above all, I must acknowledge the work of David Loades. His many publications include a major study of Mary's life, and the only detailed examination of her reign as well as other works focussed on the 1500s. My final assessment of Mary differs from his, but without the benefit of his many works, this work would not have been written.

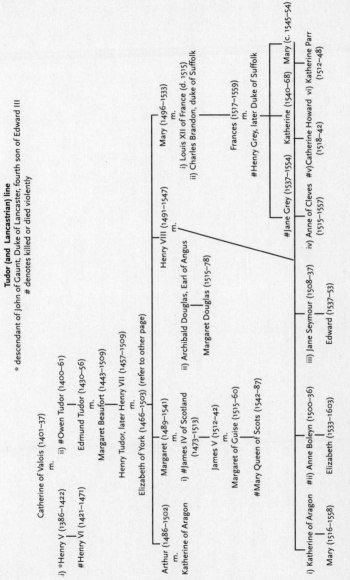

Tudor (and Lancastrian) line

* descendant of John of Gaunt, Duke of Lancaster, fourth son of Edward III

# denotes killed or died violently

Catherine of Valois (1401–37)
m.

i) *Henry V (1386–1422)   ii) #Owen Tudor (1400–61)

#Henry VI (1421–1471)   Edmund Tudor (1430–56)
m.
Margaret Beaufort (1443–1509)

Henry Tudor, later Henry VII (1457–1509)
m.
Elizabeth of York (1466–1503) (refer to other page)

Arthur (1486–1502)   Margaret (1489–1541)   Henry VIII (1491–1547)   Mary (1496–1533)
m.   m.   m.
Katherine of Aragon   i) #James IV of Scotland (1473–1513)   i) Louis XII of France (d. 1515)
                       ii) Archibald Douglas, Earl of Angus   ii) Charles Brandon, duke of Suffolk

                       James V (1512–42)   Margaret Douglas (1515–78)   Frances (1517–1559)
                       m.   m.
                       Margaret of Guise (1515–60)   #Henry Grey, later Duke of Suffolk

                       #Mary Queen of Scots (1542–87)   #Jane Grey (1537–1554)   Katherine (1540–68)   Mary (c. 1545–54)

Henry VIII married:
i) Katherine of Aragon   #ii) Anne Boleyn (1500–36)   iii) Jane Seymour (1508–37)   iv) Anne of Cleves (1515–1557)   #v) Catherine Howard (1518–42)   vi) Katherine Parr (1512–48)

Mary (1516–1558)   Elizabeth (1533–1603)   Edward (1537–53)

Figure 1 Tudor (and Lancastrian) Line

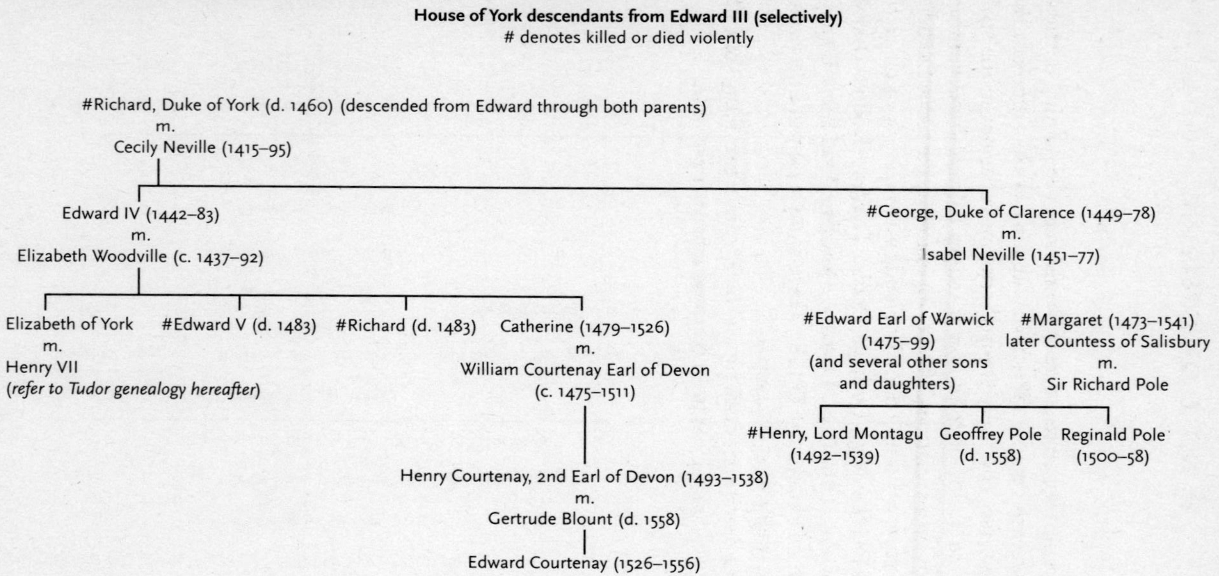

House of York descendants from Edward III (selectively)

\# denotes killed or died violently

Figure 2 House of York descendants from Edward III (selectively)

A NOTE ON SPELLING

Modern readers are trained to aspire to a consistency of spelling unthinkable in the sixteenth century. Whatever the force of the argument that early modern writers positively enjoyed creative variations in the spelling of any given word, there is now a strong cultural barrier for any reader to accept such variations. Hence, for example, the name Dudley – an important name in mid-Tudor England, was variously spelt at the time as Dodeley, Dodely, Dodlay, Dodle, Dodley, Dodly, Dodlye, Doudley, Dowdlay, Dowdlaye, Dowdly, Dowdlye, Duddeley, Dudeye, Dudlay, Dudlei, Dudleye and Dudly. There is no reason to believe that list of possible spellings is exhaustive.

All spelling has been modernised to a consistent form, but the language and word usage has been retained wherever possible.

ABBREVIATIONS

APC: Acts of the Privy Council, ed. J. R. Dasent (London, 1890–1907).

BL: British Library.

L&P: *Letters and Papers, Foreign and Domestic, of the Reign of Henry VIII, 1509-1547*, ed. J. S Brewer, J. Gairdner and R. H. Brodie (21 Vols, London, 1862).

CSPSp: *Calendar of State Papers, Spanish*, ed. W. B. Turnbull (London, 1862, 1964).

CSPV: *Calendar of State Papers, Venetian* (London, 1864–98).

CSP.Edward: *Calendar of State Papers, Domestic Edward VI 1547–1553*, ed. C. S. Knighton (London, 1992).

CSP.Mary: *Calendar of State Papers, Domestic Mary I 1553–1558*, ed. C. S. Knighton (London, 1998).

TRP: *Tudor Royal Proclamations*, ed. Paul L. Hughes and James F. Larkin, 3 Vols (New Haven, 1969) 1964–69.

INTRODUCTION: THE REPUTATION OF MARY TUDOR

THE PROBLEM WITH MARY TUDOR

When I first told friends – and some colleagues – that I was writing a historical biography of Mary Tudor, many thought I was referring to Mary Queen of Scots, a quite different and much more popular figure. Those who knew better usually said 'Oh! Bloody Mary! Why ever are you doing that?' Perhaps the most instructive reaction came from another historian. When I told him I my topic was Mary Tudor, he spluttered, 'Not rehabilitating her I hope!' I cannot judge whether this work rehabilitates Mary in the way he feared, but I hope it explains why, if she is known to people at all these days, she is usually seen as either 'Bloody Mary' or in this more ecumenical age, redefined as 'Boring Mary', a new way of suggesting there is little deserving study in her reign.

There are now a number of writers reassessing Mary's reign. My hope is that this new study of her life and reign might encourage that wider reassessment of who she was and the grounds on which so many historians have been so critical of – if not openly hostile to – her. Perhaps it might also encourage a better understanding of the range of problems she faced. At least it seems unlikely that this work could do more harm to her popular reputation. Her historical identity was shaped in the heat of the sixteenth-century wars of religion, and has endured because she fought on the losing side of those wars in England. As W. H. Auden wrote, in 'Spain 1937':

> History to the defeated
> May say Alas but cannot help or pardon.

In this study Mary will be reconsidered not just as England's first crowned queen, but also as one who set many precedents as female monarch which her sister was content to follow.

MARY TUDOR AS 'LAWFUL QUEEN OF FAMOUS MEMORY'?

Mary Tudor was the first English queen actually to reign unchallenged in her own right. As queen regnant, her reign (1553–8) preceded that of her much better known half-sister, Elizabeth (1558–1603). Despite being the first English woman to be crowned as monarch, Mary's reign has received little historical study, and within the English historical tradition the attention she has received has been overwhelmingly hostile. Her Scottish cousin Mary Stuart, Queen of Scots, habitually receives many more references in books about sixteenth-century England than the woman who ruled the country for five years. If they are pushed to identify *England's* Queen Mary, the term by which most people finally recognise her – 'Bloody Mary' – is the one invoked by Protestants, well after her death, to reinforce inherited hostility to her reign and to her religion.

Given the novelty of female rule, a reader might reasonably have expected that Mary's rule would have been explored from many angles to see just how she managed the transitions involved in the move from male to female rule. Instead, until recently there has been little detailed interest in her reign. Two of the more important exceptions are David Loades and Jennifer Loach. There was also a very important – but too little regarded – essay published by Elizabeth Russell in 1990. But in the last few years that situation has begun to change and more studies of Mary are being undertaken. Many still prefer to write about Mary's half-sister, Elizabeth I, almost as if *she* was the first queen to reign over

England. Few have considered whether Elizabeth's most enduring advantage could be that she was the second female ruler, with a ready-made model of how a queen reigned which she could reject or build on. Not only was the very idea of a female ruler more familiar when Elizabeth reigned, but she had the extra good fortune to live long enough for a clearly defined public image to be fashioned about her.

A major theme of that Elizabethan propaganda celebrated her as the great Protestant ruler who reversed her sister's Catholicism and stead-fastly resisted every attempt to restore it. In doing so, Elizabeth was also destroying the legacy of her predecessor, for Mary had worked hard (and with considerable success) during her reign to restore Catholicism. During the reign of Edward VI (1547–53), the younger brother of both queens regnant, the teachings and practice of the Church of England had moved closer to the teachings of more advanced continental reformers, and well away from Henry VIII's church. Mary followed, as the last effective Catholic ruler of the kingdom, and it was inevitable that later historians of the dominant Protestant tradition should decry her.

As a result, Mary was to be remembered not as the first queen, but as the ruler who briefly restored 'popery' to England, one indication of the extent to which she was really 'Spanish' in her sympathies. Her reputa-tion, that is, was always embroiled in the changing fortunes of the religious beliefs in England. In Mary's time, the religious divide between Catholics and Protestants was also caught up in the power politics of competing European powers. The resulting struggle for religious truth was one in which the Christian 'faithful' (of whatever persuasion) almost universally accepted that stubborn heretics, resisting the 'Truth' being set before them, should properly face death by burning. (The last here-tic to be burned in England suffered his fate in 1612, some 50 years after the death of Mary.) To most modern eyes –which do not see the differ-ences within Christian teaching as matters of life and death – perhaps the real surprise is that her appalling reputation as 'Bloody Mary' has lasted quite so long, and is still in use in both popular and more scholarly language.

The word 'popery', first used in the 1520s, was increasingly used by the 1530s to represent everything nascent English Protestantism dis-liked about the traditional Roman Catholic religion, and much more. 'Popery was not just the name of a set of false theological dogmas; it was the systematic usurpation of public and intellectual life by the priests.'[1]

'Popery' remained a very powerful word, summarising and simplifying all that English Protestants most disliked about the Catholic religion until well into the nineteenth century. Since Mary Tudor had been the ruler who devoted much of her energy during her five-year reign to restoring papal authority to an officially Protestant England, she was for several centuries treated as a case study in how appalling were both the measures for, and the consequences of, the choices she made to suppress Protestantism. The reign of Mary Tudor was quickly transformed into – and long remained – a fearsome Protestant warning of the terrors of Catholicism.

Above all, she was the ruler who burned heretics. So did many others, and the circumstances were unusual, a matter to be discussed more fully in Chapter 10. But almost all other aspects of her reign were usually subsumed into that one issue, the persecution of Protestants and the restoration of a religion that most later English historians deplored. Therefore, the most prominent feature of her Catholic reign is that some 300 of her subjects – men and women – were burned at the stake as heretics. That was indeed an unusually large number of burnings but death by burning was the traditional punishment for 'stubborn' heresy. It will be argued that across western Europe large numbers of Christians were burned by other Christians in the extensive wars of religion which marked the sixteenth century. Moreover, many Protestants agreed heretics should be burned – only the definition of heresy was contested.

Mary was, to some extent, written out of English history by the claim that, although born an English princess, she was by inclination more Spanish than English (with the strong implication that the Spanish were by nature or religion much crueller than the English). The case is seen as made stronger because not only did Mary have a Spanish mother, Katherine of Aragon, but once on the throne, she chose to marry Philip II of Spain. On such grounds as these, Mary I of England has for a long time been a despised and deplored historical character, conventionally identified as 'Bloody'.

BLACKENING MARY'S REPUTATION

When Elizabeth came to the throne (in November 1558) her accession proclamation was entirely conventional, announcing that she was now queen because of the death 'to our great grief, [of] our dearest sister of noble memory'. Just how formulaic was that expression of grief for 'our dearest sister' became increasingly clear within weeks. In the following January, during the traditional pre-coronation procession through the streets of London, the closest the celebrations came to mentioning Mary was with dark references to the great dangers Elizabeth had been in when imprisoned in the Tower – where she had been held for some weeks during her predecessor's reign, under suspicion of plotting against her sister's regime.

The last time Mary was referred to in the conventional terms of 'lawful queen of famous memory' was probably in 1570, and that was in a papal bull by which Pope Pius V excommunicated Mary's Protestant half-sister Elizabeth I for being the 'pretended queen of England and the servant of crime'. He absolved all 'nobles, subjects and people' of her realm from any oath of loyalty to her, and to reinforce that he threatened excommunication to any who obeyed any command of Elizabeth.[2] Unfortunately (from the Pope's point of view) he had to recognise that because those he wanted to excommunicate were fully in control of the country, it was to impossible actually to make the bull formally known throughout England. A few copies were circulated, and one appeared nailed to the door of the residence of the Bishop of London. It is hardly surprising that the Pope recalled the Catholic reign of Mary's time with considerable approval. The wider effect of the bull, as its existence became known, was to confirm the general view of Protestants that papal authority was a powerful threat to everything that the Protestant English held dear.

The process by which Mary's evil reputation has been modified has been tortuous. In the centuries following her reign, there have always been some Catholic apologists for her rule, but their accounts were usually no more analytic or detached from the author's religious affiliation than were those of vehemently Protestant historians. One of the more interesting works is that of Philip Hughes, who offers a careful analysis of that most central issue in Marian historiography, who was burned, and on what grounds. He offers some examples of those whom both Protestants and Catholics agreed were indeed heretics, fully deserving their fate.

From the Protestant polemicists, attacks on Mary's reputation had begun early. The Protestant exiles of her reign had frequently called her a modern-day Jezebel, referring to the biblical Jezebel, who joined with her husband Ahab in restoring false religion (1 Kings 16–21). Just five years after Mary's death, John Foxe, who became the pre-eminent and enduring exponent of Protestant sufferings, defined Mary's reign as the 'horrible and bloudy time of Queene Mary'. Nevertheless, Foxe frequently ascribed the Protestant suffering to the work of such Catholic activists as Bishop Bonner of London – frequently referred to by Foxe as 'Bloudy Bonner' – and other 'persecuting prelates'. He presented it as a persecution pursued much more by 'popish' clergy than by the monarchy itself.

There are places where he even showed some sympathy for Mary, though never, of course, for the persecutions carried out in her name and with her sanction. In the decades which followed, however, the distinction Foxe had implied between monarchy and clergy became blurred, and the late queen became 'Bloody Mary', as a contrast to the great advantages of being ruled by Protestant Elizabeth – whose religious victims were usually Catholic, and therefore more usually treated as deserving their punishment. It may have helped protect Elizabeth's reputation that many of them, especially the missionary priests, were hanged as seditious traitors for seeking to restore Catholicism rather than burned as heretics.

The power of anti-Catholicism as a spur to political activity was repeatedly demonstrated in seventeenth-century England. Foxe's *Actes and Monumentes*, familiarly known as his *Book of Martyrs*, was still so widely read that it was second in popularity only to the Bible. Thus the gruesome details of Foxe's version of the Catholic persecutions – and the quite as gruesome woodcuts – were kept alive and real for a significant part of the population. The fear that a party around King Charles I was plotting the reintroduction of 'popish' religion was a potent factor in the English civil wars in the mid-seventeenth century, which culminated in the public execution of King Charles in 1649. In his reign, to the horrors of 'popish' persecutions was added the fear of absolute monarchy. The nexus between Catholicism and absolute monarchy was confirmed for seventeenth-century English Protestants by the rule of Louis XIV, especially by his persecution of French Protestants after the revocation of the Edict of Nantes in 1685. The original Edict had provided French Protestants with some legal protection; its withdrawal was taken as another demonstration of Catholic perfidy. So for English historians,

Protestantism became increasingly identified with liberty, as (foreign) Catholicism was with oppression and cruelty.

It is therefore hardly surprising that the histories written in those years were effectively the continuation of the religious wars of the sixteenth century by more peaceful means. In 1680, Bishop Gilbert Burnet completed the second volume of his comprehensive *History of the Reformation of the Church of England*. Foxe's *Actes and Monumentes* was still a major source for Burnet, as for other historians – and treated as uncritically as ever. He wrote that 'the sourness of her temper' made it the easier for Mary to follow the principles of her bishops and their 'severe counsels' in the treatment of heretics. And so, he concluded, at the end of 'her unhappy reign and unfortunate life' as 'queen of England by inheritance and of Spain by marriage', she died unmourned by any but her 'popish clergy'. In the eighteenth century, David Hume wrote of Mary: 'Obstinacy, bigotry, cruelty, malignity, revenge, tyranny; every circumstance of her character took a tincture from her bad temper and narrow understanding.' She was, he concluded, 'a weak bigoted woman, under the government of priests'.[3]

By the nineteenth century, following the French Revolution, English fear of French Catholic absolutism had been replaced by quite as great a fear of French republican godlessness, but Mary's public reputation showed little sign of changing. One historian, Agnes Strickland, struck a very different note in her popular multi-volume *Lives of the Queens of England*, first published in 1840–9. She offered a more dispassionate account of Mary's reign, made possible because scholars like Maddern (in 1831) and Tytler (in 1839) had begun to publish fresh selections of historical sources for Mary's reign. That was the first new material to become available since the sixteenth century. Almost all of those documents, Strickland noted, 'are in direct opposition to the popular ideas of the character of our first queen-regnant, and dangerous, because the desire of recording truth may be mistaken for a wish to extenuate cruelty in religious and civil government'.

Despite the passage of the Catholic Emancipation Act of 1828, such a concern to balance the surviving information against the inherited traditions remained unusual. Published in 1860, George Eliot's account of the rebellious young Maggie Tulliver records that 'she knew little of saints and martyrs, and had gathered ... that they were a temporary provision against the spread of Catholicism and had all died [by burning] at

Smithfield.'[4] Foxe's work recording those Protestant martyrdoms was republished many times in the nineteenth century, with detailed accounts of yet more Protestant martyrdoms, but with the Marian burnings a major feature.

Throughout the nineteenth century, Mary's reign was still generally treated as meriting little attention, except as an object lesson. The only point commonly made about England's first queen in English histories was, as Lord Macauley exemplified in his *History of England* (published 1848–9), the many 'cruelties' of Mary's 'evil' reign. For J. R. Green, author of perhaps the best known of the later nineteenth-century general histories – *A Short History of the English People* first published in 1874 – the only significant theme in Mary's reign was its part in the history of Protestant persecution by Catholics. Early in her reign, 'the Protestants were at her feet, and she struck without mercy.' By the end, her cruelties and oppression were such that only the death of Mary 'averted a general revolt, and a burst of enthusiastic joy hailed the accession of Elizabeth', a judgement which would appear to owe more to Bishop Burnet's work than to the increasing range of new sources becoming available.

In the early twentieth century, the scholarly evaluation of Mary's reign became more complicated. One example of that is James Gairdner's *The English Church in the Sixteenth Century from the Accession of Henry VIII to the Death of Mary* (London: Macmillan, 1902.) Writing within the Anglo-Catholic tradition of the Church of England, Gairdner provided an unusually sympathetic account of Mary's regime. Indeed, his most pejorative terms are often reserved for the many reformers he viewed as authority-defying troublemakers who taught a reliance on individual judgement which led to 'the violation of order and disrespect to all authority'. He did not condone, but he sought to excuse, many of the persecutions of Mary's days. But other historians remained much more ambivalent. A. F. Pollard, for example, in his 1910 study, *The History of England, from the Accession of Edward VI to the Death of Elizabeth (1547–1603)* judged her as 'the most honest of the Tudor rulers' but he still also saw her as 'pitiless' in a non-English way: 'The Spanish strain in her blood gave her religion its fierce unbending character, which unfitted her for dealing with the delicate problem of the English reformation; and her Spanish marriage cast her athwart England's secular aspirations' (p.174).

Until very recently, the traditional popular view of 'Bloody Mary' has changed little. For decades the extraordinarily successful *1066 and All*

That (first published in 1930), that most popular parody of English history, reminded all those nostalgic for their old history lessons that Edward VI had forced all his subjects to become Protestant 'so that Broody Mary would be able to put them to death afterwards for not being Roman Catholic'.[5] Carolly Erikson's (very readable) biography (1978) was simply titled *Bloody Mary*. The continuing resonance of the original epithet for Mary is encapsulated in the title of a recent work: *Bosworth Field to Bloody Mary*, published in 2003.[6] As this was being written, a television 'history' series included Queen Mary among the 100 bloodiest tyrants in the world.

At the more academic level, however, interest in Mary's reign has broadened in focus from simply treating the burning of so many Protestant heretics as just another demonstration of the dangers of Catholicism. The work of Philip Hughes, already mentioned, is one example. He made the conventional case that burning heretics was the traditional response to them, but concludes that it was, in Mary's time, an inappropriate policy, given that the victims were being burned for adhering to what they had been taught by their authorities for the past two decades.

That now seems to be the accepted position, but Mary is still seldom treated as a significant historical identity for other reasons. Until very recently, serious historians have reiterated that her reign was, like her body, sterile, achieving nothing – a boring queen? Most recently she has been described by one Tudor historian as: 'politically self-deceived. Her piety and unmarried state gave her the intensity of a nun.' On the other hand, there is wide agreement that when she did marry, she married very unwisely, so both maidenhood and marriage were apparently part of her problem. Another has noted that Mary 'had received the best humanist education' but doubts that Mary had the intelligence and astuteness to benefit from such education as ruler. Yet another has criticised her for being a bad feminist since, by her marriage and the restoration of papal authority Mary 'announced herself as subject in both her persons – as woman and as queen – to the authority of male superiors'.[7]

The grounds shift but Mary, it would seem, remains for most a regrettable interlude in the history of England which is best passed over quickly, but that may now be starting to change. David Loades' two studies, of Mary's life and her reign, are valuable starting points, and

Jennifer Loach's careful study of the parliaments of her reign is an indispensable work. At the time of writing other works are also under way.

SO WHY THIS BOOK ON MARY?

To this point, I have not been discussing the reign of Mary Tudor, but rather other writers' shifting understandings of her reign. For me, the most interesting aspect is the extent to which, for centuries, almost all historians of England settled for a repetition of previously stated views rather than a reconsideration of them. Although many more documents from the Tudor period have become available in the last 150 years, there has been little fresh work on Mary until recent decades. This becomes much clearer if a comparison is made with the many historical writings about every other Tudor monarch.

There are, therefore, many questions still to be asked about Mary and her regime. As first English queen, Mary faced many problems in establishing her authority over her most powerful male subjects. The office which she inherited was profoundly masculine in expectations and assumptions, and it was she who made the necessary adaptations in ritual and government process, adaptations which Elizabeth frequently followed. Mary was prepared to fight her own way to the throne – in the face of an attempted usurpation in the name of Lady Jane Grey – and provided leadership, apparently lacking in her some of male advisers, against another attempted rebellion, six months after her accession, to retain it. She survived the many French attempts to subvert her regime, and as events proved, she managed her affairs so that England remained an independent entity, with any Spanish influence vanishing with her death. The marriage treaty she had sanctioned had provided for just that. She died in her bed, as queen, and the throne passed peacefully to her nominated successor.

Until recently, Mary Tudor has seldom been celebrated for her remarkable achievements as the first English female monarch. In the face of many challenges she maintained her rule for the rest of her life, and set many useful precedents for the much-celebrated Elizabeth to follow. This was the more important because Elizabeth succeeded to the throne at a much younger age. Moreover, unlike Mary, who was never the subject of such gossip, Elizabeth had notoriously acquired a more dubious reputation from the age of 15. It was well for her that Mary had set so many precedents in how to be queen regnant – Elizabeth's youth and suspect reputation would have made her a much more contestable first queen.

This book, then, sets out to re-assess conventional attitudes to Mary Tudor, and to re-examine her reign as the first female monarch of England. It will be argued that, contrary to the usual view, she ruled the country with some success at a very difficult and divided time. It is for the readers of this book to decide whether Mary deserved the reputation she has borne through the ages or whether, when studied in the contexts of her times – and of her predecessors – she deserves something rather more sophisticated.

Perhaps, in this much more ecumenical age, it is time for there to be at least some consideration of whether she might again be remembered as Mary Tudor, a 'lawful queen of famous memory'. What follows seeks to set out the grounds for further such reconsideration.

1

ESTABLISHING THE TUDOR REGIME

Mary Tudor was born on 18 February 1516, the eldest surviving child of the third generation of Tudors. She was born some 30 years after her grandfather Henry Tudor had defeated Richard III. By that victory, Henry Tudor had transformed himself into King Henry VII and set a new dynasty on the English throne, and when Henry VII died in 1509 his 17-year-old second son, Henry VIII, succeeded him. Such a peaceful transition from father to effectively adult son was rare in recent English history, and when it was followed by the peaceful accession of Henry VIII's under-age son Edward VI in 1547, the Tudor dynasty might have seemed securely established. But such confidence in the security of the Tudor dynasty rests entirely on historical hindsight. Neither of the first two Tudors ever felt entirely safe from the threat of alternative claimants, and Henry VII, having fought his way to the throne, had to fend off a number of aspiring pretenders.

Because the Tudor dynasty was seen by many nobles as an upstart family, it was important for both Tudor kings that they establish a strong line of succession, with heirs and sufficient 'spares'. At first Henry VII seemed to have met that need; by 1499 he had three sons and two daughters who had survived infancy. But when he died in 1509, he had only one surviving male heir, his second son Henry. The mortality rate for infants and children was high in early modern England, with as many as one in four infants dying in the first year, and another one in four before the age of ten. Moreover, statistically speaking, male children were more vulnerable than female. In each generation of the nobility, up to 20 per cent of all families produced no direct male heir. For the Tudor dynasty it was always hard to negotiate the consequences of the prevailing infant and childhood mortality rate, although the high rate of loss was not unusual.

After he became king, Henry VIII's marriage to Katherine of Aragon in 1509 also seemed fertile enough, with Katherine experiencing numerous pregnancies. But they included an uncertain number of miscarriages and in the earliest years only one child survived his birth – but died just weeks later. In 1516, the survival of Mary as a healthy baby was a possible sign of better things to come, only for no more live births to follow. It was precisely the absence of any male children from that marriage which gave rise to many of the trials of Mary's life, but also provided her with the unique challenge of becoming England's first queen regnant. This chapter sets out the defining contexts of Mary's childhood, by outlining the problematic origins of the Tudor dynasty, and the reasons both Henry VII and Henry VIII confronted so many threats within England to their security as rulers. Those fears of possible rivals for their English throne set the terms not only of Mary's life but also that of many of her closest associates.

THE FIRST TUDOR: HENRY TUDOR TO HENRY VII

A minimal requirement for a stable succession for any ruler was to have a clearly recognised heir – and in England, successful heirs had always been male. Englishmen knew that elsewhere there had been – and were – female rulers, but in England only one woman had ever been recognised as a legitimate heir. That was Maud (commonly known by the Latin form of her name, Matilda), daughter to Henry I. As one son of William the Conqueror, Henry had become king of England in 1100. In 1120 his only legitimate son, William, was lost at sea, along with many of England's next generation of leaders. (The wreck of William's ship, the *White Ship*, and William's fatal attempt to rescue his drowning half-sister, became a popular subject of medieval tales.) By 1127 Henry I believed he had solved his inheritance problem by having all his nobles swear allegiance to his surviving legitimate child, Matilda. They did so, but after Henry's death, many supported her cousin Stephen instead. The ensuing civil wars ended with an agreement that after Stephen's death, Matilda's son would succeed him in England. That son was Henry II, the first Plantagenet ruler, who reigned from 1154. Thereafter, it was recognised that the crown could be transmitted through the female line – and was on other occasions – but it was never actually held by a female heir before 1553, when Mary succeeded to it.

Until 1485 and the death of Richard III at the Battle of Bosworth, different branches of the Plantagenet family had ruled England ever since Henry II. By the mid-fifteenth century, any semblance of family unity had disappeared through increasingly intense competition between two branches – the house of Lancaster (descendants of John of Gaunt, Duke of Lancaster) and the more recently emerged House of York. To compound the problems of inheritance, over time some Plantagenet kings – most notably Edward III – had been remarkably fruitful both within and beyond their marriages. Edward III left five legitimate sons, five legitimate daughters and an uncertain number of illegitimate offspring. One of his legitimate sons, John of Gaunt, himself fathered three families, the third one illegitimate. It is hardly surprising that, with such a prolific lineage, over the generations royal and noble blood had become deeply meshed by intermarriage. Several of the greatest landholders could trace multiple lines of descent back to offspring of previous kings of England and/or their close relatives. Edward IV (died 1483), himself with three mature brothers and three sisters, also had eight children who lived long enough to be of some historical significance. Six were daughters, and several of them produced even more possible claimants to the Tudor throne. In brief, England's nobility included a considerable number who could make plausible lineal claims to the throne should the opportunity arise. The first two generations of Tudors, therefore, had good reason to be anxious that descendants of the older royal family would reassert their claims against them – as, indeed, various claimants did.

THE ORIGINS OF THE TUDORS

Unlike the Plantagenets, the house of Tudor had emerged very recently indeed, and out of almost nowhere. King Henry VII (1485–1509) was born Henry Tudor, a descendent of Katherine of Valois, the widow of Henry V and mother of Henry VI. Some ten years after she was widowed when only 21, Katherine had secretly married a Welsh member of her household, Owen Tudor. His family had played an important role in the Glyndwr rebellions against Henry IV, but it was a family in decline until Owen went into royal service. Little is known of Owen Tudor before his marriage to the Dowager Queen of England. Katherine's second family (of which three sons survived to maturity) was kept secret even from her royal son until just before she died, but Henry VI apparently accepted his half-brothers gracefully enough, and promoted their interests. Owen Tudor himself died serving the family he had married into, being captured and executed while fighting for the Lancastrian cause in Wales in 1461.[1] One son, Edmund Tudor, married Margaret Beaufort, then England's richest heiress. She was a descendant of John of Gaunt through the illegitimate family he fathered with Catherine Swynford. Since these children were all born before their parents married (in 1396), that illegitimate family formed a new line, named Beaufort after one of Gaunt's castles.

When it was finally legitimated, the Beaufort line was explicitly debarred from making any claim to the throne. Henry Tudor, the only son of the Edmund Tudor–Margaret Beaufort marriage, was born after his father's death. He was indisputably of French royal descent through his father's line, but his mother's illegitimate lineage was the only ground Henry Tudor had for a claim to the throne of England. Against his legal exclusion from the throne, Henry could trace his unbroken descent back to John of Gaunt, Duke of Lancaster. When the senior line of Lancastrians (Henrys IV, V and VI) failed after the death of Henry VI in the Tower in 1471, the young Henry Tudor therefore had as good a claim as any to lead any Lancastrian resistance to the reign of Edward IV. As a result, although initially on good terms with the Yorkist Edward, king from 1470, Henry Tudor soon found it wiser to retire from the realm and go abroad for his own safety.

Supported by his surviving uncle Jasper Tudor abroad, and schemed for in England by his mother, Henry's best chance to succeed to the throne followed the death of Edward IV in 1483. The dying Edward had named his brother, Richard Duke of Gloucester, as protector of his young son, Edward V, until the boy should be old enough to rule. But within months, Richard had both the late king's sons (Edward and

Richard) declared illegitimate and assumed the throne himself as Richard III. He faced some opposition from the start of his reign, but the opposition intensified after the two boys disappeared into the Tower of London, and rumours began to circulate that they had been murdered.*

Henry Stafford, the second Duke of Buckingham, owner of vast lands and with much Plantagenet blood in his veins, was one important noble who, at first a strong supporter of Richard, later turned against him. Many others urged Buckingham on to rebellion, including Margaret Beaufort. Her reasons for supporting his rising are not clear, but it is quite possible that she was urging him on to his destruction to help clear the way to the throne for her own son, since Buckingham was in a strong position to claim the crown himself. For whatever reasons, he finally declared against Richard III in late 1483. That rebellion was quickly crushed, and the duke was ignominiously executed in a market square. Henry Tudor had arrived in England from Brittany, but too late to support Buckingham and rapidly departed again to exile, having achieved nothing except, perhaps, the loss of a major rival. But despite King Richard's victory over Buckingham, his fortunes did not improve, and Henry Tudor returned again to England, for his second attempt to overthrow the king. He landed in Wales, but received little support there, despite the Welsh component of his Tudor descent. On 22 August 1485 he met up with Richard's much greater forces at Bosworth, near Leicester, and won the day, probably because of last-minute defections from Richard's army.

It was a brutal battle, even by the standards of that time. Richard III was probably hacked to death in the marshes by a group of unknown Welshmen, and few details of the battle were ever recorded. There sur-

---

* Who was actually responsible for the deaths of the two princes in the Tower, let alone when they actually died, is still a subject of much historical speculation – and is likely to remain so. Possible candidates have included Richard III, Henry VII, the Duke of Buckingham, and others possibly acting on behalf of some unnamed third party. The only thing universally agreed is that it is most unlikely they died from natural causes. Whatever the truth of their disappearance, the mystery would make it much easier for impostors claiming to be either of the two – but more commonly the younger one, Richard – to be put forward as figureheads by opponents to the Tudor regime!

vived, however, rumours of sinister behaviour, of treachery among King Richard's greatest followers; the behaviour of, for example, Richard's trusted supporter and Henry Tudor's step-father Lord Thomas Stanley was at best ambiguous. There was very little said about a significant number of French troops and even a Scots contingent helping Henry Tudor to the English throne. For whatever reason, there was no coherent English account of what happened at Bosworth until much later, although several foreign accounts survive.

During the previous decades, defeated monarchs (and contenders for the throne) had been known to die in mysterious circumstances. It was, however, unprecedented for the battered, naked body of an anointed king to be left lying in a tavern trough in Leicester for three days. That was the fate of Richard III, but even Shakespeare, in his reworking of nearly a century of Tudor vilification of Richard III, made no reference to the shameful treatment of the corpse of the last Plantagenet king. Curiously, some ten years after his victory at Bosworth, Henry VII was moved finally to arrange for a proper burial and tomb for Richard III; by that time he presumably felt sufficiently secure to allow himself a little courtesy to his wife's uncle. It may also have been a gesture to placate ongoing Yorkist resistance to his reign.

THE REIGN OF HENRY VII

Although Henry VII decisively defeated the forces of Richard III, the founder of the Tudor dynasty spent much of his reign shoring up the throne he had seized. His claims to the crown were never persuasively defined. The 1485 parliamentary act confirming his rule declared that he was king:

> To the pleasure of Almighty God, the wealth, prosperity and surety of this realm of England, to the singular comfort of all the king's subjects of the same, and [for the] avoiding of all ambiguities and questions.

That was an argument from convenience rather than any declaration of right. The same parliamentary act confirming him as king was also explicit that the crown lawfully lay 'in the most royal person of our now sovereign ... and in none other'.[2]

That last phrase is significant since, well before his successful invasion of England, Henry had won more support by agreeing to marry Edward IV's eldest daughter and surviving heir, but he was to do so only belatedly. He was adamant that his betrothal and later marriage to the heir to the House of York was never part of his claim to the throne. Indeed, the endorsement by Pope Innocent VIII of Henry VII's right to reign, widely disseminated through England, forcefully reiterated the Tudor case that Henry was the sole legitimate royal heir, and repeated the king's own argument that he was on the throne by 'his undoubted title of succession, as by the right of his most noble victory, and by election of the lords spiritual and temporal' as well as by the parliamentary statute quoted above.[3] It is intriguing to note how willing Henry VII was to shore up his regal claim by drawing upon that same papal power to make and unmake kings which his son, Henry VIII, was so vehemently to repudiate in the 1530s.

We cannot now know how many of his subjects were persuaded by Henry VII's claims, but there is evidence that a significant number were not. The previous three kings – Edward IV, Edward V and Richard III – had all belonged to the house of York. Henry VII, with his tenuous claim to a Lancastrian inheritance, faced resistance to his reign from some of the old Plantagenet blood in general and from Yorkists in particular for the rest of his life, despite his marriage to Elizabeth of York. Henry had married her only after his own coronation, as yet another sign of his denial that he owed his throne in any way to his marriage with her. It was only after Elizabeth of York had presented him with a son and heir, that Henry gave her a magnificent coronation. Then she received the full four days of coronation ceremonial, including a procession the day before the coronation, resplendent with white roses, the symbol of her house of York. Henry, however, never allowed her any degree of political power, but she was always a popular figure. One foreign ambassador even remarked that she was so beloved *because* she had no power.

Whatever the reason for Henry's attitude to his wife, he always showed the greatest respect for his mother, the formidable Margaret Beaufort. Throughout his reign, she remained his most consistently close associate and co-worker. With her he travelled round the kingdom for months on end, reviewing the good order of the realm and erecting monuments to emphasise the regality of their family line. Although she never mistook her role for that of a counsellor, she was unusually important to him, and entrusted with judicial authority unprecedented for a woman. Chosen for that role because of her large landholdings in any area where the king had few other reliable allies, she was the first woman known to have presided over a regional court.

Although there are no other known examples of a woman wielding quite that authority at that time, it is a noteworthy example of just how much authority women, when they did have the appropriate resources and status, could wield. Son and mother were constantly in close communication. It was Lady Margaret, moreover, who took over supervision of that important aspect of Tudor display, the planning of public ceremonials. Together mother and son ensured that the Tudor court rivalled and even surpassed the Yorkist courts in its splendour. Decades later, Mary Tudor was given some very striking descriptions of the household and estate maintained by her formidable great-grandmother, and the authority she wielded over all the men about her. It was a helpful precedent.

Henry VII is often presented as a rather parsimonious king, but he spent lavishly enough to ensure that his palaces, and other indicators of his regal estate impressed his subjects. As Sir John Fortescue (c.1394–c.1476), chief justice in the reign of Henry VI, wrote, a king needed a rich store of money to meet unforeseen and extraordinary expenses, to send ambassadors abroad, despatch an army to war or maintain his own magnificence. By that last phrase, maintaining the king's magnificence, Fortescue meant a king should have enough resources (he called it 'treasure') so that:

> he may make new buildings when he will, for his pleasure and magnificence; and as he may buy himself rich clothing, rich furs ... rich stones, fine linen, belts and other jewels and ornaments.[4]

In brief, if a king could not make such a public show, he was no true king but a poorer man than his subjects. As Fortescue knew only too well, Henry VI had never been sufficiently interested in maintaining his magnificence; by losing his throne he paid the price for that neglect. His successor and supplanter, Edward IV, never made that mistake and nor did Henry VII. The later Tudor rulers, including Mary, all demonstrated how well they had learned that lesson, that the status of each individual was most obviously maintained by his or her clothing and richness of visual presence.

By the late 1490s, Henry VII felt sufficiently secure, and had amassed sufficient 'treasure', to undertake an ambitious building programme as one way of demonstrating the permanence of his dynasty. The building that may have most impressed his contemporaries was Richmond Palace, built to replace an older one at Sheen. It was partly modelled on the more modern French and Burgundian palaces, and was an important place in the lives of both Mary and Elizabeth Tudor even after their father, Henry VIII, set about the acquisition of many more palaces and houses than any previous English king had ever dreamed of owning. Richmond was of particular interest for the emphasis on its grounds, parkland and provision of facilities for many forms of leisure. The palace had superb gardens, a good collection of wild beasts and one of the earliest tennis courts in England, foreshadowing the courtly pleasures so prominent in the reign of Henry VIII.

But Richmond Palace has long since vanished, and the building for which the first Tudor is now best remembered is the elaborate chapel he added to Westminster Abbey. From the first, it was designed as a worthy monument to the new Tudor dynasty. Significantly, given the religious upheavals of the next reign, it was conceived within the terms of an entirely orthodox late-medieval piety. To build the new chapel it was necessary to pull down an older, smaller one and a nearby tavern, which appropriately enough, given its demolition to make way for Tudor grandeur, was called the White Rose. Henry's ornately decorated and furnished chapel was still incomplete when he died in 1509, although by then it had already cost some £14,000 – a very considerable amount to spend on a chapel, however serious its dynastic aspirations.

This particular use for Henry VII's 'treasure' was politically very important. The project was designed to reiterate the links between the Tudor dynasty and the last Lancastrian king, Henry VI. The new Lady Chapel was planned so that Henry VII's tomb could be as close to that of Henry VI as possible, thereby reinforcing the fragile Tudor claim to the throne. The familial importance of the project was signified by the request of Henry VII for prayers to be said for his soul 'while the world shall endure' and prayers for his father, his mother, his wife, and the souls of their children and issue. The first Tudor tomb was placed before the altar, with superb effigies of Henry VII and his wife above their shared tomb, anticipating their final bodily resurrection with Christ. (The tomb is still there and intact but the effigies, provided by order of Henry VIII, are difficult for visitors to see clearly.) The whole design speaks forcefully to the complex of religious and dynastic imperatives which had driven the first Tudor on. His three regnant Tudor grandchildren, Edward, Mary and Elizabeth were also buried there, although only Elizabeth has a tomb and effigy.

Because of his ongoing need to secure the new dynasty, Henry VII had particular need of international recognition. His greatest diplomatic coup was in matching his elder son, Arthur, Prince of Wales, with Katherine, the fourth and youngest daughter of Isabella of Castile and Ferdinand of Aragon. A Tudor alliance with the Spanish court, confirmed in 1489, meant also an alliance with the oldest royal house in Western Europe, that of Castile. When Henry VII ordered celebratory masses to be said for the Christian capture of Granada, the last Moorish kingdom in Spain, it is hard to know whether he was more concerned to join other Christian monarchs in celebrating a reversal of Islam or in celebrating the success of his good allies and the family of his prospective daughter-in-law.

The strength of the new Tudor regime was confirmed in several ways before the marriage of Arthur and Katherine in 1501. The least appealing was probably the execution of Edward, Earl of Warwick, held prisoner in the Tower of London since 1485. It is likely that Spanish interests had demanded his death before Katherine was permitted to sail for England As the only son of George, Duke of Clarence, a brother of Edward IV, Warwick was the last available heir to the throne with unbroken descent through the male line from Edward III and, therefore, with the strongest Plantagenet claim to the English throne. He had taken no part in any conspiracies, and his death in 1499 was widely seen as an act of judicial murder, not least by its most obvious beneficiary, Katherine of Aragon. Perhaps as an act of contrition, Henry VII paid for Warwick's funeral.

That death would be remembered at intervals for the next three decades as one explanation for various disasters which befell the Tudors. Warwick's end is the more striking when compared with the fate of two other Yorkist pretenders to the throne, both actively engaged in raising rebellion. In 1487 Lambert Simnel, who had briefly masqueraded as the Earl of Warwick, and been crowned King Edward VI in Dublin, was put to work in Henry VII's kitchens after his capture. From 1491 Perkin Warbeck, who presented himself as Richard (the younger of the two sons of Edward VI and apparently miraculously escaped from the Tower some time in 1483), received support from both internal and foreign opponents of the Tudor regime. That made him a much more significant threat. Once captured, in 1497, he was sent to the Tower, but hanged only after he tried to escape to resume his resistance to Henry VII.

The death of the real Earl of Warwick, however, was not the end of the descendents of the Duke of Clarence. Warwick's only sister, Margaret Plantagenet, had been married off to Richard Pole, a man whose only claim to such a high-born wife was that he was nephew to Margaret Beaufort's half-sister. Befriended by Katherine of Aragon, who always felt some responsibility for the death of her brother, Margaret Pole later received the title of Countess of Salisbury, and became governess and close associate to the young Mary Tudor. But as will be discussed later, her Yorkist descent finally helped render her yet another victim of Henry VIII, along with one of her sons. Her third son, Reginald Pole, in exile for many years, was to become one of Henry VIII's most trenchant critics after his divorce from Katherine of Aragon, a cardinal, and the last Catholic Archbishop of Canterbury during the reign of Mary Tudor.

But that was all in the future. In 1501, all the immediate barriers to Arthur's wedding to Katherine of Aragon had been overcome. The arrival of Katherine in England, her reception and the ensuing marriage of Henry VII's heir and the Spanish princess were all celebrated as great landmarks for the Tudor dynasty. The planning had been under way for 18 months before the princess actually arrived in England; one purpose of the celebrations was to display the Tudor court to an international audience as being as splendid as any other in Europe. Katherine brought with her a household of 60 attendants. Her retinue was immediately joined by English lords, and their retinues, to meet their every need, and soon after by the Duchess of Norfolk and a company of countesses, baronesses and leading gentlewomen, all with their attendants. Henry VII still felt the attendance on her was insufficient and rode south to meet her with his own company of dukes, earls, barons, knights and gentlemen, and all their attendants. The young Prince Arthur and his retinue then rode from his residence at Ludlow Castle to meet the princess as well.

When Henry VII, who had little Latin, first met the Spanish princess, communication was difficult, since Katherine was so nervous that her

French failed her. So the king spoke English and the princess spoke Spanish for, although she had been addressed as Princess of Wales since she was first betrothed at the age of three, Katherine had never been taught to speak English. As Katherine's journey to England approached, messages were sent from both Queen Elizabeth and Margaret Beaufort, asking that, since she knew no English, Katherine should practise her French with fluent speakers. Neither of the English ladies understood Latin, much less Spanish, but both were fluent in French. Knowledge of French was widespread among early-Tudor women at the highest social levels, but there is no evidence of any English laywoman, however well born, who had learned Latin before the reign of Henry VIII. The English royal women were well aware that Arthur's bride was fluent in Latin, and Margaret for one regretted she had never been able to study that language. Katherine, brilliantly educated in Latin, was thereby familiar with Christian classical poets, the Church fathers such as Ambrose and Augustine, such pagan writers as Seneca, and many historians and legal writers. Also fluent in several languages, it seems very probable that she provided the model on which the famously well-educated aristocratic women of the next generation of high-born Tudor women was based.

Katherine's entry into London in late 1501 was an occasion for very elaborate celebrations; it has been described as perhaps the greatest ever masterpiece of English civic pageantry.[5] It also reiterated the Tudor inheritance into which the Spanish princess was about to marry. There were many red roses, as a further reiteration of Henry VII's Lancastrian inheritance. There were, however, no white roses for Arthur's Yorkist inheritance; this was a time for promoting the new Tudor dynasty. The public ceremonies surrounding the welcome for Katherine and the ensuing wedding were also among the first occasions when Arthur's younger brother Henry appeared in public. The then ten-year-old prince rode in a prominent position in the various processions and danced at the wedding celebrations with a vigour and grace which caught many eyes, and delighted his parents.

It was, on the other hand, an ominous sign for the future that during those wedding celebrations Arthur was not permitted to take part in the jousting because, although now 14, he was deemed too young and fragile to do so. There was also some debate about the question of whether the young couple should cohabit, Arthur being two years younger than Katherine and not robust. But the married couple set out together for

Ludlow soon after, pausing to spend some time at the home of Lady Margaret Beaufort. The royal heir's grandmother had spent money prodigiously, even by Tudor standards, on cloth of gold, silks and velvets for her residence overlooking the Thames at Coldharbour, to provide an appropriate setting for the new royal couple. Arthur had little time to resume learning the arts of government for he died at Ludlow, it was said of consumption, some four months later. Katherine, now the Dowager Princess of Wales, was too ill to be part of her late husband's funeral ceremonies.

The following years were increasingly difficult for her. One matter which was to become a question of wide public debate three decades later was that of whether the marriage between Katherine and the sickly, younger Arthur had ever been consummated. On that question depended the settlement of her dower rights in England and payment of the remainder of her dowry from Spain. Katherine told her parents that, although she and Arthur had shared a bed on several occasions, the marriage was unconsummated. With that statement the ladies of her household all agreed. Such a consummation was more unlikely because of the ill health and immaturity of Arthur; it was also unlikely that Katherine would lie about the matter, particularly to her mother. It was, however, in the interests of the English to believe otherwise, both then – since it determined whether they were to be paid the rest of her dowry, or be required to repay to Spain the portion they had received – and many years later, when Henry VIII wished to repudiate his marriage to her on the grounds of her imputed consummated marriage to his brother.

In the following years, Katherine remained in England while issues of her dowry and possible marriage to Henry VII's next heir were debated. After the death in childbirth of Elizabeth of York in 1503, the king even briefly contemplated marrying Katherine himself. By 1504 international alliances were shifting as two of Henry's most important international allies, Ferdinand of Aragon and the Emperor Maximilian, fell out over which of the two should control Castile on behalf of Isabella's nominated heir, her daughter Juana. (The nominal queen herself was quickly thrust aside, and soon confined as insane.) As his own international alignments shifted, Henry VII adopted very different attitudes from those of his original welcome towards his widowed daughter-in-law, detaining her because of his continuing disputes with her father over her dowry, and maintaining her in increasingly reduced circumstances.

Despite the increasing stability of his regime, Henry VII could never feel entirely secure against potential claimants to his throne. Indeed, that insecurity, and the associated imprisonment or deaths of potential rivals, continued well into the reign of Henry VIII. As one example, after the execution of the Earl of Warwick in 1499, the strongest surviving Yorkist pretender to the throne was Edmund de la Pole, a nephew of Edward IV. About 1503, one John Flamank reported to Henry VII the gist of a conversation he had taken part in at Calais some months before. It was a striking indication of how much uncertainty there still was about the probable successor to the then king. Flamank reported that various of the king's leading men at Calais had been discussing possible successors to the present king. The names under consideration included the third Duke of Buckingham, who traced his descent back to Edward III, some saying 'that he was a noble man and would be a royal ruler'. Other candidates included Henry's 'traitor' Edmund de la Pole, then still at large; 'but none of them ... spoke of my lord prince (the young Henry).'[6] Presumably, from Henry's perspective, the most disturbing aspect of this troubling conversation was that no one present showed commitment to a continuing Tudor dynasty. As it happened, De la Pole, a refugee in Flanders, was surrendered to England in 1506, with the proviso that the Yorkist heir would not be harmed. He was, indeed, kept safely cloistered in the Tower, for the rest of the reign of the first Tudor king. Henry VIII, however, as a safety measure before he invaded France in 1513 had the man summarily executed. The deaths of other possible, and sometimes improbable, claimants were to follow later.

THE ACCESSION OF HENRY VIII

When Henry VII died in 1509, he had no significant enemies still at large abroad, and he had progressively subdued the opposition at home. He left his heir, another Henry, a relatively settled realm and an abundance of 'treasure', but he felt increasingly uneasy about the way some of those riches had been acquired. In the last weeks of his life, his mind had turned much to ensuring the salvation of his soul; his will addressed the same concerns. After the death of Henry VII, one of his closest confidantes,

Edmund Dudley, declared himself also concerned to help redress past injustices 'for the help and relief of [the late king's] soul'. Dudley himself, now describing himself as 'the most wretched and sorrowful creature', accordingly set out many details of Henry VII's most troubling scheme, in which Dudley and Richard Empson had served him faithfully. He described in detail Henry VII's far-reaching practice 'to have many persons in his danger at his pleasure', which he had achieved by frequently threatening – and levying – arbitrary fines on any subjects who incurred his displeasure or suspicion.

It is not surprising that this had been a very unpopular policy, and as the scholar who recovered Dudley's petition remarked, scapegoats were needed. 'The reputation of the dead king was of some importance to his son; the reputation of the new king, as the enemy of injustice, was of even more importance.'[7] And so one of Henry VIII's first acts as he entered upon his inheritance was to offer up two of his father's closest and most trusted associates as sacrificial victims to the reputation of the Tudors. Both Dudley and Empson had been imprisoned within two days of the new king's accession, and were soon found guilty of treason and subsequently executed as the villains of Henry VII's administrative practices.

Henry VIII's ruthlessness in defending his interests and the interests of his realm as he understood them was thereby demonstrated at the beginning of his reign and would often be demonstrated again. Both his daughters were to suffer from a similar ruthlessness towards their mothers, and towards themselves when they might be challenging his will. Her father's nature and his capacity to apply relentless pressure, where he more usually demonstrated considerable affection, was to be a formative influence in shaping Mary's character. It is time to turn to from the wider background to a more detailed discussion of Mary's family life.

2

THE EARLY YEARS OF MARY TUDOR

THE MARRIAGE OF HENRY AND KATHERINE

The accession of the second Tudor king began with many forecasts of a splendid reign. His father, Henry VII, died on 21 April 1509, and the rapid execution of the two main instruments of his most unpopular policy only increased the popularity of the new king. Within weeks Henry VIII, not yet 18 years old, had married Katherine of Aragon, thereby dramatically ending her seven years of uncertainty and tribulation. Within another fortnight the newly married pair celebrated a joint coronation. Like his wife, the new king had been well educated in the humanist tradition. One of his earliest tutors had been John Skelton, the pre-eminent English poet of his day, and by the time Henry was eight he had met several of the leading international scholars, including the greatest northern European humanist, Desiderius Erasmus. Although a younger son until Arthur died in April 1502, Henry had received many high offices. By the time he was two, he was titular Constable of Dover Castle and Warden of the Cinque Ports. Soon afterwards, he was inducted into the Order of the Bath, and proclaimed Duke of York within months of his third birthday. Although little is known of the details of his education, as he matured Henry combined his interest in the newer values of humanism with the more traditional chivalric ideals.

Interest in chivalry had been revived by the publication in the new print medium of medieval chivalric romances such as Malory's *Le Morte d'Arthur,* one of the earliest English works published by William Caxton. Malory's work not only promoted romantic chivalric interests but also explicitly promoted the ideals of obedience and service to the monarch, values the new king had every reason to encourage. Chivalric exercises also gave full rein to the many forms of physical exercises Henry enjoyed – wrestling, hunting, shooting and hawking, if not tennis – but his interests and talents ranged very widely to include both composing and playing a wide range of music. As well as being a promising Renaissance prince, Henry was always a more acceptable king for his subjects than ever his father was, because through his mother the new king was descended from the Plantagenets. What is more, Henry VIII had succeeded peacefully to the throne – only the second adult monarch to do so for over a century.

Nobody really knows, however, why Henry married Katherine of Aragon. There had been some doubts about his marriage to his older brother's widow when it was first proposed in 1503, because it violated religious restrictions on marriage within family and kinship groups. As was common for European royal marriages, such doubts were apparently overcome by a papal dispensation in 1503. Possible explanations for the marriage finally taking place in 1509 have included Council pressure on the young king to ensure none of Katherine's dowry need be repaid to Spain. This explanation is the more likely because there were other diplomatic advantages in a renewed alliance with Ferdinand, his father's old ally and rival. Henry's early decision to renew war with France as soon as possible meant assured allies would be useful. Perhaps, in part, the marriage was the result of a chivalric impulse by the young prince to rescue a princess in distress. Perhaps.

Henry himself said that he married her at the wish of his dying father. That is possible, but equally possible is that it was a move encouraged by Henry's grandmother, Lady Margaret Beaufort, who had good reason for wanting to see the new king in a settled environment as quickly as possible. His grandmother had always helped his father supervise the young Henry's life and education. She took great pride in his developing prowess at jousting and running the ring, but persistent rumours indicate that she had many misgivings about his capacity for sound judgement. After the death of Henry VII, Lady Margaret had moved to the Tower of London where her grandson also was, and helped in many aspects of the administration of his household. There is also a tradition that she helped select his first counsellors which, given the number of men from her household who moved to that of Henry VIII, is plausible. There was a marked closeness between grandmother and grandson – and his new wife – until the old lady died on 29 June 1509, possibly from something she ate (contemporaries thought it might have been a badly-prepared cygnet) at Henry's coronation feast.

The new royal pair was probably the best-educated and most culti-vated couple ever to have occupied the English throne. In 1518 Erasmus richly praised Henry's support of learning, and described Katherine as 'a miracle of learning' and 'not less pious than learned'. He listed the lead-ing humanists at Henry's court and concluded that it 'is a museum [of learning] more than a court'.[1] In the early years of his reign, Henry's fre-quent chivalric gestures to his wife reiterated his deep attachment to her and, as well as being his main bedfellow, she was one of his chief advis-ers. In those years, ambassadors to the court frequently reported back to their own governments their admiration and respect for the king's wife, and her deep involvement in political and international matters.

The new king and queen were extensively courted by the leading scholars of the age and, more unusually, engaged with them, reading their works (sometimes) and even offering them patronage (occasion-ally). Katherine probably paid their works closer attention, but both could sustain conversations with leading scholars in terms which all involved reportedly found entirely satisfactory. The queen was particu-larly attracted to the works of Erasmus, the pre-eminent humanist of his generation, but also found particular pleasure in reading and promoting the works of the leading Spanish humanist, Juan Luis Vives. His best-known work, *The Education of a Christian Woman*, was commissioned by Katherine several years before it was first printed in 1529, and the English version remained influential throughout the sixteenth century, with at least another eight editions being published. Vives played an important part in England in promoting the idea that well-born women who were capable of it should study Latin, like their male social equiva-lents. Such women should read not only the Christian poets and the Bible, but also selected works of Plato, Cicero, Seneca, Plutarch and Aristotle. It was an education very like that which the new Queen Katherine had received, and had her enthusiastic support.

Henry VIII was very willing to adopt a much more aggressive foreign policy than that of his more cautious father. Although surrounded by humanists who almost universally deplored the destructiveness and extravagance of war, Henry's own ambitions, those of his companions in his chivalric pursuits and, frequently, of his father-in-law all urged him on to foreign adventures. Henry was anxious to have a leading part in the first foreign expedition, the 1513 invasion of northern France, in which he joined with the Emperor Maximilian. Henry seems to have thought of this expedition as a renewal of the Hundred Years War between the two realms, and perhaps even dreamed of making good again his French title. Against the Council argument that the king's life was too precious to be hazarded in war, Henry argued that many more wars were won when the king himself was present on the battlefield. There was even a remarkable rumour current in June 1513 that not only the king but the queen as well would shortly join the 25,000 English soldiers already in France.

That rumour is an interesting indicator of the high esteem in which Katherine was held by men around the court, but was false. Instead of going to France, the queen was appointed regent in the king's absence, and then supervised the English preparations for renewed war against the Scots. A decade earlier, when he married Henry's elder sister Margaret, James IV of Scotland had sworn 'perpetual peace' with England. By mid-1513, however, he had been persuaded by the French king to renew the 'Auld Alliance' with the French against the English and declare war against Henry while he was absent from his realm. Such joint Franco-Scottish wars against England, with armies to the north and south, were a traditional part of the 'Auld Alliance'. The Earl of Surrey set out at the head of the new army for Scotland, after the regent Katherine bade them farewell with, it was reported, a stirring speech to the troops, 'in imitation of her mother Isabella', reminding them that 'English courage excelled that of all other nations. Fired by these words, the nobles marched against the Scots ... and defeated them.'[2]

That victory was a much greater victory than any Henry had been involved in, but his exemplary wife was far too tactful to mention that. Instead she reported to him his great victory over Scotland, resulting in the death of the Scottish king, 12 of his earls and many other Scottish leaders at Flodden. Henry's soldiers in France had been involved in one skirmish which led to the capture of a French duke, whom he had triumphantly sent to Katherine as a trophy hostage. (She sent him in return the coat of the dead Scottish king.) Henry did briefly add the city of Tournai to his continental possessions on his campaign, but the most enduring result of his time in northern France was the painting he later commissioned, commemorating the great chivalric array of himself and the Emperor Maximilian which had led to the episode where the duke, a marquis and the vice-admiral of France were all taken prisoner.

The main cloud hanging over this unusually successful royal marriage was the difficulty that the couple faced in producing an heir, and preferably some 'spares' – for as well as being insurance against early sibling deaths, royal children were always useful diplomatic instruments. The difficulties inherent in successful child-bearing in early modern Europe, and the high incidence of infant mortality, have already been outlined. Katherine of Aragon's record of childbirth suggests even greater difficulties than most women faced. After an initial miscarriage of a female child in 1510, in 1511 she gave birth to a son, christened Henry. His birth was followed by many days of celebrations: a lavish christening, a pilgrimage by the king to the famous shrine of the Virgin Mary at Walsingham to offer thanks for his heir, a spectacular round of jousts and feasts. Before the celebrations had quite ended, and before the infant heir was two months old, he died. The grief for the loss of that royal son was deep. There followed for Katherine at least another three miscarriages before finally the queen was safely delivered of a healthy daughter. Several more unsuccessful pregnancies followed, until by about 1520, although she was still only 35, it was increasingly apparent that no more children could be looked for from that marriage.

THE INFANT PRINCESS MARY

And so the only child of Henry VIII and Katherine of Aragon to survive the perils of infancy was the daughter born on 18 February 1516. She was not the looked-for son, but she was still a welcome child. Two days after the princess's birth, the Venetian ambassador reported the royal event, and that he planned to make a congratulatory visit to Henry VIII soon. If the child had been a son, he assured his superiors, the visit would already have been made. Four days later he did make his visit and reported his subsequently much repeated comment to the king that the

Venetian rulers 'would have been yet more pleased had the child been a son'. Henry's response, that 'by the grace of God, the sons will follow', has also been much quoted to reinforce the traditional argument that royal daughters were a disappointment.

It is hard to see how else Henry might have responded. The ambassador, it is worth remembering, represented a republic, a political form which being formally without hereditary principles, could more easily be restricted to masculine rulers. Monarchies, being essentially hereditary, were much more subject to the vagaries of childbirth and infant mortality. Of course a male heir was always preferable, but just how desperate Henry was for a son in the first decade of his reign is difficult to establish. From 1519, he did have an acknowledged son, Henry Fitzroy, born to his mistress Elizabeth Blount, but the illegitimate boy was raised in relative obscurity in the following years. Several of the surviving comments on that subject were unsolicited observations from the Venetian ambassador, commenting frequently to his superiors and occasionally to Henry on the Venetian preference for a Tudor son.

The infant princess was given a splendid christening, appropriate for the putative heir to the throne, at least until, in Henry's phrase, 'by the grace of God' a son and brother was born. There were none of the jousts and other public celebrations which had marked the arrival of the first infant Henry in early 1511, and so quickly turned to lamentations. Her christening on 21 February 1516 began in a specially built wooden structure, hung with great tapestries, at the doorway of the church. There the infant was named Mary before the party moved into the church. The church itself was hung with embroidered cloth, enriched with pearls and precious stones. Most of the greatest men in England and/or their wives were present. As her procession moved up the aisle, the infant was flanked by two dukes, of Norfolk and Suffolk, and before them went the Earl of Devonshire. Her godfather was Thomas Wolsey, well established as the king's chief adviser and already a cardinal, indisputably the greatest power in the land after the king. After the ceremony, Mary was publicly defined as 'the right high, right noble and excellent Princess Mary, Princess of England and daughter of our most dread sovereign lord the king's highness'.

The politics of inclusion and exclusion at this great royal occasion provided an important indication of the directions in which Henry's policy was moving. In 1516 the king was seeking to bring a number of hereditary nobles, about whose loyalty he was uneasy, under much greater control than his father had deemed necessary. In that context, the absence of the Duke of Buckingham from the christening was a particularly striking omission. Buckingham, son of the duke defeated by Richard III, was the greatest landowner in England, the senior duke of the realm and descended from Edward III through both his paternal grandparents. As already discussed, he was among those whom Flamank had named to Henry VII as possible royal successor. Despite that, and although he allowed him little political power, Henry VII had consistently honoured Buckingham at the great celebrations of his reign. The splendour with which the duke necessarily surrounded himself as a sign of his greatness was always a welcome addition to the magnificence of the Tudor court. At the coronation feast of Henry VIII, Buckingham had played a spectacular part, as he did at the meeting between Henry and the Emperor Maximilian in northern France in 1513. As political alliances shifted, Buckingham was there again to help celebrate the betrothal of Henry's younger sister Mary to the elderly Louis XII of France. His absence from the royal christening could therefore easily be read as a sign of growing royal unease about the power of that great magnate, whose strong claims as Plantagenet heir to the throne were still alive.

The christening, however, also served as an occasion for publicly celebrating the royal line from which Henry VIII descended through his mother, and which had not often been celebrated in public by the first Tudor. The females of Edward IV's family provided all Henry's closest females relatives, and therefore those of his daughter, since Katherine had no relatives of her own in England. Two of Mary's godmothers were the Lady Catherine, Countess of Devonshire, surviving daughter of Edward IV and aunt to the king, and Margaret Countess of Salisbury who, as sole daughter to the Duke of Clarence, was niece to Edward IV and Richard III. She was also present because Katherine of Aragon, believing herself indirectly responsible for the judicial murder of Margaret's brother the Earl of Warwick before her first marriage, had actively sought and won the friendship of Warwick's sister. Indeed Katherine was probably a major influence in having Margaret Pole created Countess of Salisbury in her own right. The third godmother was the Duchess of Norfolk, wife of the senior duke present. Mary was carried to her christening by the Countess of Surrey, daughter of the (absent)

Duke of Buckingham and also wife to Norfolk's heir. Observers noted the unusual absence of any foreign godparents, concluding that the king was avoiding giving offence to any of his brother kings by honouring none of them with that office. Whatever the reason, those present served to reaffirm the union of the houses of Tudor and York throughout the christening.

After her christening, the infant Mary disappeared into the relative obscurity of her royal nursery. If she had been the male heir Henry continued to long for, her initial establishment would have been a more splendid one; Henry however, would not explicitly acknowledge her as his probable heir. Katherine did experience a further pregnancy, but there were to be no more children from that union. In the meantime, Mary was not sent far away from her parents; she did not acquire her own household, as a son would most probably have done. But all the evidence points to Henry's immediate and continuing appreciation of his daughter, including – but not exclusively – an awareness of her value as a new tool in his international diplomatic negotiation.

Neither Mary nor any of those around her were ever allowed to forget her distinctively royal status. From her infancy, the king required that every man doff his cap to her, and women make an appropriate curtsey. The only men permitted to kneel and kiss her hand were nobles and their equivalents. Very few were permitted greater familiarity than that. Not even dukes were permitted to kiss her cheek for that was a greeting appropriate only to her equals, of whom there were none in England beyond her most immediate family. Despite the rigid formality with which the princess was surrounded, there is no room for doubt about the affection, even perhaps indulgence, with which the king sometimes treated her. In February 1518 the child, barely two year old, was brought into the chamber where her father was meeting among others, the Venetian ambassador. He, Cardinal Wolsey and the lords present all kissed the little girl's hand. The princess's attention was so caught by the striking beard of one of the Venetian party that she called out 'Priest!' until he was 'obliged to go and to play for her; after which the King with the Princess in his arms' went up to the ambassador to request that his royal commendations of such an honest and very estimable man be passed on to his master.[3] The king, the ambassador noted with some distaste, indulged his daughter's whims so much that more honour was given to her than to the queen.

From the first, the infant princess's staff was overseen by a 'lady mistress', subsequently titled governess, and included rockers, a nurse, an unspecified number of servants and a laundress. Her first lady mistress was Lady Elizabeth Denton, but the position soon passed to Margaret Bryan, who was to serve in the same capacity in the nurseries of both Princess Elizabeth and Prince Edward. By 1519 Mary's nursery had expanded to become a more princely household, as the probability that she would be Henry's sole heir increased. Thereafter, apart from four years after 1521, Margaret Countess of Salisbury headed her household. From the earliest days her nurse had been Catherine Pole, perhaps from the same family into which Margaret Plantagenet had married. In the first year the cost of Mary's household, excluding extra payments and rewards, was some £1,400 – a considerable sum indeed in early Tudor England and enough to sustain a large and wealthy household. (The cost of the king's household for a year, however, was more than £9,000.) By the time the princess was three, and following her betrothal to the infant Dauphin of France, her household furnishings included a cloth of estate with two cushions of cloth of gold and red velvet, a cloth of gold and a velvet chair, and much else in the way of sumptuously rich hangings. The surviving records reveal much less about the more childish furnishings, let alone toys, the princess might have enjoyed. By 1520, when she was four, her household had expanded to include six gentlemen, nine valets, four grooms of the chamber, as well as her governess and more personal attendants. The household was potentially, and frequently actually, an independent entity, being for much of the year quite separate from her parents' court, and often based at Greenwich. The immediate royal family was usually reunited at time of high festivity and surviving reports of such occasions consistently described happy family occasions.

For the first decades of his reign Henry was much more interested in foreign affairs than domestic concerns. Consequently the early years of Mary's life were marked by his shifting marriage plans for her, marking the shifting fortunes of his alliances. This was one reason such close attention was paid to providing her with the appropriate setting. The very rich furnishings, the numerous personnel and the carefully prescribed rituals within her household ensured that neither the princess nor anyone else was ever allowed to forget either her royal status or her diplomatic potential. Late in 1516, for example, there was a rumour in diplomatic circles that some English 'lords' were pressing the youthful

Charles of Spain (grandson of the Emperor Maximilian, nephew to Henry's wife and in time himself the Emperor Charles V) to repudiate his French connections and take as his betrothed the English princess. She was, at the time, nine months old and therefore more than 16 years younger than her proposed spouse.

No more was heard of that proposal for nearly a decade, but Mary's importance was in no way diminished. Her status was endlessly reiterated in small ways and large. By the time she reached 16 months, Mary was godmother, along with her mother Queen Katherine, to the first-born daughter of King Henry's younger sister Mary and her second husband, the Duke of Suffolk. Neither mother nor daughter attended the actual ceremony. It happened that, for that occasion, Queen Katherine was represented at the christening by Lady Boleyn, mother to Mary and Anne Boleyn. Both daughters were to be subsequently ladies in waiting to Katherine, and respectively mistress and second wife to Henry VIII.

The complexities of the competing needs of royal status and an infant's physical and emotional development were omnipresent in the life of the young princess; it is therefore difficult even to begin to guess just how her environment affected the little girl. There are some glimpses of a sweet-tempered child, frequently described as 'merry'. In the midst of all that splendour (and with no surviving evidence of frequent contact with other children for her in her early years), there was some security in the continuity of adults closest to the princess. Catherine Pole, who was her nurse before the end of 1516, appears to have remained in Mary's household in various capacities until at least 1525. (She reappeared at the court of Queen Mary in 1553, as Lady Catherine Brooke, so it seems probable the relationship had continued, however intermittently, in the intervening years.) Like her younger half-sister Elizabeth, Mary would have had a wet nurse for the first two years of her life. A number of other names appear regularly in the household accounts or lists, so although the little princess saw her parents only intermittently, and was often at a considerable distance from them, there were a number of familiar faces always around her. Nevertheless, since the nominations to Mary's household came from the court and were always referred to the king for approval, some of them were inevitably caught up in the politics of the time and removed from the princess. Even at that age Mary appears in surviving records more often as a diplomatic tool than as a royal infant.

By July 1517, a number of Europe's Christian rulers, perhaps influenced in part by their humanist advisers, were exploring the idea of declaring a 'Universal Peace' in the Christian west although, as the Venetian Ambassador tersely noted, without the usual ultimate goal of declaring war against the Turks. In fact, this did occasionally become part of the rhetoric, but there is no sign that any of the main players were seriously considering another crusade against the Ottoman Empire. It was by then established throughout the Balkans and stretching to Hungary, as well as controlling the southern Mediterranean coast to Egypt and well beyond. But the Christian rulers had other more pressing concerns.

For Henry, the proposed Universal Peace provided a chance to renegotiate relations with his French neighbour, whose territories he had invaded in 1513. In 1514, Henry's younger sister Mary, previously betrothed to the young Charles of Spain, was married off to the aged Louis XII as part of the peace process. Within years, his infant daughter became another means for furthering this project, since Henry had fallen out badly with his previous Hapsburg Imperial and Spanish allies. Negotiations accordingly began for the betrothal of Mary and the Dauphin of France, even before it was confirmed that the Queen of France had indeed been delivered of a boy in March 1518. In April, negotiations were well under way despite some scepticism being expressed that a betrothal of two such very young partners could have any binding status. That was hardly the point of the enterprise, since the betrothal was primarily a marker of the changing Anglo-French relations. Later in the same year, marriage negotiations included the return to France of Tournai, the one trophy of Henry's costly invasion of northern France in 1513.

The curious mixture of the personal and the political, inherent in early modern conceptions of personal monarchs and their relations to their brother rulers, was repeatedly exemplified by the promise of intermarriage as a negotiating tool. Official French diplomatic contacts with the English court about alliances and international policy were interspersed with courteous royal enquiries about the health of Henry's little daughter. Exchanges on behalf of the betrothed pair included a portrait of the infant Dauphin despatched by his mother, and such domestic gifts as smocks for the little princess; it is likely that these were reciprocated in kind, but the relevant records (let alone the portraits) seem not to have survived. Like the Perpetual Peace between England and Scotland which had marked the marriage of Henry VIII's elder sister to the King of Scotland, these negotiations expressed widespread, if tenuous, ideals and were always opportunities for magnificent display, that essential component of Renaissance court life.

So it was that the English celebrations marking the proclamation of the general peace and the associated marriage negotiations began with a high mass sung with 'unusual splendour' according to Guistinian, then Venetian Ambassador. After the formal ceremonies to mark the Universal Peace there was 'a most sumptuous supper, the like of which, I [Guistinian] fancy, was never given either by Cleopatra or Caligula'. Cardinal Wolsey who took great pleasure in demonstrating his power by just such lavish occasions provided this one. Guistinian added that the banqueting hall was 'so decorated with huge vases of gold and silver, that I fancied myself in the tower of Chosroes, where that monarch caused divine honours to be paid him'. It may well be that others beside some resentful members of the English nobility thought that Wolsey was acquiring notions of his importance well beyond his reputed origins as an Ipswich butcher's son.

Two days after that remarkable feast, a fresh round of ceremonies marked the formal betrothal of Princess Mary and the Dauphin in London. One feature of the treaty was the formal recognition that if Henry were to die without a male heir, his daughter Mary would indeed succeed him. Such an explicit acknowledgement of a daughter as royal heir had last been given in England in the twelfth century, when Henry I had nominated his daughter Matilda to succeed him. But there were other European precedents, most notably in the immediate family of Katherine of Aragon. She was, after all, the daughter of a queen who had inherited the throne of Castile in her own right, and bequeathed it to her daughter Juana rather than to her husband and co-ruler, Ferdinand. Whatever her future prospects might be, the princess, not yet three, seems to have played her part well during the lengthy betrothal ceremonials. Dressed in cloth of gold, with a bejewelled black velvet cap, Mary, in the arms of her nurse Catherine Pole, was beside the queen throughout the ceremony.

That Mary understood a little of what all the ceremonial represented is suggested by another report which described the princess asking the Admiral of France, 'Are you the Dauphin of France. If you are, I wish to kiss you.'⁴ She had already learned the lesson her father had insisted upon: only with her very few equals was she to exchange kisses on the cheek. It is not clear just how many of the associated activities the princess was required to attend, but obviously not all of them, for there were yet more royal celebrations at Greenwich, including 'pageants of a sort rarely seen in England'. Despite widespread doubt about the long-term prospects for the treaty or for the projected marriage, the celebrations provided more splendid opportunities for extraordinary displays of royal magnificence and liberality.

It is impossible, however, to know how literally to treat the oath Henry took in the presence of some of his closest advisers, and before Cardinal Wolsey. The king instructed the cardinal that if he failed in his royal promise to fulfil the contract he, Henry, should be excommunicated. That might sound very serious, if only anyone could believe that Wolsey, who owed everything to the king's support, would ever have done such a thing. But it is another reminder that the intersections between royal power, public intrigue, private ambition, religious belief, the practice of power politics and sheer cynicism were – and remain – profoundly difficult to unscramble.

In June 1520, even more splendid (and competitive) ceremonial and display accompanied the further negotiations conducted at the fabulously costly meeting of the two kings of England and France at the Field of Cloth of Gold. Although the ostensible reasons for this meeting included further discussion of details about the betrothal of Princess Mary and the infant Dauphin, Mary did not accompany her parents to the last remnant of England's European holdings around Calais. For those who did attend, discussion ranged easily enough from the exchange of courtesies, in many forms, between the two monarchs to marriage arrangements, money to be paid to England by France, and the future of Scotland. From England came reports, in the midst of this extraordinary meeting, from the King's Council, that the princess was 'right merry, and in prosperous health and state, daily exercising herself in virtuous pastimes'.⁵

A few days later, three gentlemen of France visited the princess at Richmond, apparently with little warning. It is possible that the French visitors were there to check that the princess so unexpectedly left behind did not have any defects, physical or otherwise, which might mar her eligibility as a royal wife. If that were the reason, the visitors should have left entirely satisfied. Not only did their welcome include 'goodly cheer', including strawberries, wafers and wine while they admired the princess. Mary, now four years old, reportedly welcomed the French visitors 'with most goodly countenance, and pleasant pastime in playing at the virginals, that they [the visitors] greatly marvelled and rejoiced' – as, one may think, well they might, given the age of the performer. With Mary was an impressive list of leading English subjects, including her governess, the Countess of Salisbury, the Duchess of Norfolk and 'divers Lords spiritual and temporal', all helping to emphasise the point that this royal child was indeed a highly valued member of England's royal family.

There are in these years occasional glimpses of the royal family all together and 'as joyous as I have seen them', as Lord Darcy wrote to Lord Dacre in November 1520. Drafted in January 1521 a surviving letter from Henry VIII reads like the words of a king completely at peace with himself and the known world: Henry pointed to the current 'amity between us and France, and our daughter honourably bestowed there, and … [the fact that] we are at peace with all Christian princes' and asked 'what need we care for further alliance with the Pope and Emperor than we have already?'[6] It could be ironic that what Henry was actually addressing was the state of the negotiations, then not going entirely as he wished, to break with France and form a new alliance with the Emperor Charles V. There was to be, however, no discussion of his excommunication for breaking his previous undertakings to France as he had required of Wolsey.

The prospective Hapsburg alliance, which may have been one reason for a brief meeting between Henry and Charles before the former joined the French king on European soil, was finally confirmed by the betrothal of the 21-year-old Charles of Spain, Katherine's nephew and Emperor since 1519, and his cousin Mary. Because of their kinship and her prior betrothal, a papal dispensation for such a marriage was required, quite separately from the proposed political involvement of the papacy in the new alliance. The new Anglo-Imperial treaty, essentially directed against French interests, and the marriage treaty between Charles V and Mary were concluded in August 1521. The French realised only slowly just how completely they had been misled by Henry.

In June 1522 the Emperor was in England for more than a month. Welcomed to England by Wolsey, he met his aunt – before whom, as an exemplary nephew, he fell on his knees and asked her blessing – and his betrothed at Greenwich amidst yet more magnificence and royal display. The display was repeated with even more grandeur when he made his formal entry into the City of London. Between the rounds of hunting, jousting, feasting and pageants, Charles was kind to his six-year-old betrothed, and admired the accomplishments she displayed for him; negotiators finalised an agreement that should Henry have no sons, his kingdom would pass to the son of the union of Charles and Mary. But Charles's mind was primarily on other matters, and before he left England again an English herald had formally declared war on France, the realm he consistently understood to pose the greatest threat to his European interests.

The age difference between Charles V and Mary was always an indicator that the betrothal was little more than a diplomatic device, and an occasion for a rare meeting of the Emperor and his aunt. Dynastic imperatives meant that Charles, then 22 years old, could not set aside all thoughts of an heir until, in ten years or so, Mary was old enough to marry. All sides seem to have understood the fictive nature of the betrothal since, while still publicly betrothed to Charles, the princess was also the focus for a quite separate set of negotiations. Since the death of James IV at the battle of Flodden in 1514 and the accession of his infant son James V at the age of 17 months, the pro-English faction, led by Henry's elder sister Margaret, widow of James IV, and pro-French interests had struggled for control of Scotland. By 1524 Margaret was enjoying a temporary ascendancy and made a firm proposal for the marriage of Mary and James V. Part of a wider peace treaty was a proposal that James be regarded as a possible future king of England, should Henry have no male heir.

In 1525, however, the fortunes of several of the leading diplomatic players were sharply reversed. The most spectacular upset was the French defeat at Pavia by Imperial interests, and the capture of Francis I. Mary was no longer such an attractive bargaining tool. With the temporary decline of France, Charles felt free to announce his betrothal to the much more suitably aged Isabella of Portugal. (If we leap forward three decades, we find that the eldest child of that marriage, who became Philip II of Spain, also became Mary's actual husband in 1554. But that was then in the unknowable future.) Henry lost interest in an alliance with Scotland, and even spurned proposals for a renewed alliance with the much-weakened France. There is no record of what Mary knew of any of these proposed and actual negotiations for her hand, or what she thought about her betrothal to Charles and his subsequent marriage to Isabella. At her age, she was not expected to have any views on whatever her father thought good to contemplate for her, but it is worth noting that on several occasions Henry seemed willing to negotiate from the premise that his daughter might well prove to be his sole heir.

However gratifying Henry found negotiating his way through the maze of international relations and the marriage alliances he could contract for his daughter, domestic issues also demanded his attention. Problems with the stability of the Tudor dynasty were never far away, even at such apparently halcyon times, and rumours were always rife. Despite his absence from Mary's christening, the Duke of Buckingham had played his usual magnificent part throughout the Field of Cloth of Gold, and again the associated preparations and display expected of him meant further heavy demands on his purse. The conventional expectation was that great nobles who helped promote royal magnificence, as Buckingham had done on so many occasions, received in return offices, perquisites and other rewards from the king in return to help meet the associated expenses. Buckingham, despite his considerable outlay over the years, had received few rewards and less political power. Because of this, he was becoming increasingly discontented and indiscreetly muttered his discontent.

His dissatisfaction may well have been fed by a Carthusian monk, Nicholas Hopkins, who predicted that since the king would have no male heir, the Duke had an excellent chance to succeed him to the throne. That indeed had been thought possible by some nearly two decades earlier. When they were interrogated, some of the duke's servants reported overhearing Buckingham claim that after the Henry VIII he was next in succession to the throne. That dismissal of Mary's claims was potentially very dangerous indeed. Others reported the duke as saying that if he ever became king he would behead Wolsey, long opposed by Buckingham in many policy matters and deeply resented by him for the precedence the lowly born cardinal claimed in all matters.

The final break between Buckingham and the court came, from the duke's point of view, quite unexpectedly. Both Henry and Wolsey had long been particularly critical of the disorder within Buckingham's Welsh holdings. The breaking point for Henry seems to have come when Buckingham requested permission to take a number of armed retainers with him to his Welsh estates since, as he explained 'we cannot be there for our surety without three or four hundred men'.[7] When he received Buckingham's request Henry recalled that the Duke's father, the second Duke of Buckingham had begun his ill-fated rebellion against Richard III by withdrawing to Wales with a similar body of armed men. On such evidence as that, in April 1521, the Duke was summoned to Greenwich, and began his journey to court with no suspicion of what lay behind that order. He was indicted for high treason one month later, and executed nine days after his trial began. The main charge was that he intended the death of the king. Much historical energy has gone into debating the legitimacy of that charge and of the trial. But Tudor legal processes for treason cases always meant that those whom the king accused of treason had little chance of being found innocent by any 'legal' process.

The interest in Buckingham's fate for this study of Mary's life is that, as Wolsey commented to Henry's ambassador in France, the duke was seen to have conspired against Mary's right to succeed her father. Henry could have no way of knowing who else might resist the accession of his daughter to the throne, although he never believed the death of Buckingham meant the end of all other aspirants to the crown. Until 1525 there was still one potent Yorkist pretender at large, Richard de la Pole, younger brother to that Edmund Duke of Suffolk who had been executed in 1513. At one stage the younger brother had even been recognised by Louis XII of France as the real king of England and Francis I later contemplated putting him at the head of an army to invade England, although how seriously he did so is not clear. Nevertheless it was a considerable relief to Henry when the younger de la Pole died fighting for the king of France in February 1525. The story goes that when he was assured de la Pole was dead, Henry cried, 'All the enemies of England are gone' and called for more wine for the messenger.[8] All the church bells of London were rung in celebration, and a celebratory religious procession wound its way through the city to mark this most welcome death.

There were two major consequences for Mary's future from the destruction of Buckingham and the death of de la Pole. The first, of less significance, was that for four years from 1521 the Countess of Salisbury was removed from her position as mistress of Mary's household. Henry knew that she had had long had close connections with Buckingham. In 1519 the duke's eldest son and heir, Henry, had been married to Ursula Pole, daughter of Margaret, and relations between the families remained so close that the Venetian ambassador mistook the Pole sons, brothers to Ursula for nephews of Buckingham. When Buckingham fell, the Pole family was inevitably caught up in the aftermath; considering all that, Margaret Pole escaped lightly since her main punishment was to be temporarily withdrawn from Mary's household.

The more important consequence, and the one with much wider ramifications was that Buckingham's reluctance to accept a female succession may have raised more serious issues in Henry's mind about the security of his dynasty. Curiously, this anxiety seems to have been intensified by the death of the last Plantagenet explicitly to aspire to the English throne in 1525. Why this was so is difficult to explain. It may be, as some have suggested, that until the death of the younger de la Pole, Henry had simply taken a providentialist view that such matters should be left in the hands of God. But even before 1525 it was quite clear that Katherine would bear no more children. Whatever the reason, in August 1525 Henry summoned his six-year-old illegitimate son Henry Fitzroy to court, knighted him before the entire court, and then created him Duke of Richmond and Somerset, echoing the titles of his father's line. In the same ceremony the boy acquired a host of other titles, and was declared premier peer of England. Few could deny the implication that the small boy was being elevated in order to prepare him to become first in the line of succession to the English throne. The unavoidable corollary was that the claim of Mary to the throne was challengeable, as indeed it was to remain for the rest of her life. Having taken these dramatic steps to elevate his illegitimate son, however, Henry swung back to promoting the interests of his daughter. Mary was, after all, to retain the status of royal princess of England for several more years. But how constant Henry might prove in that resolve was something only the future would demonstrate.

3

THE EDUCATION OF A PRINCESS: LEARNING LIFE AND POLITICS, 1525–1536

MARY AS PUTATIVE PRINCESS OF WALES

In 1525 Henry's only legitimate child was nine years old and, whatever her status vis-à-vis her illegitimate half-brother, she retained her potential as a diplomatic bargaining point She was always educated to be at least a royal wife, if not a queen regnant; her mother Katherine of Aragon, as daughter to the redoubtable Isabella of Castile, never shared Henry's apparent hostility to the idea of female rule. That he would always have preferred a male heir is hardly remarkable; Katherine also understood that male heirs were, in principle, preferable. Even Henry's opposition, however, to female rule is easily overstated – he toyed with the idea of Mary as his heir several times and in 1536, after reiterating the illegitimacy of both Mary and Elizabeth, he considered declaring his elder sister's daughter, Margaret Douglas, his heir. His second Act of Succession included the provision that, should he have no surviving legitimate sons or daughters by Queen Jane Seymour, Henry was free to name whomsoever he chose to succeed – which, as her supporters pointed out, always left the way always open for Mary to return to her original status of heir apparent, lost in 1533.

Henry was always proud of his first daughter, and particularly proud of her prowess with virginals and lute; he sometimes supervised her playing himself. Mary's highly educated mother supervised her wider education as much as was possible, given her many other responsibilities. Despite the care exercised, surprisingly little detail has survived of Mary's early schooling, but it is clear that the well-known humanist Juan Vives influenced her early education even more than he did the education of many élite Englishwomen for the rest of the sixteenth century. At Katherine's invitation, Vives wrote a general treatise on the education of women. That work had considerable influence on the education of high-born Englishwomen throughout the sixteenth century.

Vives was well aware that his treatise provided no more than the barest outline of an education necessary for a princess. He shared with other humanists of his time the belief that a sound moral education was the primary goal for the education of each individual, male *and* female, and that such an education should always be modified according to the individual capacity and the social role of the pupil. A daughter who was destined to be the consort of a monarch or, at least in her mother's eyes, perhaps a monarch in her own right (a queen regnant), was expected to receive a sound moral education but also needed explicit preparation for a life of political decision-making. To further this, in 1524 Vives produced a collection of moral axioms and advice explicitly directed to a royal education. *Satellitium sive Symbola*, which he prefaced with a lengthy epistle to Mary, was sufficiently highly regarded to be used later in the education of both Princess Elizabeth and, more strikingly, Prince Edward. It impressed Mary so much that one of her earliest actions as Queen was to have her first Great Seal struck with the legend *Veritas temporis filia* (Truth, the daughter of time) on it, taken from Vives' collection.

In October 1527, Vives returned to England to fulfil an earlier promise to Katherine by becoming Latin tutor to Mary. But his plans were revised because of the impending divorce of Henry and Katherine. Vives, approached by Katherine for his help, advised her to offer no resistance to Henry, since he considered it would be a total waste of time and serve a part of Henry's 'sinister game'. Katherine furiously rejected his advice, and in November 1528 Vives, although on excellent terms with many English scholars, left England for the last time. Almost inevitably, however, Mary's education continued to be conducted along classical humanist lines, not least because both her parents were interested in humanist studies, and both were particularly admirers of Erasmus.

There are occasional glimpses of another emergent Erasmian human-ist in the young Mary. Giles Dewes, then almoner to the Princess recalled her, perhaps in 1527, quizzing him about the Mass. She worried that although the common people were commanded to hear the mass and 'harken to the words that the priest [shall] say', because it was all in Latin, they could not understand what was happening. Dewes gave an orthodox Catholic answer, that: 'They shall behold, and shall hear, and think, and by that they shall understand.'[1] It was indeed traditional not only to require the congregation to attend without participating but to expect that the priest should know the exact words of the office, 'so that his communication is to God, and not to the people'.[2] But Mary's con-cern, at the age of 11, that all the congregation should have a better understanding of the central religious ceremonies might be seen to fore-shadow her concern as queen to promote a broad education of the laity in the Catholic religion.

By 1527, however, the education of Mary as princess was widening to include much beyond book learning. Previous heirs to the English throne, Prince Edward, eldest son of Edward IV, and Prince Arthur, eldest son of Henry VII, had spent some years as nominal heads of a Welsh Council, based at Ludlow Castle, as part of their political train-ing. In early 1525, preparations were afoot to establish a new Council of Wales, with Princess Mary as nominal head. In that year the most influ-ential remaining figure of royal Welsh administration, Sir Rhys ap Thomas, died. The remarkable range of offices and dignities he had accu-mulated were redistributed away from Thomas's own heir, and two key offices, justice and chamberlain of South Wales, went to Walter Devereux, Lord Ferrers. From an important Marcher family, Ferrers became steward of Princess Mary's household and an unusually active member of her council, a signal of its importance in extending English influence more widely in Wales.

As the newly created Duke of Richmond (aged 6) was sent north with a splendid household, so the nine-year-old princess Mary, now nominal head of the Welsh Council, was sent to Ludlow Castle, with her own much-expanded household of some 340 people. Wolsey, as Henry's main adviser and often seen as the king's *eminence grise* in the first two decades of his rule, needed not only to ensure suitable conditions for the education and training of this eminently marriageable child, but also a council designed to ensure the administration of the law in what was undoubtedly still one of most challenging parts of Henry's realms. A comparison, however, of the scale of the respective households of Mary and Richmond suggests Henry's continuing ambivalence about which of the two was his preferred heir at the close of 1525.

THE PRINCESS IN WALES

Originally one motive for Mary's move may have been to emphasise the political importance of the princess, apparent heir to the realm of England, and promised bride to the Emperor Charles V. But by the time she left the royal court to take up her new position, Mary's most recent betrothal was at an end, and Henry's latest foreign policy schemes in tatters. Her presence with the Welsh Council was, however, still required to ensure – as mere councillors could not – that Ludlow Castle would become an important regional centre, distinguished by its displays of royal hospitality. So Mary's departure for the Welsh Marches in August 1525 served several explicitly political purposes.

It also marked Mary's longest separation yet from her mother. It is not easy to assess the importance of that for the young Mary. Katherine, who until that point had kept close oversight over her daughter's education, wrote to her on her departure, expressing relief that Mary's ill health had 'amended'. Her mother added that:

> as for your writing in Latin, I am glad that ye shall change from me to Master [Richard] Fetherstone, for that shall do you much good. ... But yet sometimes I would be glad when you do write to Master Fetherstone in your own terms, when he has read it that I may see it. For it shall be a great comfort to me to see you keep your Latin and fair writing and all.[3]

Such an interest indicates how much her mother, highly educated herself, was a most significant influence on Mary's training and patterns of belief. Her influence continued indirectly even though Mary was often separated from her, for her mother's closest English friend, Margaret Countess of Salisbury, was governess of Mary's new household. The countess was thereby restored to the position she had lost in 1521 when her family connections with the disgraced Duke of Buckingham made her an object of Henry's suspicions. She remained in charge of Mary's household until it was dramatically reduced in 1533; and at Ludlow she oversaw a household in which Mary's multitude of senior servants now wore a livery of the princess's own colours of blue and green. The princess, aged 9, was indeed head of her own household.

At Ludlow Mary appeared to the public in her carefully ordered, sumptuous royal setting, designed as a focal point for 'good hospitalitie', apparently as the king's true and acknowledged successor, the 'Princess of Wales' as both English and foreign observers sometimes called her.[4] (It might, however, be noted that some – foreigners in particular – had bestowed that title on her since 1524, when Vives had dedicated his *Satellitium* to Mary as 'Princeps Cambriae' – 'Prince of Wales'.) Such a belief must have been reinforced, for those who knew of it, by the king's expressed intention of allowing her extensive grants of land – a privilege unusual indeed for any young Tudor woman. It is, however, unknown when or whether these lands ever came under her control.

From her base at Ludlow, Mary travelled across the region to other residences in Shropshire and Worcestershire. She also made a number of progresses, often to return to her father's court, usually at Greenwich, but also paying her own visits to such centres as Coventry and Langley, where she experienced the customary civic receptions for royalty. From Langley, in 1526, she travelled with her father to Ampthill spending nearly a month there in his company.

Once he began seriously to contemplate a second marriage for himself, however, Henry began to consider Mary's vice-regal household to have been too successful in elevating her political status. Yet some ambiguity remained in Henry's plans for his daughter well after 1528 for, as Loades has pointed out, some members of her Welsh household were retained at local expense and in expectation of her possible return at least until 1532.[5] Perhaps he was keeping open an easy way of enhancing her status as a marriageable diplomatic tool. Or perhaps, even, he felt a genuine reluctance to diminish irrevocably the status of his first daughter, for whom he had frequently shown considerable affection.

THE KING'S 'GREAT MATTER'

What *is* certain is that when Mary was recalled from her Welsh household in 1528, Henry was committed to divorcing her mother. It is not clear just when Henry had decided to set aside his first wife, but he finally justified his decision to separate from Katherine on the grounds that he should never have married his older brother's widow. He claimed strong scriptural support in Leviticus 20 verse 21, which forbad just such remarriage. There were other scriptural texts, most notably Deuteronomy 25 verse 5, which prescribed the opposite, actually instructing a brother to marry the widow of his deceased childless brother, but Henry found that much less persuasive.

From the start, Katherine took a straightforward ground for resisting the Leviticus text; she reiterated, as she had since the death of Arthur, that the first marriage had never been consummated. Since an unconsummated marriage was not a complete marriage, the preferred strategy of Henry's supporters in the face of Katherine's denial was to state that she was a liar. The only person other than Katherine who ever knew what the facts of the case was Prince Arthur himself, and he had died in 1502. As all power flowed from the king an ever-diminishing number listened sympathetically to Katherine's protestations. In 1533, a Convocation of clergy solemnly resolved that Katherine's first marriage had been consummated. But until her death, Katherine insisted she had gone to Henry's marriage bed a virgin; when Katherine challenged Henry to swear on oath she was not a virgin at their marriage, he left the room rather than do so.

As long as Henry permitted, Katherine remained beside her husband, and to the endless fascination of courtiers and foreign observers, in public at least their relations remained entirely cordial. For a remarkable time, Henry lived in a curious *ménage à trois* with Katherine sewing his shirts and Anne Boleyn, his prospective new wife, manifestly remaining a potent attraction for his attention. Katherine upbraided Henry occasionally, Anne frequently. The latter's will finally prevailed when in mid-1531 Henry ordered his queen to remain behind on a hunting trip while the rest of his entourage – including Anne Boleyn – moved on.

As soon as they learned of the planned divorce, Henry's confidantes saw diplomatic opportunities as well as personal ambitions in the turn of events. Since the collapse of Henry's alliance with Charles V in 1525, his most powerful adviser Cardinal Wolsey had dreamed of a renewed alliance with France, ideally to be cemented by marriage between Henry and a French princess. By 1527 the plan had given rise to a second set of negotiations for a marriage between Mary and either the French king's second son or, alternatively, the king himself. Mary passed most aspects of the scrutiny by the French embassy well. She spoke to them, they reported, 'in French and in Latin ... they also made her play upon the harpsichord.'[6] But they also reported that Mary was so physically small and immature for her age, now 11, that she would not be ready for marriage for at least three years. That was only one of several problems with the French marriage proposals, but the Anglo-French entente was, for a while, still convenient for both sides. In 1532, members of the French court even attended a visit to Calais by Henry with Anne Boleyn, now created Marquis of Pembroke in her own right, as premier lady of his court. The French king, however, ensured that his own queen was not able to attend any of those festivities where Anne, adorned with rich jewels which had recently belonged to Katherine, led the ladies of the English court.

Although Mary caught smallpox in 1528, it seems she suffered no lasting effects since a Venetian visitor to court in 1531 was particularly struck by Mary's 'very beautiful complexion'. He found her to be 'not very tall, has a pretty face, and is well-proportioned'. Nor were the French the only ones to admire Mary's accomplishments. With no obvious vested interest shaping his judgement, the same Venetian visitor praised her command of languages, and found her very musical. In brief he thought, 'she combines every accomplishment.'[7] She was, it would seemed accomplished, well educated and possessed of the talents both her parents would have hoped for.

MARY AS HENRY'S OTHER DAUGHTER

Little is known about Mary's life during the years after she returned from Wales, although she did nominally retain her own household until 1533. Nor is it known just when she learned of her father's determination to divorce her mother. In December 1530 she was living at Richmond, and reportedly 'with a suitable establishment and is heard to be already advanced in wisdom and stature'.[8] In March 1531, she was permitted to spend several weeks with her mother. In April Mary was seriously ill with what, in a nineteenth-century translation, reads as 'the physicians call hysteria'. That has been a gift to those historians who have been dismissive of Mary, and has fed a longstanding tradition of her 'hysterical' behaviour. What the ambassador actually wrote was that Mary was believed to suffer from a malfunction of her womb (the Greek word for which is the source of 'hysteria').[9] Ancient Greek medical texts had attributed some 500 distinct disorders in women to womb malfunction. The continuing strength of that comprehensive diagnosis can be seen in a seventeenth-century manual which reported that the 'evil qualities' of an 'ill-affected womb' could affect 'the heart, the liver and the brain', causing such problems as 'convulsions, epilepsies, apoplexies, palseys, hectic fevers, dropsies, malignant ulcers, and, to be short, there is no disease so ill but may proceed from the evil quality of it.'[10]

In June, apparently recovered from her most recent illness, Mary spent time with her father at Richmond, and in July, after her parents' final separation, she was permitted again to spend time with her mother at Windsor, where they travelled together across the countryside, and enjoyed their hunting, that most royal of sports, And all the time, the two parties in the projected divorce waited upon the papal decision. Henry urged a response to his request that the papacy should admit the original papal error in approving his marriage to his brother's widow. Katherine, on the other hand, waited for endorsement of her appeal to confirm the propriety of that papal decision and therefore of her second marriage.

In late 1531 Henry struck a serious blow against both Mary and her mother when he forbade Katherine to see her daughter again. Mary was also increasingly kept from court, primarily because of Anne's hostility to her, so there is little more reliable information about her at this most difficult time. The most recent proposal for her marriage – with the King of France – had lapsed as French interests changed; moreover, with Henry apparently bent on repudiating her mother and marrying Anne Boleyn, Mary's own status as legitimate princess was becoming increasingly uncertain. As her popular mother's daughter, she had considerable public sympathy, but little interest – let alone support – from courtiers or diplomats.

In the following years, anyone close to Mary or her mother was an object of considerable suspicion to Henry's advisers. One consequence was that his daughter makes few appearances in surviving records. For more details of her life during these years historians are unusually dependent for information on the reports of the Emperor's ambassador Chapuys, one of the very few who still had access to her. His reports were coloured by concern to maximise Charles' sympathy for the Emperor's aunt Katherine and cousin Mary in England, for by 1535 he was actively seeking to persuade Charles to invade Henry's realm to rescue his female relatives and save the Catholic Church. This became an increasingly serious concern as Henry's drive for separation from Katherine increased the attacks on papal authority in England.

By mid-1532, it was increasingly clear that the anti-papal and pro-divorce forces were in the ascendancy at court. In May that year Sir Thomas More resigned as Lord Chancellor and retired to private life with a promise from Henry that the king would not pressure his conscience. For many other religious conservatives the choice between obedience to the king and obedience to the papacy was a more difficult issue to resolve, although it foreshadowed much more difficult choices to be made in the following years.

HENRY'S BREAK WITH THE PAPACY, AND ITS AFTERMATH

A decade earlier, in 1521, Henry had been awarded the title 'Defender of the Faith' for his written attack on Luther's teachings, and other services to the papacy. But now he was increasingly questioning the extent and legitimacy of the papal authority now thwarting his marriage plans. The real breakthrough in the divorce issue came for Henry when William Warham died in August 1532. Archbishop of Canterbury since before Henry VIII's accession, Warham had been unhappy about the wider implications for the church of Henry's divorce proceedings. Thomas Cranmer, Anne Boleyn's chaplain, who had been busily working to promote the case for Henry's divorce, quickly replaced him as the premier English archbishop, with full papal endorsement.

Henry's need for a second marriage became much more pressing when Anne Boleyn declared herself pregnant. In January 1533, the king secretly married her, and turned in earnest to ensuring his new heir would be indeed legitimate. This required the new Archbishop of Canterbury to pass final judgment on the legality of his first marriage, to pre-empt any danger of Katherine's appeal to Rome winning support there. She, however, refused to attend Cranmer's court, let alone accept its legitimacy, and in May 1533 Cranmer declared Henry's marriage to

Katherine null and void. The coronation of Anne as Queen of England took place on 1 June, and the pageants in the London streets for that occasion made much of the son Henry believed she was bearing. The traditional authority of the papacy in such matters had been repudiated, although the final legislation to do so was not passed until 1536.

In July 1533 Katherine was proclaimed Dowager Princess of Wales, as the widow of Prince Arthur. Any person addressing her as 'Queen' was threatened with the loss of property and/or imprisonment. But popular unease was not easily assuaged. Charles Wriothesley, in his invaluable contemporary *Chronicle*, may have been typical of many when he wrote of Katherine as 'the good Queen' now deposed and 'to be called Lady Katherine'. Similarly, in 1536 he recorded the death of 'the honourable and noble Princess, Queen Katherine'.[11] But when finally, in March 1534, Clement VII gave his judgment in favour of Katherine's appeal, it was far too late to affect anything, not least because his findings were not published in England for many years.

In England, meantime, parliamentary statute and royal decree were increasingly used to settle all outstanding matters. In 1534, the first Act of Succession wrote into law Cranmer's finding that Henry's first marriage was invalid. All subjects were required to swear allegiance to Queen Anne and to Elizabeth, born 7 September 1533, as Henry's heir. (Unusually, however, enough parliamentarians refused to include a clause explicitly debarring Mary from the throne for such an exclusion not to be enacted.) His refusal to subscribe unreservedly to this Act of Succession led to the imprisonment of John Fisher, Bishop of Rochester, once the close confidant of Henry's grandmother Margaret Beaufort. Sir Thomas More, now in private life, joined Fisher in the Tower of London for the same reason, before both were executed. Those two deaths in mid-1535, may have caused considerable revulsion in Europe, but had no obvious impact on the course of events in England or on Henry's choices.

Henry was finally declared supreme head of the Church of England in 1534, and in 1536 another statute comprehensively repudiated all papal authority as 'pretended power and usurped authority' used to promote 'superstitious and erroneous opinions'.[12] The 1534 law which had enacted that Katherine was not, and never had been, Henry's wife carried the implicit corollary that Mary was not, and never had been, a legitimate princess, although it did not explicitly say so. No legitimate appeal could be made against these legal conclusions, and it was legally treason to defend in any way, let alone invoke, the authority of the Pope. The Treasons Act of 1534 also made it treason to threaten physical harm to the monarch, his consort, Queen Anne, or their child, and treason to describe any of the three 'heretic, schismatic, tyrant' or any other terms a committed Catholic might think appropriate.

The choices facing Mary and her mother were either complete submission to Henry's wishes or committing treason against the husband to one and father to the other. And still Katherine refused to be involved in any rebellion against her husband, despite strong urgings to do so from Chapuys and others, and some indications that her nephew Charles V would be supportive. She was unmoved by repeated assurances of considerable support at home and abroad. It is impossible to gauge now just how plausible such assertions of support for Katherine and Mary were, but Henry was to remark more than once in those years how much he feared mother and daughter together acting against his new order. He reminded others that Katherine's mother had fought for and won the throne of Castile for herself. But in that fear he misjudged his first wife. Through all the years protesting against the ending of their marriage, Katherine repeatedly insisted on her total obedience to her husband and refused to countenance any talk of armed resistance. As she said to companions and wrote to Clement VII, any such action would be a sin against the law and against her lawful husband. Nevertheless, given the widespread and very public uneasiness about the king's new order, the apparent popularity of his first wife and the widespread unpopularity of his second, Henry's anxiety was understandable.

THE KING'S ILLEGITIMATE DAUGHTER

During the earlier stages of the divorce and remarriage, Mary had spent much time at Richmond in relative obscurity, isolated from her mother and on the margins of court life. At first she retained a household appropriate to the king's legitimate daughter. Margaret of Salisbury remained as governess, and her household was joined by Mary's cousin, Lady Margaret Douglas, daughter of Henry's sister Margaret Tudor by her second marriage. During 1533, anticipating the birth of a male heir, Henry appears to have planned a reduced but still splendid household for Mary, still to be headed by Margaret of Salisbury and still including Lady Mary Douglas. When Anne's child was born, however, despite the confident prognostications of doctors, midwives and astrologers it proved to be another daughter for Henry.

The king soon overcame his initial fury – for fear of which, it is said, the offending astrologers fled the country – and the child was christened Elizabeth in a ceremony quite as splendid as that which had been held for Mary some 17 years earlier. With the much-promised son proving to be another daughter, Henry was immediately under pressure from his second wife to draw clearer distinctions between the respective standing of his two daughters. All members of Mary's household were ordered to replace her badge on their liveries by the badge of the king – a very public signifier of her declining status. Henry then sought to exact total submission from his elder daughter to his new religious and his new marital order. Either would have been a very public repudiation of her mother's virtue and honesty, and an acceptance of the invalidity of papal authority. It is likely that defending her mother's virtue and reputation was her primary concern, so it is hardly surprising that Mary refused to acquiesce in either of her father's demands. In late September the Earl of Oxford and others visited Mary at Newhall to warn her of the consequences of continuing to flout the king's wishes – and the law of the land. Two days later, Mary once again repudiated the new order. Her father disbanded her household, and Mary herself was transferred to the household of the 'real' princess. That the new princess was just some three months old would not – and did not – prevent Elizabeth's household, headed by Lady Shelton, from demonstrating on a daily if not hourly basis, just where the king's bastard daughter came in the order of precedence.

In December 1533 the Duke of Norfolk, who was repeatedly used by Henry for the more disagreeable tasks (he was to preside at the trials and condemnation of both his nieces who became queens – Anne Boleyn and Catherine Howard) was sent to Newhall to supervise the disbanding of Mary's household, and her transference to that of the princess, now established at Hatfield. Mary, still 17, stubbornly insisted that she knew of no princess but herself. It is little surprise that initially all she was allowed to retain were two of her own women, even though the Countess of Salisbury, dismayed by Mary's degradation, offered to remain, with her own retinue and at her own expense, as Mary's companion. She was refused permission to do so, and Lady Margaret Douglas was also transferred to the household of Elizabeth.

The following year was difficult for both Mary and the household in which she had been placed. Lady Shelton, who was now lady governess to both the king's daughters, was instructed by Thomas Cromwell, once in Wolsey's service and now leading the royal campaign for Queen Anne and the royal supremacy, to keep a particularly close eye on Mary. Others of the household, indebted to the Boleyn interest, were often unsympathetic to her concerns. Mary's correspondence, however apparently innocent, was carefully scrutinised, and its nature reported back to Cromwell. She usually travelled when Elizabeth's household decided to travel, and almost always in their company. Henry's infant daughter was accorded all the ceremony and deference once directed to Mary, with the corollary that the elder daughter was generally required to give public precedence to her half-sister. Once at least she was allowed to ride ahead of the litter in which her half-sister travelled, but usually she was forced to submit to the public humiliation of less rich dress, less rich accoutrements, fewer attendants and a subordinate place in the retinue.

Nevertheless, and despite Anne's explicit hostility to mother and daughter, Henry never exacted from either Katherine or their daughter the due penalties for failing to swear acceptance of the legislation denying the validity of all their claims. That would have meant their death, and that was no part of Henry's plans. Rather, Katherine was granted an independent income sufficient for a seemly (if not queenly) household, and the various strategies adopted towards Mary to enforce her submission to her father's will always preserved her status as an important – but no longer pre-eminent – person.

When the 17-year-old was first thrust into Elizabeth's household, Mary had had little preparation to bear such slights and insults as were directed at her, and above all at her mother's reputation. Although there is little direct evidence of what she really thought, a good deal is recorded, usually by hostile sources, about the initial bluntness with which she defied her father's laws. Despite the household's surveillance, she was able to maintain a covert correspondence with her mother, but of that only a few letters from Katherine survive. One undated letter is probably written as advice to her daughter about her behaviour towards the king, and in the household to which she was about to be or had just been transferred. The advice can be seen as being something of a blueprint for Mary over the following years. She was 'to obey the King, your father, in everything save that you will not offend God and lose your own soul'. But the maternal advice also ranged more widely: 'for the love that you do owe unto God and unto me ... keep your heart with a chaste mind, and your body from all ill and wanton company.'[13]

Historians remain substantively dependent on Chapuys for accounts of how Mary fared in these years, but the Imperial ambassador always had a number of different agendas in mind when he stressed her discomfort, maltreatment and humiliations. His primary concerns, after all, were to protect Charles' interests, safeguard the well-being of the Emperor's aunt and cousin, and promote papal interests within England. But enough is known from Chapuys's reports to be confident that, during this period of her refusal to subscribe to her mother's disgrace and accept her own degradation, Mary experienced some prolonged bouts of illness, and on occasion her father sent his own physicians to attend her.

Her illnesses may well have been compounded by the stresses she endured. She had no independent income, and most of the royal jewels (she had always cared a great deal about jewellery) had been removed from her. She was, however, gradually permitted to regain some servants and sufficient allowance to maintain a status 'suitable' for illegitimate royal daughter. Perhaps even, as David Loades has suggested, one of the most prevalent emotions for Mary during these years was simply boredom as her access to friends was very limited, her school masters departed, her visitors few, her freedom to take the long walks she always enjoyed severely circumscribed, and the household in which she lived filled with women who were primarily friends of Anne Boleyn. Henry and his new queen avoided interviews with Mary on their infrequent visits to Elizabeth's household at Hatfield, and her most regular contact with the outside world may well have been through Chapuys. On several occasions, probably as part of his wider brief, he reported on Mary's wish to be spirited out of the country, but it is hard to see exactly what future Mary had in mind, if that was indeed her wish. Nor was her father unremittingly harsh – he sent gifts of money, and at least once permitted her to remain behind at Greenwich after Elizabeth and her attendants had moved on. Her life was never unmitigated misery, but her continuing defiance of her father took its toll on her, as it did on those around her.

An interesting glimpse into the complexity of the situation in which all the main players found themselves is found in the correspondence of Chapuys. Writing on 25 February 1535, the ambassador described a meeting with Henry, in which he passed on a request from Katherine that her ailing daughter should be sent to her, her physician and her apothecary, since her mother understood better than anyone the nature of Mary's ailment. Henry expressed his own concern for Mary's health, but reminded Chapuys of the associated much greater danger that Mary might make her escape from her mother's household 'for he perceived some indication that [Charles V] would be glad to withdraw the princess'. Charles had previously, however briefly, considered schemes for extricating Mary, probably at Chapuys' behest, but there is no sign that the Emperor was ever seriously committed to such an action. Henry suggested he also knew of secret arrangements between the King of France and the Emperor for the marriage of Mary; and commented that Katherine was the main cause of Mary's obstinacy, and therefore of her isolation. There were indeed many reasons for Henry to be anxious to retain his daughter under his own control.

Chapuys dropped that topic, but asked instead that the Countess of Salisbury might attend Mary, who 'regarded [her] as her second mother'. Henry denied that request also, claiming the countess was 'a fool, of no experience, and that if his daughter had been under her care ... she would have died whereas her present governess is an expert lady even in such female complaints.'[14] Nonetheless, very soon the Countess of Salisbury was back with Mary, as apparently were others of her household. On 25 March Sir John Sheldon, explaining the expenses of the royal daughters' household, noted the part that 'my lady Salisbury' and the lord Hussey (previously Mary's chamberlain) now played in ordering separate meals for Mary's diet. Despite his daughter's repeated recalcitrance, Mary's father showed convincing if intermittent signs of concern for his defiant daughter.

THE TURNING WHEEL OF FORTUNE

In early 1536 Mary's mother died, attended by a few close friends and attendants. Chapuys was permitted to visit her in her final illness, but the king refused Katherine's dying request, that she might see her daughter again. In a ceremony supervised by William Paulet, who as Marquis of Winchester was years later to supervise her daughter's funeral, she was given a funeral appropriate for a Dowager Princess of Wales, and buried in Peterborough Cathedral, with as little pomp as propriety permitted. A curious tradition has survived however, that 'for her sake the Church of Peterborough fared the better at the dissolution of Abbeys, and was turned into a Cathedral, as if King Henry ... should favour his Wife's grave in this place.'[15] Mary was deeply distressed at Katherine's death, but court gossip reported that Anne Boleyn was delighted.

If that report was true, Anne's was an unwise response. Her best insurance for the crown she had so long worked for was the continuing life of the former queen, for Henry could hardly admit any kind of mistake in his second marriage as long as his first 'wife' survived. But Anne had recently endured at least two miscarriages, one certainly of a male foetus. Why Henry ended the marriage is still a matter of considerable debate, but there is general (though not universal) agreement that the charges on which she was convicted – including having sexual relations with one of her musicians, her brother and several other men, and plotting to kill Henry Fitzroy and Mary – were false. Before she died, Anne's marriage to Henry was annulled by the accommodating, but regretful, Cranmer on grounds which were later declared to be lawful, but were never made public. All the reasons subsequently offered have drawn on contemporary rumours. Anne's last privilege was to be beheaded not with the rather cumbersome and unwieldy axe usually favoured by the English, but by a French sword which removed her head with one blow. She died just six months after Katherine, on 19 May 1536.

The next day Henry was betrothed to Jane Seymour, and he married her ten days later. Unsurprisingly there was considerable (but muted) comment on the king's remarrying so quickly, and speculation, but little evidence, about the possible role of Jane Seymour in Anne's downfall. She had been an attendant at the courts of both Katherine and Anne, but certainly showed little concern for her immediate predecessor. The new Queen Jane had held Katherine in high esteem, and had considerable regard for her daughter Mary, only seven years the new queen's junior. But Mary had still not accepted her own illegitimacy or the invalidity of her mother's marriage, and until she did Henry would not allow her back in court. She resisted a delegation of Henry's councillors, headed by

Norfolk; one said that if she were his daughter, he would knock her head against a wall until it was as soft as baked apples. In the eyes of Henry's advisers, Mary's continuing resistance to her father made her an ever more attractive instrument for international Catholic plots against the existing regime.

Thomas Cromwell, now the most powerful of Henry's confidantes, intervened to command Mary on the king's behalf to sign the articles of submission. He alternately threatened and cajoled her, and she knew her friends and sympathisers were coming under increasing pressure. Her long-time friend Lady Hussey had been sent to the Tower, and both Anthony Browne and Sir Francis Bryan were closely questioned about the degree and nature of support they believed there was for Mary. Suggestions of treason, actual or implicit, were all about her. Although pursuing her death was in nobody's interest at that stage, in the end nothing would do but her complete surrender, in terms of a comprehensive submission, most likely drafted for her by Cromwell, who had become her chosen intermediary.

Emotionally exhausted, concerned for the safety of her friends and apparently fearing an ever-increasing danger of death as a traitor, Mary finally succumbed to her father's demands in mid-1536. The final form of her submission is abject indeed, and a complete denial of all she and her mother had struggled against for so long. She submitted herself unreservedly to 'his highness and to all and singular laws and statutes of his realm', including all those which had destroyed her and her mother's legitimacy. It may well be that she found least difficulty in acknowledging 'the king's highness to be supreme head on earth under Christ of the Church of England'. Many conservative English Christians such as Stephen Gardiner, Edmund Bonner and Cuthbert Tunstall before her had found it possible to repudiate papal authority in a context where the central tenets and rituals of their Christianity remained intact. Given the stark choice between papal supremacy and obedience to their own king, they chose the latter.

Mary's submission may have been made easier since after the fall of Anne Boleyn and the retreat of the 'reform' party in religious policy, Henry had very publicly reaffirmed his commitment to the centrality of the mass in religious life. That was, for Mary, always a paramount important issue. Almost certainly much more painful for her was that she 'freely' acknowledged that the marriage 'between his majesty and my

mother the late Princess Dowager was by God's law and man's law inces-
tuous and unlawful'.[16] She had twisted and turned, trying to evade such
a total repudiation of everything her mother had fought for, but Henry
would allow her to evade none of his demands. He could, after all, hardly
afford to receive back into favour a daughter who had repeatedly and
treasonably refused to accept his laws.

At the time, Chapuys's version was that Mary had signed the final set
of articles without ever reading them, and had privately asked him to
obtain a papal dispensation for having done so. Mary may have behaved
like that; her acquiescence in the maligning of her mother's reputation
must have been painful, and she may well have clung, however briefly,
to a commitment to a papal supremacy which had done so much to
legitimate the resistance of both mother and daughter. No such papal
dispensation was ever forthcoming, and in the following years there is
remarkably little evidence that Mary felt a continuing need for it.
Rather, her reconciliation with her father seems increasingly to have
embraced her reconciliation as well with her father's church. After the
years of Mary's trial and rejection, the imminent reconciliation of father
and daughter was, by all the available indicators, mutually satisfactory.
But it is impossible to know just how much Mary finally violated her
conscience to achieve that outcome or, indeed, whether she believed she
had violated it at all, given the pressure under which she had been placed
and given her father's reiteration of much orthodox Catholic doctrine.

4

THE RESTORATION OF
LADY MARY, 1536–1547

MARY'S REHABILITATION

Some historians have suggested that in the years between her separation from her mother in late 1531 and her marriage with Philip II of Spain in 1554, Mary was starved of affection and, indeed, 'lonely and embittered'. While reliable information about her for that period is intermittent, known details of her life from mid-1536 to 1547 do not bear out that view. Any biographer of her faces the recurrent problem that much of the available evidence is primarily from observers with differing political agendas or from deductions based on the actions of her supporters. What is known is that following Mary's sufficiently abject submission to Henry at the age of 20, in 1536, close contact between father and daughter was resumed, and never again seriously threatened.

It was common knowledge at court that on 6 July, Mary rode from her house at Hunsdon 'secretly in the night' to join the king and Queen Jane, where as Wriothesley noted:

> the King spoke with his dear and well-beloved daughter Mary, which had not spoken with the King her father in five years before, and there she remained with the King til Friday at night, and then she rode to Hunsdon again secretly.

Although legally still a bastard, Mary was once again the king's elder and 'well-beloved' daughter. She received more, and more generous, presents of money from her father, a horse from Cromwell, and much attention from courtiers. By late 1536 her position was apparently that she was fully reconciled with her father, content with his alterations to the church, and on excellent terms with her father's new wife, the only woman to whom she gave precedence.

Mary was now attended by female companions of her choice, several of whom were to remain with her for the rest of her life, a testimony to her capacity to inspire affection. One of the best-known examples is that of Susan Clarencius. A widow when she joined Mary's household in 1536, she became after Mary's accession one of the ladies of her privy chamber and was with her as the queen lay dying. Mary was permitted to move freely between the court and other royal houses as she wished, except when her father required her presence at court – as he frequently did. Observers agreed that in appearance, dress, education and behaviour she was an ornament to the court. In the years that followed there are many signs that she delighted in the renewed affection of her father, a feeling which apparently survived the many occasions he was to use her as a marital bargaining chip in his diplomatic games, and the several times he attacked the more conservative of her friends.

MARY AND THE CHANGING ROYAL COURT

Henry now viewed both his earlier marriages as invalid. Accordingly, in mid-1536 by the second Act of Succession (28 Henry VIII, c. 7) Mary was, for the first time, explicitly barred from succeeding to the throne – as was Elizabeth – in favour of whatever heirs Queen Jane Seymour should provide. Mary's standing at court was not obviously affected by that statute; indeed, it was probably enhanced by the disappearance of two of her more plausible rivals for the throne. In July 1536 Henry's illegitimate son the Duke of Richmond died – a victim it was believed of a slow poison, the usual explanation for any royal death. Wriothesley went even further recording the remarkable rumour that his death was 'by the means of Queen Anne and her brother Lord Rochford'.[1]

In the same month the king's niece Lady Margaret Douglas and Lord Thomas Howard were imprisoned for becoming engaged without the king's permission – a treasonous act, since she was of royal blood. Howard died in the Tower the following year, and after his death a subdued Lady Margaret was set free. In 1544 Henry married her to Matthew Stuart, Earl of Lennox and a strong claimant to the Scottish throne, as part of a complicated Scottish project he had in hand. In the longer term it worked, since their son, Lord Darnley, became the second husband of Mary Queen of Scots and father of James VI of Scotland. In 1603 the Scottish James VI became James I of England, effecting that union of the two crowns for which the Tudors had so long schemed. But it seems unlikely Henry had quite such a long-term result in mind for his project.

Nor was the young Elizabeth then a challenge to Mary. The traditional presumption of bad relations between the king's daughters after Anne Boleyn's death owes more to later tradition than it does to contemporary evidence. In late 1536, for example, Mary reported to her father that her younger sister was 'such a child … as I doubt not but your Highness shall have cause to rejoice of in time coming'.[2] There are a number of instances of Mary's kindness to her much younger sister. The 17-year age difference between the two sisters meant that although officially theirs was still a joint household, practically they had separate ones. Elizabeth lived mostly in the country and pursued her studies, while Mary was more frequently at court. There was little reason for tension between them until after the accession of Edward VI, when they were both significantly older.

Mary's reconciliation with her father was undoubtedly made easier because with the fall of Anne Boleyn the religious reform movement, also known as the evangelical party, had lost one of it key supporters. The view that Mary was always a conservative Catholic, committed to all the old ways, especially to the centrality of papal authority, does not sit easily with the surviving evidence from this time. For Mary, celebration of mass was and always remained the central religious rite, but during his reign Henry VIII countenanced no significant challenge to the theology of that sacrament.

Her Erasmian humanist background, shaped by her parents' long-standing inclinations, meant that Mary had never shown much interest in most forms of popular religious expression, including pilgrimages and 'miraculous' images. Although both her parents, when younger, had undertaken pilgrimages to the famous shrine at Walsingham, Mary was apparently unmoved when the image of Our Lady of Walsingham was brought to London and burned. Her response is also unknown when the tomb of Thomas Becket was demolished on the grounds he had been declared a saint by the 'usurped authority' of the Pope. When she became queen, Mary did have Becket's tomb restored, but that was after her brother's reign, which had demonstrated to her just how dangerous to her religion royal supremacy over the church could be.

She was even less likely to be hostile to the 1538 requirement that the English Bible should be widely available. Rather it will be shown that, as Henry gradually modified the face of the official English religion in his later years, his elder daughter became an active participant in the process of making commentaries on the scriptures more available. In her own reign, she encouraged the preparation of another English Bible translation and, indeed, the use of the Henrician English Bible was never banned by her government. On the other hand, the 1539 Act of Six Articles (31 Henry VIII, c. 14) reaffirming such central Catholic doctrines as the 'real presence' in the mass, that celibacy of priests, and the 'expedience and necessity' of confession all confirmed Mary's own positions.

MARY AND CONSERVATIVE REACTION

Two of the better known features of the reign of Henry VIII are his six marriages and his dissolution of the monasteries of England. The second needs some discussion here. By the sixteenth century religious houses, monasteries, nunneries and priories had been an important part of western Christendom for almost a thousand years. As older orders lost their initial spiritual purposes, newer ones had appeared across many realms. The great monastic buildings of many religious orders were a familiar and often impressive sight in late medieval England, as elsewhere. They provided places apart from the distractions of the secular world where men or women could cultivate piety, pray for the wider community (then considered the most potent form of activity), foster scholarship, and offer hospitality and charity. Scattered across the English landscape, the religious houses had accumulated such considerable wealth in possessions and land that frequently, as one historian remarked, 'spiritual corporations had, over the centuries, become economic corporations.'[3]

Although the familiarity of monasteries ensured a great deal of popular support, there was nothing new about disbanding 'decaying' religious houses. Indeed Wolsey had done so in the 1520s, partly to fund a new university college, and Erasmus was only one of many increasingly sceptical about the merits attributed to enclosed religious houses. In the dissolutions of the 1530s, Thomas Cromwell, who had been in Wolsey's service in the 1520s, may have borrowed from his practices. Smaller and little-regarded foundations were dissolved first. Henry supported the dissolution of the monasteries in part because they provided bases of conservative resistance to his religious changes; furthermore the acquisition of their considerable land holdings offered him great economic resources. Among the most notable of the dissolved establishments was Katherine of Aragon's favourite, Syon, which many, including Wriothesley, saw as 'the most virtuous house of religion that was in England'.[4]

Another was Fountains Abbey in Yorkshire, founded in 1132, and by the sixteenth century the richest Cistercian house in England. Popular protests broke out in the north as the spreading closures of abbeys reinforced existing hostility to wider religious changes and more local resentments. The uprisings, which began in October 1536 in Lincolnshire and spread in the following months across most northern counties, culminated in the Pilgrimage of Grace. The rebels against the new religious policies proved collectively too numerous for the royal forces, headed by the Duke of Norfolk. He advised Henry that short-term compromise was necessary; in the longer term a judicious mixture of government guile, deception and betrayal defeated the rebels, whose leaders were taken captive and executed, as were an unknown number of lesser participants.

Even her very suspicious father was, however, satisfied that Mary had done nothing to encourage those protesters who, as well as calling for the restoration of monasteries and of papal supremacy, also called for the restoration of Mary to the status of legitimate daughter and heir to the throne. There is no indication that Mary showed any interest in such calls, even though some of those once closely associated with her household were implicated in the risings. She also behaved with complete filial propriety when she wrote to Charles V, perhaps at her father's behest, explaining her change of view about the legality of her mother's marriage and the status of the papal claim to supremacy. Her tone was such a contrast with her earlier messages appealing for his help that Charles needed considerable reassurance that the letter was indeed written by Mary. By March 1537, active resistance to Henry's religious innovations in England was defeated.

THE ARRIVAL OF HENRY'S MALE HEIR

An even more pleasing development for Henry in 1537 was the pregnancy of his new wife. There were celebrations for the queen's 'quickening of child' in May, and public prayers that the child should be a prince. On 12 October 1537, St Edward's Day, Jane Seymour gave birth to a healthy son. His arrival was grounds for a spectacular bout of public rejoicing, which included great religious processions, bonfires and feasting in the streets of London, and magnificent, ostentatiously delighted celebrations across the social spectrum. The tiny cause of this excitement was christened Edward three days later, with more emphasis on the splendour of the occasion. His godfathers were the Archbishop of Canterbury (Thomas Cranmer), the ubiquitous Duke of Norfolk and the Duke of Suffolk. Edward's only godmother was the Lady Mary, a relationship which was to become increasingly ironic as their religious beliefs drove them into considerable conflict. His other sister, the four-year-old Elizabeth, carried the special baptismal robe in the procession.

The day he was christened, Edward was proclaimed the king's sole heir and granted the titles of Prince of Wales, Duke of Cornwall and Earl of Chester. As befitted the undisputed heir to the throne, Edward had his own household from March 1538, and the lady mistress of his household was, once again, Margaret Bryan, who had held that position for the infants Mary and Elizabeth. Clearly, she gave satisfaction in that role to the king, although it probably helped that her husband, Sir Francis, had long been the king's close companion. She had care of that household until, at the age of six, Edward was, in his own words, moved from 'among the women', and transferred to the supervision of learned men.

The delight in a male heir was, apparently, not diminished by the unexpected death of Queen Jane 12 days after giving birth to her son. Childbirth was always hazardous, but for the first ten days she had seemed to be recovering well before a rapid decline set in. Jennifer Loach has suggested that the queen died *because* she was queen. That is, her rank and the importance of the occasion required she should be attended at childbirth by esteemed royal doctors, rather than by midwives who had much more practical experience. Female empirical knowledge was not enough for a queen, who required the services of 'book-learned' male advisers.[5] When Jane's funeral was conducted, on 12 November, Lady Mary was chief mourner with a considerable company of ladies and gentlewomen in attendance on her.

Mary never indicated any doubts about Edward's greater claim to be Henry's first heir, just as she never doubted the legitimacy of Henry's marriage to Jane Seymour. All this was despite the reservations of many conservative Catholics at home and abroad. Indeed, from 1536 on she appeared quite unmoved by Catholic arguments that Henry's third marriage, conducted beyond papal authority, was invalid. This provides further evidence that after her submission to her father, and for the rest of his life, she accepted his repudiation of papal supremacy. In that she joined such leading churchmen as Gardiner and Bonner, who accepted Henry's leadership in religious matters during his lifetime, but were alienated by subsequent Edwardian innovations.

MARY THE CAUTIOUS, OR MARY THE INSCRUTABLE?

Mary's importance at the court as the king's favoured daughter was secure after the birth of her brother, but she still had a delicate path to tread as her father's once dissident daughter, albeit now restored to his affection. As the northern risings had again demonstrated, she remained popular within the realm. It was usual for large crowds to greet her public appearances, as they had when she was putative Princess of Wales. Her potential influence within the realm had also been demonstrated by a proposal discussed between Chapuys and the Duke of Norfolk that the duke's son should marry Mary. Henry would never willingly have agreed to that increase of influence for the man already pre-eminent among his powerful subjects – and frequently out of favour – but the discussion suggests just how readily Mary was seen as a means of advancing the interests of others. Not just her cousin the Emperor Charles V, but all Catholics concerned to end Henry's schism with the Catholic Church saw her as a potential figurehead for their interests. Her popularity and standing was therefore, as she must have realised, a potential danger to her, given the continuing religious divisions within Henry's realm, and his own suspicious nature.

So Mary's high standing at her father's court never meant she was entirely secure, and 1538 was a particularly dangerous year for her. As Henry's most influential biographer, J. J. Scarisbrick, has shown, in 1538 when Henry fell seriously ill, two factions quickly emerged at court, one backing Edward and the other backing Mary. Each grouping was of sufficient strength for it to be likely a serious contest could have ensued.[6] In the event Henry recovered, but had received a forceful reminder of how uncertain the line of succession still was, not least because Catholics still committed to papal authority regarded Mary as Henry's only legitimate child, from his only legitimate marriage.

The anxiety this generated was only intensified by rumours during the summer of 1538 that Pope Paul III would finally excommunicate Henry, thereby rendering any who still subscribed to papal authority free to overthrow him. In the aftermath of uprisings of 1536 and 1537, successive members of Mary's earlier households and several good friends fell victim to Henry's suspicions. If she suffered for them, however, she suffered in silence. The victims included Lord John Hussey, once Mary's lord chamberlain; his wife had been Mary's good friend and companion, spending some time in the Tower for continuing to address Mary as a princess after Henry had declared she had no such status. Hussey had previously discussed with Chapuys the possibilities of foreign invasion on her behalf, and was implicated in the Pilgrimage of Grace. He was only one of the more notable of her associates who suffered the standard penalty for treason, of being hanged, drawn and quartered. Mary may or may not have been distressed for those men or the plight of their wives – no evidence has survived as to her responses. She may well have been a kindly person, but she had also become skilled in the art of prudent concealment. She had, after all, been trained since infancy in the art of royal inscrutability.

Even in the case of Henry's attacks on two families most closely associated with her own earliest years, the Poles and the Courtenays, there is no sign of Mary's own response to their fall until after she became queen in her own right. This may be the strongest indicator we now have of just how constrained Mary felt herself to be by her father's actions. In late 1538, uncertain of his support at home, and fearing a combined Catholic attack from abroad, Henry renewed his attacks on surviving Plantagenet descendants. The Poles were a major target. Readers will recall that Margaret of Salisbury, daughter of the Duke of Clarence and niece to Edward IV, and subsequently married off to a relative of Margaret Beaufort, had been a close companion to Katherine of Aragon before being made governess to her daughter. Margaret had three sons, of whom the third, Reginald Pole, had been such a promising scholar that his cousin King Henry had financed his studies at home and abroad, and granted Pole several benefices in the English church. In 1530 Pole had worked for support for the king's divorce in France before he returned to England, but soon started to show signs of unease over the king's Great Matter. Rather than explicitly oppose Henry's proposed divorce he had withdrawn, with Henry's permission, to Italy.

As Catholic resistance strengthened, dangerous suggestions were circulating that Pole might be a suitable future husband for Mary and a suitable King of England. There is no evidence that was ever *Pole's* aim, let alone Mary's. By 1536, however, he had written a strong attack on Henry's divorce, in a work he insisted was intended for only Henry's eyes. Recent legislation meant that any expression of opposition to the royal actions was now treasonous. Moreover, by early 1537 Pole was in Flanders, trying to build on the unrest of the Pilgrimage of Grace by winning foreign support for that movement from Francis I and/or Charles V. There was, therefore, no doubt that he was now a traitor to the king.

Pole's elder brother, Henry (Lord Montagu), on the other hand, was always an active supporter of the king, raising his men to support him during the Pilgrimage of Grace in 1536. Later, both Montagu and his mother wrote to Reginald reminding him of his duties to the king who had done so much for their family. Driven by anxieties about foreign intervention and by continuing uncertainty about ensuring an incontestable heir, Henry finally moved, seemingly, to eradicate all surviving descendants of the White Rose of York (which was, of course, also his mother's house). Reginald Pole was safely out of reach, but his brother Geoffrey was arrested and interrogated, in the Tower after the manner of the day, until, after two months, he 'remembered' critical comments by his mother and brother about some of Henry's decisions. Under the treason legislation, the fact that the comments were private and that no associated action was ever attempted did not prevent them from being treason. Lord Montagu was soon in prison and his mother detained.

Still under pressure, Geoffrey Pole also implicated the Marquess and Marchioness of Exeter, who were also both soon in the Tower. Henry

Courtenay, the Marquis of Exeter, was the grandson of a daughter of Edward IV. After his death, it was claimed that his dynastic ambitions had included plotting not only to marry his son to Mary, but also to destroy young prince Edward. Montagu and Exeter were both tried and beheaded within a month of their detentions. Some argue that Henry VIII was not waging a war against Plantagenet descendants, but dealing with actual and potential traitors. What this exoneration could not explain, however, is why the Marchioness of Exeter and her young son, Edward Courtenay, were held in the Tower until Mary was able to release them in 1553, let alone why Lord Montagu's small son and sole heir disappeared into the Tower as his father was taken, and was never heard of again. It is even more puzzling why the Countess of Salisbury, now well into her seventh decade, had to die. Henry may well have threatened to wipe out the entire brood, but she was well past child-bearing age. It proved impossible to find evidence against her, but she was held prisoner until renewed activity by the more conservative forces led to her being found guilty by an act of attainder (for which no evidence needed to be supplied or tested) in 1539. She was executed in 1541.

The ways in which Mary tried to compensate these families for their trials after she became queen will be discussed in another chapter. There is some evidence that Mary herself was also under careful surveillance during these years, by his advisers even if not by her father. In May 1538 Mary acknowledged a warning from Cromwell against 'the lodging of strangers' (i.e. suspect visitors) at Hunsdon, promising even more caution on her part, and asking Cromwell to continue guiding her in the right path and 'eschewing the contrary'.[7] Indeed, she may have spent much of the year at Hunsdon, and her correspondence with Cromwell shows a keen awareness of the benefits of maintaining good relations with her father's chief counsellor. Given that those targeted were among her closest friends, had been supporters of her mother's interests and shared very similar religious views, her caution is understandable. She had long been surrounded by warnings of the possible fate of those who opposed – or were thought to oppose – Henry's political will. There were further warnings in the fate of two other men in 1540: her tutor for some eight years, Dr Richard Featherstone, who was first sent to the Tower in 1534 for refusing to subscribe to the oath of succession (the one which named Elizabeth – by 1540 firmly excluded from succession – as the one true heir) and Dr Thomas Abel, who had written in defence of Katherine of Aragon as well as refusing the same oath. Featherstone had remained a confidante of Mary's, even after he had been sent to the Tower. In a bizarre example of the complexities of Henry's religious changes, both were executed in 1540 with another priest, while on the same day three 'Protestant' heretics were also punished. As one foreign observer remarked, it seemed that in England people who supported the papacy were hanged, and those who opposed it were burned.

Throughout all these troubles, Mary publicly remained Henry's trophy daughter, well regarded at home and abroad; her standing was what gave Henry such leverage with her name in marriage negotiations. How much Mary was involved in any of these discussions is unclear. One of her possible suitors, Philip of Bavaria, apparently took his prospects seriously, but the attitude of the king and Cromwell is less clear. Despite her initial hesitations because Philip was a Lutheran, Mary was quick to assure both Cromwell and her father that of course she would always be a ' most humble and obedient daughter'. In late 1539, the suitor arrived in England to offer the king his military service and Mary his hand in marriage. The couple even met in late December and talked together in German through an interpreter, and in Latin directly. After the meeting, Philip declared his hope of persuading Henry to agree to their marriage. Although he visited her three times in all, Henry finally decided against losing his favourite bargaining chip, and Philip returned to Germany, where in 1559 he became Elector, Count Palatine of the Rhine. More immediately, Henry returned to his more usual role of seeking to play Hapsburg and French interests off against each other over the following years, using Mary still as a useful tool. We know nothing of Mary's own attitude to any of her wooers.

Once Henry wished to re-enter the marriage market himself, after the death of Jane Seymour, he offered himself, his elder daughter and sometimes his two other much younger children, as players in diplomatic games across much of Europe. In late 1537, he contemplated marriage with Mary of Guise (who married James V of Scotland) and then the recently widowed Christina of Denmark, niece of Charles V. (Holbein's portrait of her, now in the National Gallery in London, is the enduring remnant of those negotiations, and was to provide a model for Eworth's portrait of Mary, shown on the cover of this book.) Inevitably, the fact that two of his three children were illegitimate, and the disputes about which was the legitimate child, were often barriers.

The French countered another Spanish proposal, which had included marrying Mary to a Portuguese prince, with an offer of the younger son of Francis I for Mary, and a sister of Mary of Guise for Henry. Soon after, Henry asked Holbein to make portraits of five French women of marriageable age, but Mary seems to have been dropped from those negotiations. Ultimately none of Henry's manoeuvres succeeded in his primary aim of forestalling an alliance between Francis I and Charles V against the schismatic Henry. The continuing destruction of the monasteries and royal appropriation of their possessions, the destruction of shrines, relics and images all only increased Catholic unease about Henry, and provided the background to Reginald Pole's 1538 papal-backed campaign to rally Catholic powers against him.

THE APPARENT TRANQUILLITY OF THE UNMARRIED PRINCESS

Henry's need for a new ally led to negotiations with the Duke of Cleves, whose religious stance was similar to his own, neither papal Catholic nor Lutheran. He was to marry the duke's sister, and Mary to marry perhaps the Duke of Cleves, or the Duke of Bavaria. Holbein was despatched once more, this time to produce a likeness of Anne of Cleves, and another of her sister Amelia, but Henry quickly settled on Anne as his preferred bride. On the new queen's arrival in England, Mary, now aged 23 to Anne's 24, headed the ladies who welcomed her. When, however, Henry came face to face with the first bride he had not personally courted, he was dismayed and disappointed, soon declaring himself unable to consummate the marriage. Although some contemporaries found her poorly educated, Anne was widely said to be handsome, even unusually so, and the most usual description of her manner was that she was 'good and gentle'. Henry never really tried to find out much about her, marrying her in January 1540, but only reluctantly and after he had been advised that there was no way to avoid it. Anne appears to have played her public part as Henry's wife well, but he had little interest in her, and soon developed a much more enthusiastic interest in a young woman placed in court as a lady in waiting, one Catherine Howard, who, like Anne Boleyn, was a niece of the Duke of Norfolk.

In June Anne of Cleves was ordered from court. She knew enough of the fate of his previous wives to be very worried. Perhaps because of that 'good and gentle nature' which Henry had previously seemed to value so little, Anne was treated quite differently. In July her marriage was annulled, but she found herself with the new status of 'sister' to the king, sometimes invited to court and ranking very highly (though lower than a royal wife). Wriothesley's comments are indicative of a wider view, that it:

> was great pity that so good a lady as she is should so soon [have] lost her great joy; nevertheless the King has given her four thousand pounds [a] year with four goodly manors in England to keep her estate during her life.[8]

Some even said she was more popular than Katherine of Aragon had been. The traditions of her as crude in manner, the 'mare of Flanders', belong to a much later period and were not part of the contemporary attitudes. In her short period as queen, she had already struck up a friendship with Mary Tudor which endured for the rest of Anne's life. It was not just her newly acquired status as the king's sister which led to being treated with respect and affection; her personality seems to have made her agreeable to a remarkably diverse group of people. This left Mary on excellent terms with the king's sister, who visited the royal court on several occasions, but her own marriage prospects had vanished as Henry lost interest in further foreign marital adventures for himself.

Catherine Howard was only 19 years old and a stark contrast with Anne of Cleves in that she was already sexually experienced. To Henry, however, she was a strikingly attractive and innocent girl, a judgement in which he was much encouraged by the extended Howard affinity headed by the Duke of Norfolk. The king married her in August 1540, showering rich jewels and other presents on his new bride. A shared interest in jewellery, dress and dancing was not enough, however, to establish good relations between the king's elder daughter and his new wife. Early in her reign, Catherine complained that Mary did not treat her with the respect she had shown to Henry's previous wives. The new queen was sufficiently resentful to order two of Mary's attendants dismissed from court. That tension was resolved, but the 19-year-old wife and the 24-year-old daughter had little in common, not least because even without any comparison to Mary's extensive schooling, Catherine was remarkably uneducated.

In January 1541 Anne of Cleves paid her first visit as the king's sister to the court, then at Hampton Court. One wonders what precisely was in the minds of the various participants as the discarded queen curtsied low to the new queen, previously in service to her. But the outward demeanour of all, as reported by Chapuys was impeccable, as Henry, his current wife and his previous wife dined publicly together in perfect harmony. It is entirely likely that Mary also behaved with complete propriety, for she was fond of Anne and would not have wished to offend her father. It is, however, surely tempting to speculate on what thoughts Mary may have allowed herself on that occasion. Regrettably we again have no evidence from that particularly discreet lady on which to base such speculation.

Henry's delight in his fifth wife continued as in the summer of 1541 they made a visit to the north, which Henry had first promised in the aftermath of the 1536 uprisings. He did, however, require that his popular elder daughter should also accompany them to the conservative north, much as he also expected her to be at court for most of Queen Catherine Howard's reign. At one level, the progress provided a magnificent narrative of sumptuous royal display, with carefully planned displays of royal benevolence towards those northern subjects who had remained loyal, while remorseful submissions were offered by those who had not. At Lincoln, the king wore cloth of gold, the queen cloth of silver, while 80 archers with strung bows went before them, and the greatest dignitaries of the realm were all in close attendance, as well as the ladies and gentlemen of the court. For their part, the citizens at all levels elaborately enacted their delight at the royal presence, their total loyalty to the monarchy and their anxiety to atone for their disloyalty in ever consenting to participate in the 1536 uprisings.

Meanwhile, the most secret knowledge at court was that the king's wife had resumed a clandestine relationship with one Thomas Culpepper. Back at Hampton Court in late October, Henry was content as ever with his wife. Not one of his courtiers dared tell him face to face about his wife's infidelity; instead Cranmer sent Henry a letter setting out the details of Catherine's reckless behaviour before and during her marriage. The king was slow to accept the implications of the report, but as more evidence and confessions were accumulated, he had little choice. After the queen was arrested, Mary, who in accordance with her father's wishes had been spending most of her time at court, was escorted by Sir John

Dudley (later to play a much more hostile part in her life as the Duke of Northumberland) to join the household of the young prince; she was to be away from court for much of the following year. Queen Catherine Howard was taken to the Tower in February 1542, and executed three days later. Her husband was reportedly depressed and morose for some months afterwards. There are no records of Mary's response to the disastrous end to that marriage. It might be understandable if she felt at least relief at Catherine's end, but if so, she was careful not to display it.

THE FINAL YEARS AS THE KING'S ELDER DAUGHTER

In December 1542, however, Mary returned to her father's court, and was once again made much of by him, as she was for the rest of his life. This is of some historical interest because some reports of her ill health also recurred throughout this period. It has been suggested that there was a markedly psychosomatic dimension to her illnesses from the 1530s onwards, a suggestion that is taken to confirm the premise that after her mother's death Mary was a 'lonely and embittered woman'. This however is undermined by more reports of poor health in the final years of her father's life when her standing was high. One indicator of her improved status was the number of children to whom she stood godparent. Since 1537 she had been in demand for infants of relatively lower social status. Since her restoration to her father's court, the standing of her godchildren went much further across the social spectrum – from Prince Edward to Henry, the infant son of Sir Thomas Wriothesley, Lord Chancellor of England and Knight of the Garter. (He was not the chronicler often quoted here, but his cousin.) The list of those to whom she was invited to be godmother continued to grow in subsequent years. From 1542 her improved standing meant she was once again the subject of diplomatic marital overtures, although her father finally rejected them all.

For a brief time, even, because of the frequency of her father's visits to her quarters, Mary was sufficiently well informed about political events to be a helpful adviser to the Spanish ambassador. There were many comments that Henry was 'calling at the princess's apartment two or three times a day'[9] probably because of the presence there of Lady Latimer, better known now as Katherine Parr. Having joined Mary's household, by February 1543 she was close to Mary and entrusted with such responsibilities as ordering clothes for her. In March, with Lady Latimer's ailing elderly husband dead, Mary was permitted to invite Anne of Cleves to court. Such visits had rarely been allowed after the death of Catherine Howard for fear of starting rumours that Henry was about to reinstate his previous wife. Now, Anne's invitation was another sign that, after Lord Latimer's death, Henry's revived marital hope were now firmly focussed on his widow.

Some four years older than Princess Mary, Katherine was the elder daughter of Thomas and Maud Parr. Both parents had served Henry and Katherine of Aragon in the halcyon early days of their reign, before Thomas died in 1517. Katherine of Aragon may even have been god-mother to her friend's first daughter. Certainly, when Maud Parr died in 1531 she left to her elder daughter furnishings and jewellery given to her by Henry's first queen. Katherine received a conventional education for a family of such standing; she was well instructed in proper comport-ment and such social essentials as French from an early age, but she probably received little classical instruction. Although there were Latin texts in Katherine's early schoolroom, however, and although the uncle who advised on her education was Cuthbert Tunstall (whom Reginald Pole once described as the most learned man in England), Katherine had not been well schooled in the classics when she came to court.

Her generation continued the family tradition of seeking careers at court. Both her brother and younger sister had already begun promising court careers before Katherine came to Henry's attention. Her sister Anne Parr was Chief Gentlewoman to successively Anne of Cleves and Catherine Howard, and married William Herbert, who was to become the first Earl of Pembroke. Her brother's rise came rather more slowly, but accelerated in Edward's reign, to decline again in Mary's. As she and Mary became close friends, as their two mothers had also been, it may have been Mary who first inculcated a serious interest in classical learn-ing in Katherine, but they already shared interests in music, dancing, fashion, jewellery and the very royal pursuit of hunting.

When Henry married Katherine Parr in July 1543, both his daugh-ters and his niece Lady Margaret Douglas attended the bride. But soon afterwards, for reasons not yet known, Elizabeth was forbidden court. In a letter she wrote to Katherine in July 1544 she lamented 'inimical for-tune' which had kept her from Katherine's company for a year, and asked for the queen's intercession with the king on her behalf since 'hitherto I have not dared to write to him'.[10] Elizabeth was back at court during the following September when Henry was abroad and Katherine was regent-general, but she had returned to Ashridge at the end of the year, whence she sent Katherine a New Year's present of her translation of *The Mirror of Glass of a Sinful Soul*. There is, clearly, little in the surviving records to endorse the view that in the final years of Henry's life, Elizabeth had become his preferred daughter. It is, however, the case that, not yet 12 years old, Elizabeth was still expected to spend much time with her schoolbooks in a suitable country house.

Whatever the cause of Henry's displeasure with Elizabeth, both daughters were finally and explicitly restored to the royal line of succession in 1544 (*35 Henry c. 1*) as Henry prepared for his last active military campaign in France. The illegitimacy of both daughters was disregarded, and they were named as heirs after Edward in birth order: an ironic comment, one might think, on all that energy which had been expended on avowing and disavowing the inheritance of each of his daughters in past years – to say nothing of the price others had paid for not unreservedly following the shifts and changes in Henry's decisions about his succession. That Mary had precedence over Elizabeth sparked no recorded adverse comment, and only reaffirmed what had long been the dominant view of the proper order of things.

Her explicit restoration to the line of succession may have been one reason why, in 1545, Charles V himself briefly considered marrying her, some 20 years after their first betrothal. As Chapuys reported, in a break from the customary purely political tenor of such discussions, the Emperor was then more lusty than he had been for some time, and his (Chapuys') description of the princess 'made the Emperor's mouth water'.[11] As so many others had concluded, however, Charles finally decided that Henry was too untrustworthy to have as a father-in-law, whatever Mary's reported attractions.

MARY, THE 'MOST WITTY' WOMAN OF THE REALM

During the final years of her father's reign, Mary received ever more recognition for 'the fame of her virtue and learning', as Mary of Portugal expressed it in November 1546. The previous year, in November 1545, the Emperor's ambassador in England reported that, as he and Mary were waiting as godparents for the christening of a daughter of John Dudley, now Lord Lisle and Henry's Lord Admiral, he had had a conversation with Mary 'in several languages which she speaks well'.[12] Whatever the differences in the religious directions they took after his death, in the final years of Henry's reign, as the young Elizabeth matured, all three royal women demonstrated an educated interest in classical texts, religious translations and religious instruction, within the defined Henrician doctrinal boundaries. The circles surrounding the queen included such humanist luminaries as Anthony Cooke, which may well explain how Mary first met his daughter Anne, who, as Anne Bacon, was to become a member of her royal household.

Exactly how much Mary and Elizabeth shared in those years is not clear, but both, educated in the humanist traditions, found common ground with Katherine on spiritual matters. One of the less considered consequences of this shared interest followed from Katherine's role in having some of Erasmus' *Paraphrases upon the New Testament* translated into English. The translation of the chosen sections, the four gospels and *Acts of the Apostles,* was under way by late 1545, and the translators she chose included Mary. Mary's work on the *Gospel According to John* was, however, reported to be much delayed by yet another bout of ill health, which led to her chaplain Francis Mallet being asked to complete the work.

We cannot now know just how much Mary had completed before her illness, but it was enough to allow Katherine, in a letter full of her affection for her, to ask Mary whether she wished it 'to go forth to the world (most auspiciously) under your name, or as the production of an unknown writer'. The latter option, Katherine thought, 'would do a real injury [to the work] ... since you have undertaken so much labour' and 'all the world' knew how much work she had put into it.[13] The outcome was that after the effusive dedication to Katherine, variations of which the editor Nicholas Udall placed before each of the five books, he included before John's Gospel an equally striking lengthy tribute to 'the most noble, the most virtuous, the most witty, and the most studious Lady Mary's grace'. Like most dedications that was markedly uncritical, but like any such comment on a contemporary, it needed to have some plausibility to have any effect. Having praised her many splendid attributes and the great pains she had taken in her translation, he also nominated

Mary as a 'peerless flower of virginity', expatiating on the rewards of such self-denial in the service of 'her father's most beloved subjects'.[14] The terms he used interestingly anticipate those in which Elizabeth was to be praised in the 1580s and 1590s for her virginity.

What Udall could not know was how Mary then lamented just that virginity fearing that, while her father lived, with any marriage proposal always postponed in the hope of another offer even more beneficial to her his plans, she would remain 'only the Lady Mary, and the most unhappy lady in Christendom'.[15] When she thought about her marriage prospects Mary may well have been unhappy, but she seems to have had little else about which to be miserable in her father's final years. She was probably unconcerned by her brother's censorious tone in a Latin exercise written for Queen Katherine in 1546. In it, the 8-year-old prince deplored Mary's fondness for 'foreign dances and merriment, which [he pronounced] do not become a most Christian princess'.

Priggish at best, this may also have been hypocritical since, as a recent biographer remarks, the prince was at the same time showing considerable enjoyment of court life himself.[16] But a tutor may have set the exercise, and the prince's attitude to his elder sister was hardly crucial in 1547. Elsewhere she was recognised and appreciated as an unusually well educated woman, with every accomplishment which could make her an ornament to her father's court, and she apparently had the happy knack of winning and retaining many friends – always providing that political interests did not come between them. What more could a dutiful Tudor royal princess want than that?

5

MARY IN THE REIGN OF
EDWARD VI, 1547–1553

REGIME CHANGE IN MID-TUDOR ENGLAND

Mary was still living in the queen's household when her father died on
27 January 1547. She, like Katherine Parr, had been prevented from
seeing the king in the last month of his life. Indeed, Henry's death was
so much a political rather than a family event that for three days neither
woman knew he had died. Henry's executors used those three days of
secrecy to refashion the king's will, and settle the new arrangements.
They made significant changes, but just how many things not in the
original will were 'remembered' as the dying king's verbal instructions
by the men now in power is uncertain. Katherine Parr's most recent
biographer has even suggested that the queen expected to become
Edward's regent, but no indication of any such plan by Henry has
survived.

Henry's will had named 16 members of Prince Edward's Privy
Council, with shared full authority to govern the young king in all
public and private matters. As one indicator of their authority until
Edward came of age, the council also had authority over the marriage of
either of Henry's daughters. In the light of subsequent events, it is significant that the Council Henry nominated included men with opinions
across the religious spectrum, from reformist (evangelical) to those who

clung to the Henrician church settlement (conservative). The latter included Sir Anthony Browne, Henry's Master of the Horse, a man who frequently demonstrated sympathy with Mary. Arrested and examined at the time Mary defied her father in 1536, and later restored to Henry's favour, he remained a member of Somerset's Council until his death in May 1548. Henry had, however, refused to include Gardiner, Bishop of Winchester, among his nominees on the grounds that his personality was too difficult.

Within days of Henry's death, however, Edward's uncle Edward Seymour, Earl of Hertford and now Duke of Somerset, emerged as Lord Protector, with much more authority than other councillors. It has been suggested that such concentration of power was an entirely rational move in such a decentralised society, but at the time others within and beyond the original 16 needed considerable persuasion. For example, Henry's Lord Chancellor Thomas Wriothesley, Earl of Southampton (and cousin to the chronicler Wriothesley), was forced from the Privy Council for resisting Edward Seymour's elevation. Since he was one of the more conservative members, his removal also affected the balance of power in the new council. Somerset's supporters acquired considerable amounts of land and prestige in those early days. John Dudley, Viscount Lisle, emerged from the changes gratifyingly enriched and now Earl of Warwick. Thomas Seymour, younger brother of Edward and now Lord Seymour of Sudeley, was less satisfied, arguing that as uncle to Edward, he should have more authority over the young prince. Denied that, he was given a place on the Council, from which the more conservative members were being forced.

A quite different beneficiary of Henry's death was the Duke of Norfolk, saved by Henry's death the day before he was to be executed. He remained, however, a prisoner in the Tower throughout the reign of Edward VI, perhaps because he was another 'conservative', perhaps because his influence were still feared, and certainly because the Council had other uses for his considerable estates. These were redistributed away from him in the new regime, and much of his personal clothing – including not only his ducal parliamentary robes and Garter regalia, but also gowns, coats, doublets and hose – were transferred to the new Duke of Somerset.

During these early weeks, Van der Veldt, now the Imperial ambassador in England and therefore seen as a protector of Mary's interests, complained that 'Madam Mary' was being kept ignorant of developing events. Once Edward's council was rearranged, however, the new regime was generous in its dealings with the new heir apparent. Such generosity was probably deemed necessary because Mary not only had considerable popular support but, more worrying for the new regime, she was regarded by Catholic powers abroad – and particularly in the Hapsburg lands – as the true heir to the English throne, since she was the one child of Henry's only marriage to have papal approval. Both Charles V and his sister, Mary of Hungary, regent of the Netherlands, hesitated before acknowledging Edward, waiting for a sign from Mary that she would make her bid for the crown. Later, there were even rumours of a proposed joint Hapsburg/French alliance to install her on the English throne. But Mary never hesitated to accept her brother as the next true monarch, nor gave any sign of appealing to papal authority. Nevertheless, the men now in power were always acutely aware that Charles V, the greatest power in Europe, regarded his cousin as being under his particular protection.

In his will, Henry had treated Mary and Elizabeth equally, leaving each £3,000 in 'money plate jewels and household stuff' as long as they remained unmarried. (If either married with council approval, she might receive another £10,000 in the same form.) But the combined cost of those grants for the late king's daughters, combined with the many grants it was 'remembered' the late king had planned for the men now in Edward's Council, were prohibitive. If fulfilled, they would leave the realm, as one councillor put it, 'unfurnished of money for defence of his Majesty, his realms and subjects'. Partly to avoid this problem, the councillors rewarded themselves their 'remembered' bequests not in money but in land. That had the added advantage of ensuring them the landed estates appropriate to their newly acquired titles. Having granted themselves land instead of money they could hardly do otherwise for the late king's daughters.

That was particularly true of Mary, who was thought likely to know the true terms of the will. She denied any such knowledge to the Imperial ambassador, but she may have been protecting her own interests. Whatever the reason, Mary acquired land holdings worth some £3,820 per annum, rather more than the Henry's will had stipulated, whereas Elizabeth received, belatedly, land worth just the £3,000 intended. The Council supplemented these resources for both princesses with loans of rich furnishings from the royal storehouses. Mary came out well ahead of Elizabeth, in terms of visible status as of estates. One example is that Mary acquired two cloths of estate, a crucial part of a royal setting, but Elizabeth received none, and Mary was given a canopy, to be hung over a bed or a throne. That was made of sumptuous materials – cloth of gold tissue, black velvet, and purple and yellow silk. Even more striking was the letter M embroidered on it, with a crown, probably for some uniden- tified royal forebear, but now a visible symbol of Mary's high royal standing as heir apparent to Edward.[1] She would have sat under this canopy when receiving important visitors – and throughout Edward's reign, there were many who wished to visit her for her status as heir apparent, or as known sympathiser with more conservative religious practices. Many families sought to place their children, particularly daughters, in her household. The canopy was a visible reminder of the potential advantages of doing so.

The consequence was that in 1547, and against her father's stated intentions, Mary became mistress of several of the more impressive homes in England, including Hunsdon. She had lived there in the 1530s; more recently it had been extensively refurbished for Prince Edward. She also acquired Newhall – also called Beaulieu – in Essex, a house capable of accommodating the entire court. Her third great possession came from the estates of the disgraced third Duke of Norfolk. He had built at Kenninghall a house described as 'a lavish palace, faced with ornamental brickwork and adorned with Turkish carpets and rich tapestries ... intended to rival Wolsey's Hampton Court and York Place'.[2] In all, Mary was granted some 32 principal manors, and a number of minor ones, most of which were concentrated in or near East Anglia. Those estates were further enhanced by later transactions, the most significant of which led to her acquisition of Framlingham in early 1553.

Once the residence of her half-brother Henry Fitzroy, the illegitimate Duke of Richmond, Framlingham was a well-fortified castle, which Mary received as part of a late exchange of properties with the king. Behind the exchange may have been a plan to move Mary further from the coast – and therefore from foreign aid – but Framlingham was to be the stronghold where she assembled the troops to back her claim to the throne of England. Given her later reputation as a Catholic reactionary, it may be significant that she also accepted several properties that had once belonged to the church, most notably the priory of St John of

Jerusalem, which became her main London residence. Some she retained for the rest of her life.

From her estates Mary received an income which rivalled that of the very wealthiest peers in the land, and indeed, Edward's Council may have intended to win her support by establishing Mary as a significant magnate. That her lands were almost entirely based in East Anglia and the Home Counties, and therefore relatively close to London, may have been meant to ensure that a discreet oversight of her activities could be maintained. But Edward's councillors, in so enriching her (or buying her acquiescence in their own aggrandisement) had also given her the resources which enabled her to live more independently than ever her father had intended. Somerset may well have congratulated himself that the king's elder daughter, a submissive and acquiescent female, had been gratifyingly sidelined. He may, furthermore, have felt more comfortable in this since she and his wife were good friends, as indicated by a letter Mary wrote to the duchess in April 1547, addressing her as 'My good Gossip', reminding her of the time when she was a member of Katherine of Aragon's household, asking for help for two of her mother's old servants, and signing herself 'Your loving friend during my life'.[3] There was real friendship there, and more immediately, other royal women were to give Somerset and the Council more to worry about.

THE LATE KING'S WOMENFOLK DIVIDED

Mary remained with Queen Katherine, in seclusion until her late husband's funeral, so she may have accompanied the dowager queen to Henry's magnificent burial and requiem mass in the chapel at Windsor. By April, however, Mary moved her new household to her newly acquired properties – St John's, then Newhall and later Kenninghall, to inspect her new estates. A marked coolness had developed between the two pre-eminent royal women, caused by Katherine's readiness to consider remarriage long before the customary mourning period of two years. Her suitor was Thomas, now Lord Seymour of Sudeley, Within days of Henry's death, and presumably unknown to Katherine, he discussed marrying Mary – he was told she would never agree – or Elizabeth – to which he was told the Council would never agree. Elizabeth had already and very properly snubbed a possible overture, on 27 February, asserting that she was too young and the proposal too soon. He had perhaps also debated marrying Anne of Cleves, before he resumed his courtship of Katherine.

Years before, Seymour had wooed Katherine with every expectation of success until Henry had declared his interest, when she had little choice but to marry the king. Her behaviour as Henry's queen had been irreproachable, but she always retained considerable affection for Seymour. They were secretly married before the end of May, and the marriage remained secret while Seymour sought approval for it. When he approached the young king, Edward first nominated Anne of Cleves as a bride, before suggesting that Seymour should marry his sister Mary, 'to turn her opinions'.[4] Edward, aged 9, was a committed supporter of evangelical reform – and, apparently already dissented from his father's religion. Finally persuaded that Katherine was an appropriate bride for Seymour, Edward was understandably resentful when he found that he had been tricked into sanctioning the wedding months after it had taken place.

When Seymour first asked Mary to support his courtship of Katherine, she refused any involvement. Once the marriage was public knowledge, she wrote to Elizabeth suggesting a joint response. Elizabeth agreed that the memory of their father had indeed been shamefully dishonoured. Nevertheless, to avoid seeming ungrateful for Katherine's past kindnesses, she wrote, she would take no action. Mary, she added, being older, might have more freedom of action.[5] Indeed, Elizabeth lived in the new Seymour household for many months, where her apparent slight to the memory of her father was followed within a year by scandal linking her improperly with Seymour. There were reports of extraordinary romping between Seymour and the girl, that Katherine had come upon Elizabeth in Seymour's arms, that Katherine herself asked Elizabeth to leave her household.

Whatever the truth of those rumours, Elizabeth did leave the household in May, first for the household of the Dennys at Cheshunt – Sir Anthony Denny had been a close confidante of her father – and then to establish her own household at Hatfield. But her move did not forestall the rumours, and common gossip soon had it that she was pregnant by Seymour. There was a Privy Council investigation of her behaviour, members of Elizabeth's household were briefly held in the Tower, and ambassadorial reports gleefully reporting the scandalous doings of Anne

Boleyn's daughter. Those rumours of Elizabeth's behaviour after her father's death may well have been the origin of Mary's enduring mistrust of her sister, since a spotless reputation was a prerequisite for any female claim to virtue. That is, mistrust of her younger sister may have begun well before their religious differences became obvious.

Mary found it hard to deny her years of close friendship with Katherine, especially when she knew that her 36-year-old friend was facing her first pregnancy. In August 1548, she wrote to Katherine, hoping to 'hear good success of your Grace's great belly'.[6] Katherine gave birth to her daughter at the end of August and named her Mary, but died some six days later, another victim of the sixteenth-century perils of childbirth. The chief mourner at Katherine's funeral was neither of her stepdaughters, but their cousin Lady Jane Grey, granddaughter of Henry's younger sister Mary and, by Henry's will, third in line to the throne. She had been in Seymour's care in 1547, and there were rumours that she was intended – at least by him – as Edward's future bride. Jane returned to Seymour's household after his wife's death, but he apparently grew impatient of achieving control of King Edward through her. He increased his efforts at more direct influence over the king, by presents and flattery, and began discussions with other discontented magnates, gathering weapons and fortifying his castle. Unsurprisingly, he was arrested, found guilty of treason, and beheaded. On his death, letters were found which he had written to both Mary and Elizabeth, urging them to resist his brother, Somerset. Obviously a difficult man but capable of considerable charm, his memory survives among some historical fiction writers as Elizabeth's one real love. His history certainly illustrates just some of the perils for any royal woman then seeking a trustworthy spouse.

By the time of Seymour's death in March 1549, the two sisters were in their separate households, undoubtedly enjoying the unexpected degree of independence which Somerset and the Council had made available to them. Very few letters between Elizabeth and Mary have survived from the period, but one strongly suggests that Mary was the more frequent correspondent. As Mary fell ever further from favour with the ruling group, Elizabeth spent more time at her brother's court, carefully remodelling herself as a demure Protestant princess, dressing with more restraint, wearing little jewellery and conforming to all the new religious requirements.

For much of Edward's reign Mary also led an outwardly pleasant life, moving between her houses, appearing at court sometimes. There are indications that Edward had been very fond of his elder sister, but his affection must have been strained as he became personally involved in trying to enforce her conformity to the new religious laws. Much of the information about her in these years comes from the reports of Van der Veldt back to Charles V and Mary of Hungary, itself a mark of how little interest she was to Englishmen active around the Edwardian court. But she had many good female friends, including the Duchess of Somerset. With them, increasing difference in religious opinion seems not to have been a significant barrier to enduring and close friendship.

Mary had all the resources necessary to maintain a life of almost royal splendour in residences that provided a suitably magnificent setting for the heir apparent. In the ambassador's accounts, there are several reports of Mary's illnesses, including one diagnosed as 'melancholy'. Some, however, were explicitly political in origin, ill health being a plea she often used to avoid going to court when she anticipated yet another confrontation over her religious practices. On her own estates, between which she could move freely, she was in an excellent position to take the long walks she enjoyed, to hunt (always a favourite pursuit), to pursue her considerable musical talents, to gamble at cards, to add to her collection of paintings, to maintain the exchange of gifts which marked both friendship and the seeking of patronage. But she was seldom unreservedly free to enjoy those opportunities, since from early in Edward's reign she was confronted by the prospect and then the reality of religious changes she could never accept.

INCREASING RELIGIOUS DIFFERENCES

Mary and Katherine may have been observers at the coronation of Edward in February 1547, but nothing confirming that has survived. So it is uncertain whether Mary heard Archbishop Cranmer calling upon Edward as the new young Josiah to ensure all 'idolatry [was] destroyed ... and images removed'. That signalled a renewed attack on religious images as the first moves to true religion; the Lady Chapel of Ely Cathedral, 'purified' by Edwardian enthusiasts, offers a striking example of how comprehensively the call to destroy all images could be interpreted.

Rather less contentious was Cranmer's reminder on the same occasion that even without any church rites, let alone approval from 'the bishop of Rome', a king 'is yet a perfect monarch ... and God's anointed'.[7]

Edward's coronation was the first formally to deny papal authority. That change was seldom explicitly challenged, and never by Mary in Edward's reign, but it was another reminder of the break with the past. Like earlier kings, Henry VII had made much of traditional papal authority to endorse his contested monarchy after 1485. Similarly Henry VIII had been crowned with papal sanction, and married to Katherine of Aragon after a papal dispensation had been granted. But by 1536 the 'pretended power and usurped authority of the bishop of Rome, by some called the Pope' had been totally abolished in Henry's realms (28 Henry VIII, c. 10), so Cranmer's point was hardly innovative.

But from the coronation onwards, other religious changes were signalled. In late July 1547, new church Injunctions was issued together with a *Book of Homilies*. The *Homilies* were to be read in place of a sermon or where there was no qualified preacher, and conservatives were quick to notice that they introduced several changes in doctrine. The injunctions also required that the (still unpublished) translation of Erasmus's *Paraphrases* should be placed in every church, which coincidentally meant that members of every parish could also read Udall's editorial praise for 'the most noble, the most virtuous, the most witty, and the most studious Lady Mary's grace' quoted in the previous chapter. There was more: 'What' he also asked in his dedication to her:

> could be a more manifest argument of minding the public benefit of her country, what could be a more evident proof of her will and desire to do good to her father's most dear beloved subjects ... than so effectively to prosecute the work of translating which she has done.[8]

If the Mary so promoted was an admirable model of piety in July, she was soon to be seen as someone much more troublesome to the realm. Among the earliest critical conservatives was Gardiner, Bishop of Winchester, who protested that one homily in the new collection taught the Protestant doctrine of salvation by 'saving faith'. Another undermined the doctrine of transubstantiation. That was not only false doctrine, he said, but flouted the existing law – as indeed it did.[9] The emerging debate about the nature of the Eucharist was in direct violation of Henry's Six Articles (1539: 31 Henry VIII, c. 14). These had declared that consecrated bread and wine were indeed 'the natural body and blood of our Saviour Jesu Christ', and stipulated that anyone who denied or even disputed that doctrine 'shall be guilty of heresy and burned'. It was months before any of the religious innovations were legally confirmed, but for his early and repeated opposition to successive changes, Gardiner was finally to join Norfolk in the Tower in June 1548. There they both remained until freed in person by Mary in August 1553, as the new Queen.

One problem, therefore, with the first religious changes introduced by the new regime was that they apparently depended on an imperial royal authority to override statute law. But there was another, even more fundamental, problem. Under Henry, the monarch had become God's vice-regent; as the title page to the 1539 Bible made clear, he was immediately responsible to God for transmitting religious truth to clergy and laity (see Plate 3). It followed that no earthly power could delegate that religious authority from the divinely sanctioned king to any council.

Although Edward's Privy Council had authority to govern the young king and his realm, many doubted that power included authority to determine religious changes. A 'perfect' king with the capacity to determine religious doctrine was hardly to be found in a 9-year-old body. Stephen Gardiner had been one of the first to comment on the problem. He had endorsed Henry's repudiation of papal authority, but in early 1547 he suggested that silence on religious questions was the best policy, 'with reverence to the authority of our late sovereign ... till our sovereign Lord that now is, come to his perfect age'.[10] Others took a similar position. In Cornwall, responding to the renewed campaign against images, an over-enthusiastic iconoclast was murdered and those responsible insisted 'they would have all such laws as was made by the late King Henry VIII, and none other until the king's majesty that now is' had turned 24,[11] itself a remarkably late age of discretion!

The first Edwardian parliament met in November 1547 to legitimate the attacks on traditional religion now well under way. The doctrine of justification by faith was already officially entrenched in religious statements, and marriage of the clergy was effectively allowed (Cranmer had been married to his second wife for some years). Many traditional rituals were under attack. Processions were forbidden as part of church liturgy, as were the recitation of the rosary and bearing palms on Palm Sunday.

For the first time there was an official denunciation of the doctrine of purgatory. (Under Henry there had been a ban on the use of the word 'purgatory' to describe a time or place of punishment for those who, although they died 'in the grace of God' still had outstanding sins to expiate. Prayers for the dead were, however, continued.)

In all, by the end of 1547, as MacCulloch pointed out, the reformers had 'robbed the Church's traditional liturgy of the drama, movement and visual impact which gave it much of its power'. They had achieved this in the face of three hostile constituencies, 'the Emperor, the majority of the lay political nation and those bishops who were not part of the inner circle'.[12] Only after most of that was already in place did the new parliament finally revoke Henry's Act of Six Articles with all existing heresy legislation, and introduce communion in both kinds for laity as well as clergy, another clear break with Catholic tradition.

In all the changes being undertaken, a major point of contention was the nature of the mass, now more commonly called communion. For Mary, the traditional mass, enacting transubstantiation was a matter on which she would never compromise. As the *Lay Folk's Mass Book* expressed her traditional position: 'the worthiest thing, most of goodness in all this world, it is the mass.' It was, after all, the 'central public ritual of the Latin church from the thirteenth century to the Reformation and of the Roman Catholic church thereafter'.[13]

It was on the nature of the mass/Eucharist/communion that Mary based her resistance to the many Edwardian changes. As the more evangelical agenda was being promoted, Mary increased the number of masses she heard in her own household. Later in 1547 she wrote a letter of protest to Protector Somerset, which is now lost, but which apparently reiterated the case that religious changes should wait until Edward was of an age to determine them. She may have felt freer to do this because of her long-standing friendship with Somerset's wife, and previously good relations with Somerset himself. Prior friendship, however, proved no protection from Somerset's scathing reply. He insisted that the changes under way were a continuation of the reforms Henry had been unable to complete, he reminded her of the earlier opposition of (tactfully unnamed) 'stiff-necked papists' to the excellent reforms her father had begun, and marvelled that 'she who had been well bred and was learned, should esteem true religion and the knowledge of the scriptures *newfangledness or fantasy'*. He urged her to reconsider the matter 'with a humble spirit'.[14]

In a surviving draft letter, undated but in Mary's own hand, her feelings were expressed with a passion she seldom expressed so forthrightly. Traditionally dated about 1551, it could well have been written almost any time during Edward's reign, even in 1547. It is a furious draft, with many crossings and insertions. She commented with 'no small grief' on how much men who owed their all to the late king her father, had broken the oaths they swore to him, and ignored his will. She noted 'what usurped power they take upon them in making (as they call it) laws both clean contrary to his proceedings and will, and also against the custom of all Christendom and (in my conscience) against the law of the God and his Church.' Unlike the late king's counsellors, she added, 'I will remain an obedient child to his laws as he left them until such time as the King's Majesty my brother shall have perfect years of discretion to order the power that God has sent him, and to be a judge in these matters himself; and I doubt not', she wrote, 'that he shall then accept my so doing better than theirs who have taken a piece of his power upon them in his minority.'[15] The draft set out the position she held for as long as possible.

What enabled her to resist Edward's Council as long as she did on religious issues was the support the Emperor her cousin gave her. Possibly from family loyalty, more likely because of the leverage it gave him in English politics, Charles V had very early constituted himself as Mary's protector. Throughout 1549, he was increasingly concerned about the pressure put on Mary to cease having mass celebrated in her household. In January he had asked his ambassador Van der Veldt whether she was under pressure to comply with the new Act of Uniformity (2&3 Edward VI, c. 1). That act, which foreshadowed the first Edwardian *Book of Common Prayer*, prescribed communion in both kinds and indicated that the traditional mass was under serious challenge. Charles advised his ambassador to tell the Council that 'as your own private opinion' the Emperor would 'suffer no pressure to be put upon her, our close relative', let alone permit her to be treated in a less honourable way. Since England was already at war with both France and Scotland, the Council had little choice but to heed the Imperial warnings, at least in the short term. So Mary was, for a while, permitted some religious latitude.

From Easter 1549, the first *Book of Common Prayer* was introduced in churches across England. It set out the form of 'the Holy Communion, commonly called the Mass' and offered the even more novel name of 'the Supper of the Lord'. The introductory statute required that the new order should replace all older forms. Mary's most pressing fear, as she remarked to Charles V, was that, being a helpless and friendless woman, she would no longer be permitted to live 'in the ancient faith and in peace with my conscience'. She added that: 'under God, and considering the tender age of the King my brother, your Majesty is my only refuge.'[16] Mary's dependence on the Emperor for protection at this time has been much criticised by subsequent historians. It is, however, difficult to see where else she might plausibly have sought protection as she saw her like-minded compatriots excluded from power, humiliated and/or imprisoned.

As matters worked out, no Catholics were to be executed for their religion, although two over-radical Protestants were burned as heretics between 1547 and 1553. Those seen as rebels in the southwest counties and East Anglia in 1549 were ruthlessly put down, but unsuccessful rebellions were always harshly suppressed. Nevertheless, Mary did have good reason to fear persecution for continuing to hear the mass, against the new laws. In June 1549, the Council warned her against her continuing defiance of the king's will, and his laws. She was instructed 'to be conformable and obedient to the observation of his Majesty's laws, [and] to give orders that the mass should be no more used in her house'.[17] But Mary ignored that advice and, following pressure from Charles and his ambassador in England, a truce was agreed between the contending parties. Mary was to be permitted 'private' observances of the mass. 'Private' covered the presence of members of her household, thereby leaving her chaplains free to celebrate those 'private' services for her large and splendid household and, perhaps, visitors. The conditions were never formally agreed; and whether the concessions were temporary or permanent, whether the service was to be 'privately' public or private 'in her closet' and precisely who might attend were all matters for future contention.

By late 1549 the regime was facing other problems; it even seemed possible that popular resistance might cause some reassessment of the new religious forms. There were risings in the southwest, Oxfordshire and Buckinghamshire, all calling for the restoration of the Henrician church order. Demands included the restoration of the doctrine of transubstantiation, the mass in Latin, and communion for the laity in one kind only. Suppressing the rebels was made more difficult because the gentry were also significantly divided on those issues. But the terms of the calls suggest that there was still a strong acceptance of the principle of royal supremacy and no desire to have the papacy restored.

The better-known Kett uprising in Norfolk, which also coincided with the issuing of the first *Book of Common Prayer*, showed much less explicit resentment against religious changes, but offered a more general critique of misrule by the local gentry. There was some suspicion that Mary had had prior knowledge of the East Anglian uprising, perhaps through some of the local men she now had in her household. The Council prudently took the view that it was improbable that she was personally involved. On the other hand, it is remarkable that, although the largest landowner in East Anglia, and resident at Kenninghall throughout the Norfolk disturbances, she did nothing to suppress that disorder. What part, if any, she played on either side is still a matter for speculation.

Somerset's foreign and social policies had helped shape the conditions which gave rise to the 1549 uprisings. He had pursued Henry's policy to unite England and Scotland by seeking to marry Edward to the infant Mary of Scotland. Apart from draining England's financial resources, the resulting war achieved very little, its main purpose being entirely defeated when Mary Stuart, betrothed to Edward since 1543, was taken to France and betrothed to the Dauphin in 1548. The wars only aggravated considerable existing social and economic dislocation that reflected rapid population increase and much slower growth in employment opportunities. In late 1549 discontented councillors moved against the Lord Protector. Warwick worked, briefly, with such conservatives as Southampton and Arundel and met with Van der Veldt, to ensure there would be no intervention from Charles V.

The general impression created was that a change of leadership would lead to a change in religious direction. There were even rumours that Mary would become regent to Edward. Somerset responded by issuing an appeal in the king's name, summoning all his loyal subjects to defend himself and his Lord Protector. He thereupon moved the king from Hampton Court to Windsor, and prevented other councillors from reaching him. After a few days – receiving no support – he gave way. Edward and his other councillors met again on 12 October and the extraordinary struggle for control of the boy king was over. The widespread reports of a conservative recovery disappeared as Warwick took full control. The politics of those events remains confused, but once again Mary may have rejected an opportunity to become actively involved in English politics. The continuing political potential of both princesses was demonstrated by the letter the Council found it advisable to write to Mary and Elizabeth to explain their actions which, they wrote, were solely to protect the king.

Confronted by considerable financial problems, intensified by the war, Warwick had to settle for peace on humiliating terms – including the loss of Boulogne, so recently won by Henry. Given little choice, he adopted a policy of amity with France – which included talk of a plan to marry Edward to the eldest daughter of Henry II of France. That French alliance, which continued almost as long as Warwick was Lord President of the Council, necessarily meant a turning away from the Hapsburg powers. The result was increased pressure on Mary to conform to the new religious laws, since her Hapsburg protector had less influence. Somerset returned to the Council within months but was finally executed in January 1552 on the improbable grounds that he had plotted to murder a number of his fellow councillors. He was also charged with being too protective of Mary – a charge that did not bode well for her fortunes while Warwick was dominant.

MARY AND THE EMERGENCE OF THE DUKE OF NORTHUMBERLAND

Far from leading a conservative reaction after 1550, Warwick, who did not grant himself the more familiar title of Duke of Northumberland until October 1551, pursued further evangelical reformation. An increased number of dissenting higher clergy were imprisoned. Edmund Bonner, Henry's Bishop of London, undertook to obey the Injunctions and *Homilies* in 1547 'if they were not contrary to God's law, and the ordinances of the church'.[18] He was imprisoned briefly, then later, having expressed other reservations, was deprived of his diocese and imprisoned again. His replacement from June 1550, Nicholas Ridley, began pulling down the altars in London churches. Cuthbert Tunstall, Bishop of Durham, struggled to protect his conservative flock, but finally he stopped attending the Privy Council. Arrested in August 1550, he was transferred to the Tower in December 1551, where he remained for the rest of the Edwardian regime. Another conservative, George Day of Chichester, stayed with his diocese until the order to destroy all altars proved more than he could endure, and he too was imprisoned.

Even before the change in Council leadership, Mary was sufficiently uneasy about future toleration for her religious practice to dream of fleeing from England. When yet another marriage proposal was under discussion in 1549, she commented to Van der Veldt that she wanted less to marry, more to find some other means of getting out of the country. Although Mary was permitted to pay her customary visit to Edward's court in March 1550, Van der Veldt was becoming as fearful for Mary's safety as ever Chapuys had been in the 1530s. Mary was increasingly anxious that she was again to be pressured as she had been when she defied her father.

It is now impossible to judge how much the ambassador's anxiety was the conclusion of a man caught between the insistence of Mary that she should have her mass, and the equal insistence of the Council that she should not. When her hearing the traditional mass was under discussion, the discussion always returned to the extent of the freedom, and its duration, initially agreed between the Emperor and the Council. As she did when the pressure was on her on religious matters, and so also on marriage proposals, Mary explicitly used the Emperor as a protective device, even declaring that she would make no marriage without his consent. Charles's main interest was always to keep France and England apart, as the best way of ensuring his troops and ships had easy access from Spain to the Netherlands. Since the English Council and Charles had such different objectives in mind when discussing prospective husbands for her, both sides were effectively neutralised. The Council was not interested in allowing Mary to marry a Hapsburg ally, for obvious reasons. Charles, however, was as adamant that she should not marry an Englishman, since he would thereby lose his means of intervening in English affairs.

Mary's situation became even more stressful as Edward began to make his own voice heard regarding her religious practices. His own views were strongly evangelical, so that he fully endorsed successive changes to religious practice in his church. He took his own initiatives against traditional practices such as evocation of the saints, and expunged all mention of St George from the Order of the Garter, the highest honour in Tudor England. (St George was subsequently reinstated by Mary and has remained there ever since.) Although Edward was known to be unhappy about Mary's religious practices, Van der Veldt was less concerned about the king's possible intervention, more puzzled that the more complete onslaught he anticipated from the Council on Mary had not yet taken place. By mid-1550 the ambassador seemed fully persuaded Mary's position was so dangerous that she should be helped to flee from England.

Charles never wholeheartedly approved that plan, because it seemed unlikely Mary would ever return to England once she had left, or be able to claim the throne except at the head of a foreign army. There were, indeed, rumours that once Charles had Mary in his power, he would marry her to his son Philip of Spain and return her as the 'true' English monarch at the head of Hapsburg forces, but these were probably nothing more than rumours. There is no way of assessing the relative enthusiasm of the main protagonists (apparently Mary of Hungary, Van der Veldt and Mary Tudor herself) for Mary's flight from her potential future realm. Any possibility, however slight, that it might have succeeded was foiled by English Council knowledge of the plot even as it was taking shape, by the opposition of the main officials in Mary's household to it when the plan was in place, and by her own ambivalence about it. Furthermore, local inhabitants, keeping close watch against the possibility of fresh social unrest like that which had broken out the previous summer, noted with extreme suspicion the foreign ships loitering near Maldon, and passed the reports on to relevant officials.

The prospect of any success was finally destroyed by Mary's own refusal to take part in the adventure, although the ships were in position and the leader landed to negotiate her rescue. He finally lost patience and withdrew. Edward noted in his *Chronicle* a failed plan by Mary of Hungary 'to take away the Lady Mary and so to begin an outward war and an inward conspiracy', which came to nothing because the leader 'was but a coward and ... durst not go forth with his enterprise'.[19] That might be said to be as plausible an explanation as any for the ill-fated scheme. The whole escapade had resolved nothing, except that later Edward required Mary to exchange some property closer to the shoreline for the fortified castle at Framlingham, in good time for it to serve her well against the proposal to install 'Queen Jane'.

Indeed, for some months it seemed there was relative tranquillity. In late November, an unnamed lord wrote to Mary about her renewed health problems. She wrote a most courteous reply, explaining that her current problem was one she frequently suffered in autumn, 'at the fall of the leaf', so there was little point in taking up his offer of 'the choice of any of the King's Majesty's houses or any other man's being meet to be had'.[20] That, it would seem, was indeed a generous offer, and courteous reply. On several occasions, however, it is clear that used the claim of ill health as a convenient excuse to avoid meetings and journeys she did not wish to undertake

Once all signs of her attempted flight died down, renewed attacks were made against Mary's chaplains for saying mass in her household, particularly in her absence. Predictably enough, Mary resisted, insisting she always conformed with the original terms of the agreement which Charles' ambassador had brokered. Her answer, the Council responded, 'required deliberation' so that 'as they might find leisure, they would send her an answer'. The answer they duly sent was part homiletic, part yet another rehearsal of the Council's understanding of a more limited agreement by which Mary alone was permitted to hear mass, and that only in her private chamber. As Loades has remarked, affairs would probably have gone on much as before if only Edward, who was following the affair, had not intervened at that point.[21] The letter was couched in the 13-year-old king's voice but in another hand. Addressed to his 'Dear and well-beloved sister', he summarised the situation as he understood it. The problem was that:

> you, our nearest sister, in whom by nature we should place reliance and our highest esteem, wish to break our laws and set them aside deliberately and of your own free will: and moreover sustain and encourage others to commit a like offence.

The last section, significantly in Edward's own hand, included the assurance that, although an exception had for some time been made for her, he intended now to see his laws carried out. He could not, he wrote, 'suffer it to be otherwise as a true minister of God; without exception of persons I could not tolerate practices that have been condemned as bad'. To avoid any misunderstanding, he ended his letter by reiterating: I will see my laws strictly obeyed.'[22]

Mary had every reason to reply that her brother's letter 'caused me more suffering than any illness, even unto death'. She pleaded for her exemption to be continued, begging 'in the humblest manner possible' to be suffered to continue as she had in the past and assured him 'that I will live and die your most humble sister and loyal subject'. She was, however, unable to argue, even to herself, that her brother was still being used as a tool against her, nor could she sustain the proposition that the religious changes had been made independently of the king's will. The dispute had entered another stage, and soon became much more public. The London merchant, Henry Machyn, noted that on 15 March 1551:

> Lady Mary rode through London unto St John's [her London residence], with fifty knights and gentlemen in velvet coats and chains of gold before her, and after her [some 80] gentlemen and ladies every one having [a set of black rosary] beads.

That was indeed a startling visual defiance of the regime's religious prohibitions. Two days later, again accompanied with many 'noble lords and knights and gentlemen', she rode to Westminster where she was received in the king's presence chamber, Machyn reported, with due ceremony before enjoying a 'goodly banquet for two hours'. The next day she returned to New Hall and stayed there 'with honour, thanks be to God and the king her brother'.[23]

Any confidence Machyn drew from this appearance that all was well between the royal siblings was sadly misplaced. Scheyfve, Van der Veldt's replacement as Imperial ambassador in England, reported that as Mary rode to London 'the people' ran five or six miles, and were 'marvellously overjoyed' to see her, but that no one had cared to ride from the court to greet her. This apparent discourtesy foreshadowed worse things. At their previous encounter, first Mary had wept when pressured about her religious practice, and Edward had wept for her weeping, before councillors had intervened to end that discussion. But of the most recent meeting, Edward noted that she was told by his councillors 'how long I had suffered her mass' but 'except I saw some short amendment, I could not bear it. ... I constrained not her faith but willed her but as a subject to obey.'[24]

At least, Mary reported to Scheyfve, she had got in some shots of her own. When a councillor claimed that by Henry's will she was subject to

Council authority, she (correctly) insisted that applied only to the matter of her marriage. She added that by the same will her father had provided for two masses each day and four obsequies to be said for him every year, provisions so far completely ignored. Honours went to Mary in that exchange about her father's will, at least by her account.

As she rode away from the court, Mary could no longer pretend that when he came of age, Edward would accept her religious practice. She may, however, have been aware that some councillors were a moderating force between the brother and sister. Edward, with all the confidence of youth, quoted Biblical verses to prove it was a deadly sin to tolerate the 'popish' mass. Some members of his Council showed sensitivity to Mary's status as heir apparent, and more sensitivity to the danger of defying the Emperor's protection of her. Edward's preferred policy threatened both the end of ready access for the English cloth trade to Antwerp, under Hapsburg control, and possibly even war. As it was, given the strength of commitment by both Mary and Edward, those distressing confrontations between the two were so nearly to culminate in civil war, that scourge of so many early modern societies. How much more dangerous the religious differences between once affectionate brother and sister could become must have been a question on the minds of many informed observers in early 1551.

6

EDWARD AND MARY: THE FINAL STRUGGLES

MARY'S FURTHER RELIGIOUS STRUGGLES

Both groups knew that the March 1551 confrontation between Edward and his councillors on the one hand, and Mary and her household on the other, was far from resolving anything; it had simply heightened tensions all round. Mary retired to her rural estates and sent detailed defensive accounts of recent events to her cousin, Charles V, but for a while nothing more happened. This was because, however briefly, and against his own inclinations, Edward had been persuaded against pursuing the matter of Mary's disobedience further. The combined efforts of Cranmer and others had convinced the 13-year-old king, as he noted in his *Chronicle*, that although 'to give license to sin was to sin, to suffer and wink at it for a time might be borne', but any such concession was only for the short term. Neither Cranmer, nor Edward nor Northumberland could afford to overlook for long Mary's continuing 'sin' and defiance. Nor could they continue to accept Mary's version of the original agreement with the Emperor, by which she, her household and even her visitors were permitted to hear mass in her houses. That was, for the governors, a clear – and provocative – breach of established law.

Edward's councillors now adopted an indirect approach to the issue as other members of her household were punished, ostensibly for their own but effectively for Mary's practices. At least two men were examined before the Council for hearing mass 'twice or thrice' in Mary's presence, and, being found guilty, imprisoned in the Fleet. One of those was Sir Anthony Browne, whose father of the same name had been Henry's Master of the Horse and Edward's councillor. Pressure was increased in April, when Mary's chaplain, Dr Francis Mallet, first indicted in December 1550, was formally charged with celebrating mass in Mary's household in her absence. For that offence he was sent to the Tower.

Another chaplain Alexander Barclay, under similar pressure, accepted Cranmer's protection and was then granted a preaching licence and a comfortable living. He was, however, the only member of Mary's household whom Cranmer was able to win away from her. The customary flurry of protests from Mary to the Council and the Imperial ambassador over the Mallet's imprisonment followed, with the usual lack of effect. Scheyfve, Charles' ambassador, glumly reported that not only were Hapsburg wishes quite disregarded at court, but in May the French ambassador received particularly flattering attention when he went to watch Edward tilt at Greenwich. Mary's religious fortunes were again, it seemed, dependent on shifting diplomatic relations.

In August 1551, the king renewed his active hostility to 'licensing sin', leading to what was to become for Mary the most alarming development so far. Responding to the king's renewed fervour on the matter, the Council decided that after 'the long sufferance of her and her family to do what they have done', it would forbid all Mary's household from hearing mass under any circumstances. Edward noted the Council's next moves in his *Chronicle*. First Rochester, long Controller of Mary's household, was commanded to appear before the Council with Edward Waldegrave and Sir Francis Englefield, also senior members of her household. At Mary's instigation they had first stretched the patience of Council almost to breaking point by their delays in attending, but once there they were ordered to ensure that no one in her household either said or heard mass. This prohibition, they were instructed, included the Lady Mary. They were to pay the closest attention to ensuring that the chaplains, their servants and their households also observed this instruction.

Rochester tried so hard to evade following his instructions that he was finally commanded 'on his allegiance to the king' to obey it. That meant that should he resist further he would be guilty of treason.

Furthermore, her officers were told, if Mary refused to hear them or tried to dismiss them from her household, they were commanded, 'on the King's Majesty's behalf' to stay in her service, and in her house, to see the order obeyed. A week later the three reported back to the Council that when they had finally tried to raise the matter with her, Mary adamantly refused to hear their message, threatening to leave the house immediately if they tried to repeat it. She had made much of the point that it was not the place of her officers or servants to instruct her in her religion. They had been, they reported to the Council, so worried by her reaction that they could not deliver the Council's message, for fear of bringing on another attack of her 'old disease'. (It might be remembered that, throughout these years, there are good reasons for suspecting that a number of Mary's illnesses were primarily political in nature.)

Her officers had tried again to convey the Council's message the following Wednesday, but Mary was, they told the Council, 'even colder than before and forbade them to deliver their charge'. Her gentlemen decided, all things considered, it was preferable to report their failure to the Council than to persist with their message. They also carried with them a letter from their mistress to the king. When the Council insisted they should try again to deliver the message they flatly refused, and were imprisoned – a result which they must have anticipated. If they really preferred prison to facing Mary, that is perhaps a fascinating glimpse of just how formidable this exemplary royal lady could be. All that early training in regality, it seems, had not been wasted.

Just how serious the confrontation between the two royal siblings had become was indicated by Edward's noting: 'Certain pinnaces were prepared to see that there should be no conveyance overseas of the Lady Mary, secretly done.'[1] There were now particularly strong reasons to ensure that Mary did not join Charles and become a more potent instrument for the Emperor's policy, for the English government was well aware how strong popular support for the old religion remained. In September, Scheyfve sent a very full report to the Emperor about the next developments. As Mary had refused to hear their message from her own men, the Council sent officials from the king with verbal and written messages of affection – and his demand for her obedience.

Mary would or could not immediately answer the king's messages, claiming again the return of her old illness. The usual debates about the nature of the promise made to the Emperor – and some councillors suggested there had never been such a promise – were inevitably revisited. Mary was, it might be noted, well enough when the council delegation departed to call after them that she needed her household officers back, not least because without them she was required to deal with such matters as how many loaves were required and what they cost. To such concerns as supervising kitchen requirements she had not been bred. (Readers might enjoy the gender reversal in her household of the usual domestic duties, but it is another sign of Mary's unusually high status.)

Mary did, however, dismiss her chaplains the following day, perhaps to save them from further attacks by the Council. Once more Scheyfve argued her case before the Council, but Northumberland insisted that the king was taking a personal interest in the case, and that there should be no exceptions to complying with the legally established religious forms. Mary of Hungary, sister to Charles V, writing to the ambassador on her brother's behalf, repeated her earlier advice that if 'the King or his ministers proceed to take the mass away from the Lady Mary, she would have to "put up with it".' In submitting to that, she would be blameless. If, however, the regime were to try to force Mary into 'erroneous practises ... it would be better for her to die than to submit.'[2]

The stakes had become very high indeed, when, unexpectedly, all participants in this drama pulled back from the brink. That may have been because of the news of Somerset's final fall. That he was charged with multiple offences took front stage, and the immediate focus of the leading councillors – and presumably the king – moved to those matters. Among Somerset's many offences was the claim that he had always favoured a more gentle approach to Mary, but if he had ever been an effective protector, events demonstrated that he was no longer indispensable in that role. This was less because other councillors had adopted a more conciliatory approach (they had not) than because other concerns became more pressing.

One fresh alarm was that, with war having broken out between French and Imperial interests, the English cloth trade with Europe was a major victim. It was therefore necessary to co-operate with Mary of Hungary as regent of the Netherlands to stabilise trade conditions, especially at Antwerp. The international situation required the same co-operation until mid-1552, which might be another reason for there being, suddenly, much less pressure on Mary to conform fully, rather than merely refrain from hearing mass. That may have remained the formal situation for the rest of Edward's reign, but it is not clear that Mary consistently observed that tacit agreement.

Mary even received a message, which may have been conciliatory, that the king had no wish to force her conscience – official deprivation of her mass was, it seemed, conformity enough. When, in October that year, Mary Guise, Dowager Queen of Scotland, visited Edward for several days, Mary was invited to Court to 'accompany and entertain' her, and Edward sent a message that he would enjoy the pleasure of her company. That may well have been another peace overture, but once again, Mary pleaded ill health, and once again she explained to Charles' representative that her health was an excuse to avoid the risks of religious pressure from her brother. Moreover, at the time of that invitation the leading three men of her household were still in prison; presumably Mary found it hard to overlook that, even if the court did not.

Another possible confrontation loomed briefly in mid-December, when the Council asked to have two of her priests sent to them, but her (perhaps evasive) reply that neither was with her seems to have ended that matter. Honour was, apparently, satisfied on both sides. By late in 1551 she was planning to make her usual visit to Edward's court after Christmas, which suggests some kind of accommodation was under way. In March the three officers of her household were released and returned to their usual duties. In June 1552 she rode through London to St Johns, 'with a goodly company of gentlemen and gentlewomen' as Machyn recorded, and went by barge to Greenwich to visit her brother. Nothing, it seems, was said about religion on that relatively successful visit, but also nothing had been done to moderate her brother's deep conviction that she was an unreconstructed follower of deeply erroneous religious beliefs, and a danger to the church he was building with such conviction.

It is hard to gauge just how much was known beyond court circles of the disputes about Mary's religious practice, but given her earlier public progress through the main streets of London with symbols of the traditional religion worn by all her entourage, there can have been little confusion about her religious sympathies. Given that, perhaps the most puzzling public projection of Mary during the Edwardian regime was the 1551 publication of an expanded edition of the *Paraphrases of Erasmus,* now edited by the strongly evangelical Miles Coverdale, and accordingly more evangelical in its translation of the previously untranslated New Testament commentaries. But despite all that had passed both very publicly and more privately between Mary and most members of the Edwardian regime, and despite Coverdale's own strongly evangelical sympathies, the same extended panegyric for 'the most noble, the most virtuous, the most witty, and the most studious Lady Mary's grace' was retained in its entirety from the first edition.

The expanded *Paraphrases* were only part of a continuing reformist push, which included the 1552 second *Book of Common Prayer*, much more explicitly evangelical that the first, particularly in the communion service. Through all these changes, as possibilities for ambiguities between the old and the new religion were successively removed, Mary remained on her estates, maintaining her high status and, officially at least, in her version of a religious limbo. Since her main protector abroad, Charles V, was suffering ill health for much of the time, and her recent supporter at home, the Duke of Somerset had been ignominiously executed, her relative tranquillity for much of 1552 was a welcome change from the previous year. That may have been one reason senior members of the Edwardian regime were soon to be shown to have underestimated her continuing political potential within England.

THE WILL OF THE KING AND THE LAW OF THE LAND

After six years, one indication of the growing confidence of the Edwardian regime in 1553 was the dissolution in March of the parliament first elected in 1547. There was talk of fresh elections for a new parliament to meet in September not least because the previous summer had been the most relaxed so far for the Edwardian regime. Although the endemic problems of financial difficulties, social discontent and religious disputes among the governors continued, for the first time its leading members felt able to go their various ways. In 1552, Edward had been deemed old enough to make his first extended summer progress; it took him through Hampshire, Sussex and Surrey. He was reportedly in good health, enjoying his hunting and developing the martial skills expected of any well-born young man. Since he had turned 14 in late 1551, he had taken a growing interest in the affairs of his realm. Although his father's will had stipulated he was to be ruled by his Council until he was 18, he – and his advisers – were well aware that his cousin James V of Scotland had been deemed old enough to exercise some royal authority when he was 14. Northumberland, probably looking to the time after Edward took full control of his monarchy, prepared him carefully in his expanding responsibilities.

Mary's life was apparently also more tranquil, though nothing further had changed in the matter of her permitted religious practice. But when she visited London and her brother again, in early January 1553, both Machyn, citizen of London, and Scheyfve, the Imperial ambassador, waxed eloquent about Mary's reception at court and the much more satisfactory ceremonial with which she had been welcomed. She had reached London on 6 January, and four days later as she rode to the king at Westminster, Machyn recorded, a great number of lords and great ladies accompanied her and her retinue through the streets. The assembled company included the Duchesses of Suffolk and of Northumberland, the 'lady marquises' of Northampton and Winchester, a number of countesses and other ladies of the court. At the outer gate to the palace, the two dukes, the Marquis of Winchester, several earls, the Lord Admiral – the greatest men of England it seemed to Machyn – met and saluted her before she passed through to the presence chamber and was greeted by her brother.[3] Scheyfve was at least as gratified in his report. Given later developments, it is tempting to see this reception as a precautionary move, given Edward's health and Mary's position in the succession, but at the time there was little reason for concern about Edward's health. The question of why Mary then received such an unusually warm welcome remains unanswered.

Edward's decision to overthrow his father's will and install Lady Jane Grey as his heir was almost certainly still in the future. Historians continue to debate just where the idea of displacing both Mary and Elizabeth from the succession in favour of their cousin began. John Guy has argued that ever since Northumberland's push against Somerset in 1549, and the threatened Catholic counter-push, which proposed Mary as Edward's regent, Mary was a potential threat to Northumberland's life and he concluded she must be excluded from the throne.[4] But other historians question the importance of Northumberland in the initial decision to exclude Mary, and are more inclined to see the decision to alter the line of succession as one taken later, by Edward himself. He had been, after all, a healthy child, and had survived the years when mortality rates were highest. There had already been some negotiations for his marriage; he had participated in his first tournament, and he was maturing into the role of a king. There seemed no particular reason to worry about the line of succession in 1551, when Somerset finally fell, or later.

Nor is it necessary to read a long-term sinister purpose into the marriage of Lady Jane Grey and Guilford Dudley (a younger son of Northumberland) in May 1553. For much of the previous year the duke had been seeking a marriage between Guilford and Margaret Clifford. Margaret's mother and Jane Grey's mother were the two daughters, by her second marriage, of Mary Tudor, Henry VIII's younger sister. In both proposals Northumberland was seeking an alliance with families of Tudor descent, but it seems improbable that he had been plotting to change the line of succession when first seeking to marry his younger son to a daughter of Mary Tudor's younger daughter. The marriage with Jane Grey was a later decision.

But in February 1553 Edward contracted a cold which proved unusually persistent; with all the benefits of hindsight, it might have seemed ominous that he had barely recovered from another cold at Christmas time, but no significant problem was immediately obvious, He had not fully recovered his health when he opened parliament on 1 March, doing so at Whitehall rather than as was more usual at Westminster. The same month, Scheyfve reported, Northumberland was keeping Mary closely informed about the state of her brother's health – which suggests that he still understood her to be the royal heir apparent. And Edward had probably begun drafting what has become known as his 'Device', by which Jane Grey finally emerged as his heir some time previously.

That he did so has been seen more as a symptom of his own conscientiousness than of any foreboding of his imminent death. Mary was still his heir apparent and it is hardly surprising that the enthusiastically evangelical monarch deplored the possibility of having his resolutely Catholic sister succeed him and overturn his religious changes. But his adjustments to the succession went much further than simply excluding her. The line of succession established by Henry in 1543, had provided that, should all Henry's three direct heirs die without successors, the crown would then pass to the heirs of 'the Lady Frances our niece, eldest daughter to our late sister the French Queen'. Since the three surviving children of Frances Grey were also female, it meant that Edward's successor would be the Tudors' cousin Lady Jane Grey, eldest daughter of Lady Frances and Henry Grey, Marquis of Dorset and Duke of Suffolk. But that was also not a satisfactory outcome for Edward when he began drafting his preferred succession.

Edward's most significant change to his father's settlement of the crown was his unqualified exclusion of both his sisters, his stated grounds being that they were both illegitimate. It became clear that his preference was for a male heir of soundly Protestant beliefs. That his preference for a male heir was also selective is demonstrated by the fact that he ignored the (Catholic) descendant of Henry's elder sister Margaret's second marriage: Margaret Douglas's son Henry, Lord Darnley, who was about 7 years old when Edward was drafting his will.

Rather, if he himself were to have no male descendants, Edward looked first to the Lady Frances Grey, Duchess of Suffolk, for an (as yet unborn) male heir. Failing that, he looked for a male heir of one of her three daughters – Jane Grey, or her sister Catherine, or their sister Mary. If none of these produced his desired male heir, then perhaps one of *their* (as yet unborn) female heirs would produce a male heir. In other words, Edward looked initially even unto the third or even fourth generation for his Protestant male heir. One can only agree with David Loades that Edward's was indeed an 'extraordinary genealogical wild-goose chase'.[5] The only two firm conclusions are that Edward's strong preference was not to be succeeded by a female – any female, but least of all by either of his sisters – and that he was not expecting to die any time soon.

But after March 1553, there were more serious fluctuations in his health. He received the new French ambassador in mid-May, but was then very weak, and troubled by a cough. In early June, the Imperial ambassador heard the king was unable to take food, forced to lie on his back, and troubled by swelling legs; soon after, it was reported that even Edward had given up all hope of a recovery. Jennifer Loach has examined the striking fluctuations in his reported symptoms to suggest that he died of acute bilateral bronchopneumonia, a condition almost impossible to treat before the twentieth-century discovery of antibiotics.[6] Inevitably, however, contemporaries suspected poison, as they did for almost any royal deaths in the sixteenth and into the seventeenth centuries.

From 12 June the king addressed the issue of his succession with a new urgency. He still completely overrode the terms of his father's will.

Plate 1 Henry VIII, *c.*1535, attributed to Joos van Cleve. By the mid-1530s the brilliant Renaissance prince of the early years was visibly becoming a more ruthless monarch. The Royal Collection © 2007, Her Majesty Queen Elizabeth II.

Plate 2 Katherine of Aragon, attributed to Lucas Horenbout (or Hornebolte). The beautiful young girl of the early portraits became much more matronly after a number of failed pregnancies and only one living child. © National Portrait Gallery, London.

The Byble in
Englyſhe, that is to ſape the content of all the holy ſcrypture, bothe
of ÿ olde and newe teſtament, truly
tranſlated after the veryte of the
hebrue and Greke textes, by ÿ dy-
lygent ſtudye of dyuerſe excellent
learned men, expert in the foꝛſayde
tonges.

Pꝛynted by Rychard Grafton &
Edward Whitchurch.

Cum pꝛiuilegio ad impꝛimen-
dum ſolum.
1539.

Plate 3 Title-page to the 1539 'Great Bible'. This sets out Henry VIII's role as
God's vicegerent on earth, determining religion for church and laity. In
Edward's time Mary argued that only an adult monarch, not his Council on his
behalf, could exercise such power. © British Library Board. All rights reserved
C.18.d.1.

ANNO DNI 1 5 4 4

LADI MARI — DOVGHTER TO
THE MOST — VERTVOVS PRINCE
KINGE HENRI — THE EIGHT

THE AGE OF — XXVIII YERES

Plate 4 Portrait of Mary I or Mary Tudor (1516–58), daughter of Henry VIII, at the age of 28, in 1544 (panel) by Master John (fl. 1544). This portrait was probably commissioned by Mary soon after she was restored to the line of succession to the throne. She was also spending much time with Queen Katherine Parr in what may well have been the happiest time of her adult life. National Portrait Gallery, London, UK/The Bridgeman Art Library Nationality/copyright status: English/out of copyright.

Plate 5 Portrait of Elizabeth Tudor, *c.*1546 (oil on panel) by Flemish School (16th century). Aged about 13, Elizabeth, also restored to the line of succession is a Tudor princess quite as much as her elder sister, but with much more explicit references to her learning, at a time when Mary's scholarly reputation was more recognised. Private Collection/ The Bridgeman Art Library Nationality/copyright status: Flemish/out of copyright.

Plate 6 Edward VI when Prince of Wales, *c.* 1546, attributed to William Scrots. A partial imitation of Holbein's most famous image of his father, Edward's stance suggests he promises a continuation both of Henry's rule and, by the placement of his hands, of the Tudor dynasty. The Royal Collection © 2007, Her Majesty Queen Elizabeth II.

Plate 7 View of Framlingham Castle, previously the property of the Duke of Norfolk, which was just one of a number of properties presented to Mary early in Edward's reign. It was to be where she gathered her forces to claim the throne from Lady Jane Grey. Reproduced with the kind permission of English Heritage.

Plate 8 Mary I, early representation of her as triumphant 'queen regnant', Michaelmas, 1553, Plea Roll of Kings Bench. This is perhaps the earliest portrait of Mary as 'sole queen', with all the indicators of full monarchy about her. The background fighting seems an exaggerated reference to the initial attempt to install Jane Grey. The National Archives, ref. KB27/1168/.

Plate 9 Great Seal of England, 1554, counter-seal showing Mary and Philip on horseback. Although Philip appears more prominent, it actually shows Mary taking precedence, slightly ahead and with Philip on her left hand.

Plate 10 Mary I exercising the royal touch – manuscript illumination from *Queen Mary Manual*, Westminster Cathedral Library. Perhaps the most striking sign of Mary's assertion of full monarchical power was her continuation of the traditional, quasi-priestly royal power to heal those unfortunates suffering from the 'king's evil' (scrofula). Reproduced with the kind permission of the Westminster Cathedral Library.

Because it had been confirmed by statute, that older will had a legal force which the determination of an underage king could challenge only with difficulty. When his judges were first consulted about Edward's decision to replace his father's will by his own 'Device' – now hastily modified to accept the absence of any male candidate and going directly to his eldest Grey cousin, now Jane Dudley – they were understandably reluctant to become involved. There was no time to write Edward's will into statute law; since the last parliament had been dissolved and fresh elections would be required, it would be months before a new parliament could assemble. All now recognised how terminally ill Edward was. So it came about that the last days of Edward's reign marked a return to the earliest struggles between those who thought the king's command enough and those who treated statute law as paramount.

At the start of his reign, until the first parliament met, the issue was that of religious changes which defied Henrician legislation, and the proponents of the pre-eminence of statute law were religious conservatives. At the end of the reign, the group giving priority to law was more varied. The issue on both occasions was whether decisions sanctioned by statute (that is, approved by both houses and endorsed by the king) were superior, or whether the legitimate authority was an imperial monarchy, 'perfectly' legitimated as Cranmer had suggested at the coronation service by God alone, and capable of overriding parliamentary statute.

The latter was the view that Edward's councillors had implicitly endorsed when they introduced novel religious practices early in Edward's reign. The ideology of imperial kingship was brought into play again at the end of Edward's reign when he sought to alter his father's will and statute by his own youthful will. His paramount concern was, he told some around him, that his disposition of the crown should preserve 'the religion whose fair foundations we have laid'. That requirement obviously ruled out Mary's succession since she had repeatedly proved so very obdurate on religious matters. Elizabeth's religious stance may have been preferable, but Edward deemed her the daughter of a disgraceful mother. Moreover, he was firm that his sisters were both illegitimate, and related to him only 'of the half blood'; they were therefore not his legal heirs.[7] On the other hand, Jane Grey was from a reliable evangelical dynasty and he had known – and liked – her all his life.

Moreover, she was now safely married to a son of his most trusted adviser and councillor, whereas he expressed deep concern that neither of his sisters was yet married. He feared either might marry a foreigner and thereby transfer control of the realm to foreign interests, perhaps even to the papacy. Edward's own will in forcing this disposition of the crown away from his own family was formidable, as his councillors and judges found. The alterations to his 'Device' as his life was ebbing were all in his own handwriting. Essentially what he did was abandon the prospect of any male heir – there was no time for that. Her mother was excised from the succession and Jane Grey herself was elevated as preferred royal candidate.[8]

Once it was clear where Edward's preference lay, both his duty to the king and his own family interests meant that Northumberland, always a forceful man, gave wholehearted backing to Edward's wishes. Gradually most of the judges, with the striking exception of Sir James Hales, concurred with the king's wishes. After that apparent signifier of its legality, the resistance of doubters was more easily overcome, although some, like Arundel maintained reservations to the end. It should, moreover be noted that such a prominent evangelical as Cranmer had serious reservations about debarring Mary from the throne; there was always for all concerned, except possibly Edward himself, more than religion at stake in the disputed succession. Both statute law and issues of legal inheritance were important, as well as the personal interests of all those involved in the decision.

Submission to the monarch's will, however, was a deeply entrenched belief in Tudor England. That had been one reason for the general acceptance of Henry VIII's repudiation of papal authority. Shakespeare was to invoke a long tradition when he had a soldier tell the incognito Henry V: 'We know enough if we know we are the king's subjects. If his cause be wrong, our obedience to the king wipes the crime of it out of us' (*Henry V*, IV i). The same belief apparently held good for the greatest men of the land, even when the crown was in the possession of a zealous 14-year-old.

Accordingly, letters patent for the new succession were prepared and signed by the leading government figures, most judges and some of London's most prominent citizens. Northumberland's preference for the French interest came to the fore, and there are strong indications that their new ambassador Noailles was well-informed – and supportive – of the move against Mary. It was never in the French interest to have a Hapsburg cousin, least of all one who had already received so much support from the Emperor, succeed peacefully to the English throne. Edward died on 6 July, and his death was officially kept secret for several days, but even Machyn, hardly a prominent citizen, noted on the same day Edward died, that 'as they say, deceased the noble King Edward. … And he was poisoned, as everybody says.'

Edward's death remained officially secret until Queen Jane was proclaimed on 10 July. It seems astonishing now, with the benefits of hindsight, that so few precautions had been taken against Mary seizing the initiative, but she was apparently dismissed as a significant consideration. But Queen Jane's accession proclamation is unique for its sheer length, much of it explaining precisely who the new queen was; after all, she had no previously publicised claim to the throne. The proclamation perforce also explained just why Henry's will, by which his daughters should succeed his son, had been discarded.

As Machyn reported, at Queen Jane's proclamation, it was explained throughout London that 'my Lady Mary was unlawfully begotten' but already, he added as an indicator of things to come, a young man had been taken up for speaking of 'Queen Mary' and saying 'she had the right title'.[9] (The offender was placed in the pillory and had both ears cut off.) That glimmer of popular discontent gave rise to little immediate concern among the leaders of the new regime, for they believed that had control of the instruments of government, the support of the established authority, control of the navy and the backing of the French. Moreover, Charles, it was soon known, had instructed his ambassadors to take no steps in Mary's cause unless she was likely to triumph; he expected so little of her that he let it be known he would not object if she were married to an Englishman. Only a public repudiation could have been a clearer signal of his abandonment of her interests.

Queen Jane took up residence in the Tower, which had long served as treasury and armoury as well as royal residence and prison. There was confidence at the highest levels that all was well with the new order. Wriothesley headed up a new section of his *Chronicle* with *Jahannæ Reginæ. Anno 1°* – First Year of Queen Jane – though he may have done so reluctantly. He recorded, as did other observers, that on the following Sunday Dr Ridley, Bishop of London, had preached at 'Paul's Cross', a public place where important sermons were often delivered. Ridley had declared 'the Lady Mary and the Lady Elizabeth, sisters to the King's Majesty departed, to be illegitimate' by God's law, and the endorsement of the English clergy and parliament. At that, Wriothesley added, 'the people murmured sore'.[10] But even before that, on 11 July, Wriothesley, still a political outsider, already knew that Mary had proclaimed herself queen in Norfolk and elsewhere, that some noblemen, knights and gentlemen had already come to her, as well as 'innumerable companies of the common people.'

MARY'S STAND FOR THE THRONE

Even before Edward's death was made public, and Jane Dudley formally declared queen, the Council had received a letter from Mary, asserting her title to the throne by act of parliament, her father's will and 'other circumstances advancing her right'. She cautioned them against resisting her 'just and rightful cause' and reminded them of the allegiance they owed her.[11] Some contemporary accounts suggest, indeed, that Mary's proclamation of herself forced the Edwardian Council into declaring for the new queen sooner than they had intended. Tradition has it that Mary first heard of Edward's death from a London goldsmith but, fearing it was a trap, waited until his death was confirmed for her by a 'medical practitioner' Thomas Hughes.[12] The news simply confirmed the plan she already had in place of retreating from Hunsdon, inconveniently close to London in such times, to Kenninghall, 100 miles from London. The attempt to keep Edward's death secret had been as ineffectual in Mary's case as it was for so many others; moreover, she was also aware of the plan to install Northumberland's daughter-in-law. Given that so many in London, including some sympathisers of Mary's cause had been informed and then sworn to secrecy about Edward's plan, she was almost inevitably also well informed.

Mary quickly let it be known that, rather than heading for the seacoast and flight abroad as the Council expected, she was preparing to make a stand for her claim to the throne. At first this caused the Council little concern, since they believed they held all the key instruments to maintain control, but they had not anticipated the rapidity with which a significant number of the leading men of East Anglia rallied to Mary. Some historians, working on the long-standing assumptions about Mary's lack of initiative and political judgement, have insisted that Mary could not have acted so successfully on her own, but that is based on two dubious assumptions. One is that her habitually submissive and desperate language to such supporters as Charles V reflected a real inability to act without advice, rather than a rhetorical strategy for ensuring the support of powerful protectors against an unsympathetic regime. The second is that without at least some of the realm's leaders always on her side, she could not have succeeded, or even made a stand.

But quite apart from her own strong convictions, Mary had important elements on her side. Historians have often overlooked how long she had lived at court, and how carefully she had been trained not just in the comportment of a pre-eminent woman, but also in the political complexities of court life. She had already, on several occasions shown a steely resolve, which even the best-connected men had found very difficult to stare down. That the new and relatively unknown candidate for the throne was the daughter-in-law of Northumberland was a definite bonus for Mary. The duke, after all, had a strong claim to being the most loathed man in England, most particularly in East Anglia where his brutal suppression of the Kett rebellion was still remembered. Even more helpful to Mary's cause was the considerable number of people in London already sworn to support Jane from 12 June on. Implicated by their office rather than by their private belief in those extraordinary events, there were some among that number of Londoners who warned Mary, always well informed about the state of Edward's health, about the increasingly public 'secret' of the proposal to put Jane Grey on the throne.

Above all Mary was by 1553 the greatest landowner across East Anglia, supplanting the (still imprisoned) Duke of Norfolk both literally and metaphorically. The estates the Council had granted her in 1547 gave her the resources and the clientage to exercise an unusual independence of action. As noted in the previous chapter, the 1553 exchange of lands which gave her Framlingham markedly strengthened her position. The clientage she had acquired since 1547 was a major source of her earliest supporters. But she also retained wider appeal because she had for so long been seen as legally heir-presumptive, first to Henry and then to Edward. This gave her a wide appeal which crossed the conservative/evangelical religious divide. After all, even Cranmer, Archbishop of Canterbury, needed sustained persuasion before accepting Edward's preferred line of succession. Sir John Harington of Exton, when pressed to join Northumberland's cause, pointed to the Henrician statute which nominated Mary as heir after Edward. Harrington did not go so far as to fight for Mary, but he quite firmly refused to fight for Northumberland, which was, it transpired, quite as important.

Just how much weight to give to the several factors in the events by which Mary won her throne – religious affiliation, the strength of support from different social levels, the value placed on a 'legitimate' succession, the strength of Mary's own affinity, the unpopularity, particularly in East Anglia, of Northumberland and the general ignorance about his daughter-in-law Lady Jane Grey, to name but some of them – is still a matter of historical debate. There are, however, two matters beyond debate. One is that Mary would have found it much more difficult to claim the throne if she had not been so widely recognised over so many years as next heir to Edward. The other is that Mary, separated from the men who were her most important advisers, and with the Imperial ambassador keeping his distance in his wait-and-see stance, acted quickly and decisively to resist the proposed new royal dynasty.

As soon as she was confident that Edward really was dead – an essential precaution, since to claim the throne while he was alive would have been high treason – Mary wrote to his Council in the terms already quoted. The same day, at Kenninghall, she assembled her household and proclaimed herself queen. The response, as one eyewitness recorded was that 'everyone, both the gently-born and the humbler servants, cheered her to the rafters and hailed and proclaimed their dearest princess Mary as queen of England.'[13] Messengers were then sent out, 'in all directions' to proclaim Mary's accession and raise her supporters.

So word was officially spread that Mary was contesting the succession, but this did not always lead to unhesitating acquiescence. Even in her 'home' counties of East Anglia there were both urban and rural areas which opposed Mary's claims. Events in Kings Lynn and Yarmouth suggest that the responses to Mary's claims were more ambivalent – and more shaped by local and personal considerations – than a broad-based narrative would suggest.[14] That was significant because it highlights the importance of the speed and decisiveness with which Mary and her advisers acted, to forestall the possibility of a Janeite reaction getting a toehold among the local leaders across the realm. As it was, within a very few days not only local gentry but also a few noblemen were beginning to join Mary's camp. The first was the Earl of Sussex who, McIntosh suggests, may have been won over less by his own inclinations than by the consideration that his son was already being held as a hostage. Whatever persuasion may have been used, he joined Mary at Framlingham, where the Marian camp had moved, mainly because it was a much more defensible position than Kenninghall. Other early adherents were important local leaders like Bedingfield and Southwell, whose estates were nearby and who shared Mary's religious preferences; but they were not obviously part of her affinity and chose freely to join her.

For whatever reasons, there was a steady stream of supporters swinging her way. On 15 July five (some reported six) navy ships, sent by the London Council to prevent Mary's flight and/or the landing of Imperial troops, were off Yarmouth (some report Ipswich, others Harwich) when a revolt by the majority of the crews ensured that all of them went over to Mary's side. The explanations for the mutiny vary – resentment of some officers, or resentment of poor pay and conditions, or even sympathy with the Marian forces – but what mattered most at the time was that they backed the aspiring queen rather than the one installed in the royal quarters of the Tower. The number coming to Mary's camp continued to increase at such a rate that by 16 July a command structure was established for the troops, and a disciplined force started to be shaped. The same day, Mary's council minuted a decision to send 10,000 men to collect armour and munitions from the palace of Westminster. A foreign observer, who had no obvious reason to exaggerate what he saw, gave an independent indication of the numbers finally assembled. Reporting on Mary's inspection of the assembled troops within days of the anticipated clash with Northumberland's troops, he described them as tossing hats in the air and shouting 'Long live our good Queen Mary'.

> And by reason of the great outcry of the people, and the many discharges of the artillery and arquebuses, the Queen was obliged to alight to review the troops, for the fright and much rearing of the palfrey she rode; and she inspected the whole camp, which was about a mile long, on foot.[15]

Within days the rumour mill was spreading the claim that she had some 30,000 fighting men with her. She was not about to submit to the loss of 'her' throne without a fight, and in a very short time, it appeared, she had assembled a formidable army. Northumberland was soon aware that the outcome of any battle would be, at best, uncertain.

THE COLLAPSE OF THE REGIME OF QUEEN JANE

Jane Dudley née Grey was first a reluctant bride to Northumberland's son, and then an even more reluctant queen. Finally she was persuaded to accept the role, but there is little evidence just what role her (evangelical) religious preferences played in that decision. There is even less evidence that religious difference rallied much evangelical support to her cause. There was split allegiance in many communities, but those who were active overwhelmingly turned to Mary. One of Northumberland's sons, Lord Robert Dudley (whose modern reputation owes much to his enduring friendship with the future Queen Elizabeth) had been left waiting for a decision from Kings Lynn about its allegiance for a week before he finally 'took the town by force' and proclaimed Queen Jane on 18 July. (Mary had been proclaimed in Norwich nearly a week earlier.) Even more ominous for the new regime was the silence of the London crowds, and increasing anxiety within the Council. On 10 July, as Queen Jane passed through the streets of London on her way to take up royal residence at the Tower, she passed through silent crowds. The chronicler, however, did not add 'And none said God save her' until some time later, presumably after Mary had assumed power and Northumberland was safely in the Tower.[16]

Northumberland had anticipated the possibility of Mary appealing once again to her cousin the Emperor for help, and taken steps to prevent any Imperial forces landing in England. That was one reason he had sent those ships to East Anglia. In turn he was sorely tempted to accept French help, and sent a relative to negotiate for appropriate terms. But he had not anticipated Mary raising troops on her own behalf, let alone winning such a substantial force as she was rumoured to have. If the new regime were to maintain its hold, clearly there would be a fight, but he had few troops readily available and almost no obvious leader for such a force. The Duke of Suffolk might have served that purpose, but his daughter, the queen, flatly refused to allow him to leave her. By 14 July Northumberland had recognised, reluctantly, that he had no choice but to lead the London forces himself, and trust his fellow councillors to hold the line in London. Some 1,500 troops were raised in London – they were to receive ten pennies a day for their trouble – and Northumberland marched out of London at their head, again, it was reported, before an unusually silent crowd.

Special representatives sent by the Emperor when Edward was dying were still in London, and worked at undermining the remaining councillors. Their most effective argument was probably that the French were offering help to Northumberland, not to support Queen Jane but to clear the way for their own candidate, the young Mary Queen of Scots, niece to Henry VIII, but now betrothed to the Dauphin of France and a committed Catholic. That may have been true, for her claim was to be explicitly advanced after the death of Mary and against the accession of Elizabeth. Having alarmed their listeners, the special ambassadors agreed to meet with a larger group of councillors the next day, when Northumberland was still in London.

But Northumberland was not informed of the proposed meeting. Instead he set off to seize Mary, proclaiming Jane, declaring Mary a bastard and burning at least one house that had given her shelter in her flight to Kenninghall as he went. But the evangelicals were not joining his cause, and it seemed the whole Thames valley was turning to Mary. Most of the Council, increasingly divided, and uneasy about the amount of support Mary was winning across the country, were turning their backs on Northumberland. One of the leading players in this was Henry Fitzalan, Earl of Arundel, once Henry's lord chamberlain and a privy councillor, who had suffered various humiliations at the hands of Northumberland. By 19 July a significant majority of the councillors had agreed that Mary should be proclaimed queen, as she was that day in London. By the time Northumberland reached Cambridge, he knew the cause was lost, and proclaimed Mary himself in the town centre, throwing his cap in the air – a traditional sign of great pleasure – as he did so. It was Arundel who rode to Cambridge, where he arrested Northumberland, the man of whom he had said a few days previously that he was a man for whom he would be happy to shed his blood. Arundel escorted Northumberland back into London where, it was said, the crowds, no longer silent, jeered and mocked him through the streets.

Some scattered resistance continued for a few days, but Suffolk had already told his daughter she was no longer queen. She and her husband apparently both remained in the Tower, but now as prisoners awaiting the pleasure of the new queen. The day Mary was proclaimed in London, Wriothesley reported that Arundel and William Paget, another Edwardian councillor, 'rode in post to the queen ... cheering the people that sat banqueting about the bonfires, asking them if they rejoiced not at their good news, which all thanked God and said God save Queen Mary'. Others recorded that *Te Deums* were sung across London, and bonfires in every street, with good cheer at every bonfire and the bells ringing in every parish church. As the Grey Friars chronicler noted, a *Te Deum* was sung at St Paul's with the organ playing. (Music had been banned from churches by the Edwardian regime.) Mary was queen, and London was determined to show its pleasure, and attachment to at least aspects of the 'old' religion. As Clarendon was to observe at the restoration of Charles II in 1660, those who felt least pleasure were among those who smiled the most. For London, having accepted the reign of Queen Jane, now had to prove its undying and unquestionable loyalty to Queen Mary. And the Grey Friars chronicler began another section of his record, always headed again at the beginning of a new reign:

Maria Regina

7

ESTABLISHING ENGLAND'S FIRST FEMALE MONARCH

SOCIAL AND ECONOMIC PROBLEMS FOR MARY

The realm Mary was now to rule was a religiously unstable society. An old subterranean tradition of hostility to orthodox Catholic teaching had been reinforced and renewed by new Lutheran and other Reformation teachings from the 1520s on. The consequences included 20 years of increasingly intense religious struggles at the upper levels of the socio-political hierarchy; and much popular unease at successive religious changes was manifest from the Pilgrimage of Grace, through riots and uprisings in Edwardian England, to similar protests in Mary's time. All those alterations in church doctrine and practice came at a time when England was also undergoing increased economic and social stress, which was the more disturbing because this was also a time of marked popula-tion growth. Successive governors of England between 1547 and 1558 found the resulting range of intensified social problems extraordinarily difficult to redress, all the more so because they became closely enmeshed with successive religious changes.

And that all coincided with unprecedented shifts in patterns of land ownership. As Henry VIII had acquired great estates from the magnates he destroyed, and from the dissolved monasteries spread across every county of England, much more land was soon available for sale. The previously very limited trade in land expanded rapidly. Many local communities, already hard-pressed, were further disrupted as new landlords, often recently made courtiers, bought and sold the holdings the tenants worked. The new landlords challenged the infinitely complex customary manorial tenures and customs in their drive to recover and augment the costs of the estate purchases.[1] The associated tensions at every level of the local communities would be difficult to exaggerate.

There was also a series of bad harvests, in 1545, 1549–51 and most drastically 1556–7. The last and most severe poor harvest was, inevitably, read by Protestants as a providential judgement on Mary's restoration of Catholicism. After those poor crops, even the better years saw high grain prices, and serious shortages of cattle and dairy products. Such hardships in turn exacerbated outbreaks of plague and the 'sweating sickness', a form of flu first reported in 1485–6. Another form of influenza swept across the realm from 1556 to 1558, its impact so dramatic that it has been described as 'the greatest mortality crisis of the sixteenth century'.[2] Like the sweating sickness, it took a form which struck at the wealthy as well as the poor, causing even more alarm at all social levels.

The most immediate of all the difficulties confronting Mary, however, was that her financial resources were very limited. This was in part because inflation had followed from successive governmental decisions between 1542 and 1551 to lower the value of the currency. As well as the resultant inflation and widespread financial hardship, Mary also inherited a debt from Edward of more than four times the expected annual surplus in royal revenue.[3] And all this confronted her first at a time of extraordinary expenses, including those of reclaiming her throne from Jane Grey, the costs of her magnificent entry into London, and her equally magnificent coronation so soon after.

ENGLAND'S FIRST QUEEN REGNANT

Almost every possible issue of establishing and enacting early modern female monarchy was addressed first in Mary's reign. Even the language needed adjustment. At Mary's funeral service, after a reign of five years, the officiating bishop still described her as 'a queen and by the same title a king also', adding that her sister Elizabeth was likewise 'now both king and queen ... of this realm'.[4] Absence of a word to describe the power of a female sovereign is one indicator of the problems with the very concept of a woman exercising all the authority of English monarchy.

Admittedly the English realm had never explicitly excluded females from the throne. Even in France, where by the sixteenth century it was against the constitution for a woman to reign, there had been no bar to women doing so before the later fourteenth century.[5] Elsewhere in Europe women had reigned: one of the better-known fifteenth-century examples was Isabella of Castile, Mary Tudor's own maternal grandmother

In England, however, before the nine-day rule of Queen Jane, there had been only one female monarch, Queen Matilda. She succeeded her father Henry I in 1135, but was never crowned. Years of civil war followed her brief rule, until the parties agreed that after King Stephen, Matilda's rival monarch, her son should rule, as Henry II. Thereafter England had several examples of women with a claim to the throne who were content to be conduits of that inheritance for their sons. Recent examples of that were Margaret Beaufort, mother of Henry Tudor, and (perhaps) Elizabeth of York, mother of Henry VIII.

In England, as elsewhere, there was always some formal resistance to female rule. The fifteenth-century struggles between Yorkist and Lancastrian again produced arguments which restated the French position, that not only were women debarred from the throne, but so were male inheritance rights to it through the female line. Always informed by the current fortunes of the protagonists, in 1485 that debate disappeared from all officially sponsored public debate after the victory of the Lancastrian heir Henry Tudor – through his mother's line – at Bosworth.

Literary men also discussed issues of female suitability to reign, making much use of such legendary figures as Semiramis (mythical founder of the Assyrian empire) and the Amazons to argue forcefully their preferred position. The varied telling and retellings of the deeds of those ancient women canvassed almost all possible stances on the suitability of women for power, but belonged more to intellectual gamesmanship than serious political debate. In the 1530s, possibly because of there being then two possible female heirs, a pamphlet war broke out in England about the nature of women, but its status as a serious debate, always unclear, has become even more doubtful since it has been shown that some authors wrote pamphlets on both sides of the argument.

Finally, whatever the dominant masculine assessment of the 'nature of women', political pragmatism and strong commitments to inheritance rights won out in the middle of the sixteenth century. It undoubtedly helped Mary's case that all the available alternative candidates were also female, most surviving male potential claimants having been destroyed by Henrys VII and VIII. That dearth of eligible males had been most graphically demonstrated by Edward's increasingly desperate search for an as yet unborn male heir before his last-minute nomination of Jane Grey to succeed him.

To the English the word 'queen' denoted a queen consort, a king's wife, who derived whatever power or authority she had from her relation to the king. As Henry progressively set aside four of his wives, beheading two of them, he graphically demonstrated the limits to that authority. So, throughout Mary's reign, and into Elizabeth's, subjects struggled to distinguish linguistically a king's wife from a female ruler. But linguistic problems were only part of the problem. Most western European societies in the sixteenth century held to the Aristotelian concept of a society constructed on the model of a family, ideally ruled by the father. The family units were bound together in an ascending hierarchy until the whole community was presided over by the head, the father of the nation, the royal *pater familias*, the king. Patriarchy as a concept informed every aspect of established authority and royal legitimation.

The prevailing ideology taught that the primary female virtues were chastity, submissiveness and obedience The law prescribed that conventionally an unmarried woman, however learned, pious and virtuous, was subject to her father, or brother, until she married and acquired her own husband as her 'head'. In practice, as Tudor men well knew, their wives and mothers were often formidable women, but, they explained, they were describing the general rule, not the atypical cases. Such exceptions certainly existed, and were much more common when high social status could override female gender. One striking example was that of Margaret Beaufort. There is a detailed account of Henry VII's mother presiding at a splendid feast; she and a surviving daughter of Edward IV sat together at the head of the table, with an appropriate cloth of estate. Her husband, Thomas Stanley, by then first Earl of Derby, was seated further down one side of the table; He was, after all, an earl, whereas her blood was royal.

Pragmatism and the sanctity of inheritance rights were also important for determining who ruled in England. And at the pragmatic level the idea of Mary as heir apparent had been familiar to Englishmen since the mid-1520s when she rode off to Ludlow Castle, as two acknowledged Princes of Wales had done before her. After her reconciliation with her father she was a familiar sight around the court, well versed in diplomatic etiquettes, drilled in the power plays of patronage, often seen in those years in the company of her royal father. After the fall of her mother, there was still considerable popular support and sympathy for both mother and daughter, from commoners as from the more conservative élite families.

When Henry died, Mary had assumed the conventionally masculine role of a land-owning magnate as well as that of the most visible defender of the Henrician forms of religion. The evangelical religion promoted by the Edwardian regime prevailed mainly in London, parts of East Anglia and the South East. Even in those areas, there may well have been only minority support for the Edwardian reforms. Furthermore, enough committed evangelicals supported Mary rather than Jane for queen for it to be clear that religious affiliation was never a straightforward determinant of political allegiance; acknowledged inheritance rights were also a powerful consideration in Tudor England.

ESTABLISHING THE MARIAN REGIME

If they were concerned about having a woman on the throne, Mary's subjects could console themselves – as they did again in the reign of Elizabeth – that at least there would be plenty of 'grave' adult males to counsel her. Indeed, her Privy Council, which would be Mary's main administrative body, took shape with impressive speed, even while she was officially a rebel against Queen Jane. From the first, it was Mary who took the initiative. Her earliest group of advisers, when she proclaimed herself queen, were all members of her own household, and therefore previously as excluded from affairs of state as she had recently been. Rochester, Waldegrave and Jerningham were the earliest known members. Englefield who, with Rochester and Waldegrave had undergone imprisonment on her behalf in 1551, joined her Council soon after.

Sir John Huddleston, who had sheltered her on her flight from Hunsdon, and whose house Sawston Hall was burned in revenge by Northumberland, was the earliest non-household member on her Council. He had also brought, perhaps as a hostage, Henry Radcliffe, son of the Earl of Sussex, thereby 'encouraging' his father to be the first really eminent man to join her, so the queen owed Huddleston a great deal. The Earls of Sussex and Bath were early members of Mary's Council, as was Sir Richard Southwell, although he had publicly committed to Jane. His 'most humble submission' was the more readily accepted, because he arrived 'amply provided with money, provisions and armed men' and because of the added benefit of his wide experience in 'counsel' at court.

FORMING MARY'S FIRST COUNCIL

When Mary moved to Framlingham, she already had a council of 19 men. As the balance of power shifted Mary's way, the Edwardian councillors still in London wrote to her that they too were her 'most humble faithful and obedient subjects having always (God we take to be our witness) [her] true and humble subjects in our hearts ever since the death of our late Sovereign lord'.[6] Mary's response to that hopeful declaration was nuanced. Of the five councillors she added while at Framlingham, four had been Edwardian councillors, and of those, Paget and Rich were effectively professional advisers and administrators, willing to serve whomsoever ruled. From one put together to meet a military emergency, her Council was already changing to one religiously more diverse and with the core of a competent, professional Council.

The men Mary gathered around her represented a cross section of experienced administrators and trusted confidantes, but few were both. Given the conventional belief that Mary was always particularly dependent on Hapsburg influence, the most striking absence from her advisers was that of Simon Renard, the new Imperial ambassador (and an invaluable but unreliable source for the early months of Mary's reign), who did not join Mary until they were both at Newhall on 29 July. She had set a great deal in place before then, but the expanding membership of the Council illustrated one of the most difficult dilemmas facing the new monarch: that she had no choice but to trust – or at least seem to trust – men who had, so recently, been actively involved in excluding her from the throne.

Despite her proclamation in London as queen, Mary remained several more days at Framlingham. One reason was the continuing uncertainty about just how secure her regime was; her council decision on 20 July that some 500 men within the castle should attend her at all times was evidence of that. As the alternative regime collapsed, Northumberland himself exuberantly proclaimed Mary queen in Cambridge, but no one found that particular declaration of loyalty persuasive. Before Mary entered her capital, Northumberland and his sons were all held in the Tower, as were others most closely implicated in the attempt to install Queen Jane.

The most surprising exception was the release from the Tower of the Duke of Suffolk on 31 July, although he was deeply implicated in plac- ing his daughter on the throne. Mary's clemency was attributed to the pleadings of his wife, Frances (daughter of Mary Tudor, Henry's sister, and therefore cousin to Mary as well as a friend of long standing), that he to be set free on parole. Robert Wingfield praised Mary as 'the most merciful queen' on this occasion but it is easy to see why Renard feared that Mary would bring about her own downfall by her mercy. As will become clear in the next chapter, if Suffolk had been a more competent man, he might well have destroyed Mary a few months later.

MARY'S ENTRY TO LONDON

Another reason that Mary lingered at Framlingham was that she needed time to prepare for her entry into London, her first formal appearance as England's queen regnant. Masculine embodiments of full royal magnifi- cence were familiar enough, but modifications were necessary for England's first female monarch, to retain her femininity as well as displaying her monarchical splendour. Her sister Elizabeth wrote to ask Mary's guidance whether, for her part in the imminent pageant of Tudor splendour, she should wear mourning for Edward's death or more colourful apparel to mark her sister's triumph. Such an occasion was, of course, also a reaffirmation of Elizabeth's own position, as now Mary's heir apparent. She may not have a received a reply (certainly nothing survives) but she chose the splendour option anyway.

Machyn recorded that Elizabeth rode into London on 29 July with 2,000 horsemen, 100 of them in velvet coats, and all in her colours of green and white, to take up residence in the Strand at what had been Somerset's great residence. Wriothesley reported her riding out of

London the next day with 1,000 horsemen as she rode to join the queen. Elizabeth obviously had a large company with her but it may well be that the conflicting numbers demonstrate that general impressions (plus or minus 1,000 horsemen) were more important to observers than precise numbers.

If Elizabeth's public procession was impressive, it was a markedly lesser one than Mary's when the queen entered London. Mary was making her formal entry as England's new monarch into her capital, a city which had so recently apparently welcomed the accession of quite another queen. Both of Henry's daughters understood very well the important political role which magnificence played in displaying and maintaining the complex social hierarchy. Countless works, from Aristotle's *Ethics* to the Renaissance proliferation of advice books for princes, explained the need for rulers to dress lavishly, live splendidly, and always embody the wealth, power and magnificence of the whole realm.

Mary's royal entry into London was magnificent by any criterion. On 3 August she rode from Newhall to a house in Whitechapel, with Elizabeth and her company among the many others already riding in her procession. Mary changed into her most royal clothes and received the mayor and aldermen of the city before the progress began. One account has it that 10,000 rode with her that day through the streets of London, the houses all hung with cloths, banners and streamers, the route lined with all the members of the various companies and guilds. At intervals through the streets stages were erected, where musicians sang and played their instruments.

That welcoming display which London provided was conventional enough, but the queen that day must have seemed particularly spectacular. Wriothesley described her as wearing a gown of purple velvet, with purple satin sleeves, and a purple satin kirtle (overskirt) 'all thick set with goldsmith's work and great pearls,' and her outer sleeves the same fabric 'all set with rich stones', as was her headdress. Even the palfrey she rode was 'richly trapped with gold embroidered to the horse's feet'. The new French ambassador, excluded from the procession, presumably because of the French support for Jane, gave very much the same description, as did the Imperial ambassadors. The monarch, traditionally masculine, had always been expected to be the most magnificent person present; a woman, the unusually detailed descriptions of the ambassadors suggested, could do it too. She was accompanied by the great men of the realm and the city. The Earl of Arundel went before her through the city, carrying a sword of state. The Lord Mayor and aldermen joined in as the procession wound through the City of London. All the way, Sir Anthony Browne, leaning against Mary's horse to brace himself, had the train of her heavily embroidered gown over his shoulder.

A striking feature for all observers would have been the number of women immediately following her: the Lady Elizabeth with her entire entourage, the Duchess of Norfolk, the Marchioness of Exeter, both suitably accompanied, and after them a 'great number of ladies, every one in their degrees'. At a time when women were more conventionally observers rather than participants in such displays, the presence of so many around the queen emphasised the accession of a female monarch. The total procession certainly surpassed the 3,000 Machyn thought he saw that day, and even the 4,000 horsemen a French observer reported.

What was also noted that day was that when the queen spoke it was with words 'so gently spoken and with so smiling a countenance that the hearers wept for joy'.[7] The weeping may be an exaggeration, but in public, as in private, it was frequently Mary's gentle manner which was first remarked. (As Nicholas Ridley had previously had occasion to note, it was only when confronted on issues of religion that Mary's sweet and gentle manner gave way to obduracy.) Renard agreed that throughout the procession, her 'gracious modesty ... her manner, her gestures, her countenance were such that in no event could they have been improved.' Rather more coolly he added: 'her face is more than middling fair.'[8]

When Mary arrived at the Tower, the shooting of guns, which had begun when she entered the City, was said to be like great thunder, or sounding as if it were an earthquake. As she entered the Tower, which Mary made her residence for the next ten days, she found Gardiner, Norfolk and Edward Courtenay, all kneeling and asking her pardon. Again her gentleness was noted as she greeted them, pardoning them for their offences against her predecessors. Courtenay was the son of the executed Marquis of Exeter and had been held in the Tower since 1538, when he was 11. Stephen Gardiner, an Edwardian prisoner for some years, celebrated mass for the queen daily for as long as she was in the Tower, and on 23 August she installed him as her Lord Chancellor. The Catholic survivors of the Edwardian era were now assuming the power of government.

WHAT RELIGION NOW?

When Mary first entered her capital, many households welcomed her by placing in their windows images of saints and of the Virgin, hidden for years against just such an occasion. That spontaneous revival of banned religious symbols – and almost immediately of banned religious services – in London was vehemently attacked by the evangelicals, who pointed out, quite accurately, that all such practices were against the law. Those displays and protests were all reminders of what everyone knew, that Mary had inherited a religiously divided kingdom. Her first royal proclamation, issued on 28 July, commanded an end to all 'naughty' talk in the streets of London by 'light persons, delighting in continual alterations and never content with the present estate'.

The proclamation had no discernable effect. More religious disputes broke out, including in the churches, and the appearance on the streets of printed pamphlets of a thoroughly seditious nature was a further alarming development. The first of many pamphlets, distributed on 15 August, appealed to noblemen and gentlemen 'favouring the Word of God' to turn against Mary, supported as she was by 'hardened and detestable papists'. Above all, it attacked Gardiner, as 'Winchester, the great Devil, [who] must be exorcized with his disciples'.[9]

On 13 August, one of the most notorious religious riots of the period occurred in London. A week earlier, John Rogers had delivered a strongly evangelical sermon at Paul's Cross, London's most popular preaching site. The following Sunday Gilbert Bourne, one of the queen's chaplains, was chosen to counter Roger's message, which he did by defending prayers for the souls of the dead and also defending the reputation of Bishop Bonner, lately released from prison and restored as Bishop of London. Uproar ensued, and Bourne had to be rescued from a shouting, furious crowd. Caps plucked from the head and thrown were common enough missiles, but a dagger which narrowly missed Bourne was quite a different matter. The Catholic preacher was rescued by from his attackers by an evangelical preacher, John Bradford, and order was restored with considerable difficulty. The Lord Mayor and aldermen were summoned before the Privy Council, and the city threatened with the loss of its liberties if such an outrage occurred again. The next Sunday the sermon at Paul's Cross was delivered in the presence of all the crafts of London, in their best livery, the lord mayor and aldermen, and 200 of the guard 'to see no disquiet done'. Order was maintained that day, and London retained its civic liberties.

Given the increasing disturbances, and the heated disputes between clergy of opposing views, to say nothing of the increasingly seditious words commonly heard and read, it is hardly surprising that Mary decided to forbid all unauthorised preaching, first in East Anglia and then more generally. Accordingly, in another proclamation addressed to religious matters on 18 August, Mary made clear that although she herself would always observe the religion in which she had been raised, yet no subject would be compelled in the matter of religion until 'further order by common consent' should be taken.

On several occasions early in the previous reign Mary and Gardiner had both resisted religious changes because they were enforced before their approval by parliament, and therefore in direct violation of the existing law. Both therefore were acutely conscious of the perils in introducing religious changes before they could be sanctioned by Mary's first parliament, scheduled to meet immediately after her coronation. In the meantime, though, the private religious liberty of both Mary and Gardiner was, however temporarily, extended to the rest of the population. Mary had very early on set an example in hearing mass again, and all over the city altars were being raised again (they had been lowered and even become communion tables in the previous regime). As the hope of mutual toleration collapsed further, the Latin mass replaced English services in several London churches well before her coronation.

It might seem surprising that in the midst of all this disputation, and despite Mary's longstanding hostility to Archbishop Cranmer – a hostility dating back to his declaration of her mother's divorce and reinforced by his role in the transformation of official English religious practice and doctrine – the archbishop remained at liberty. His biographer suggests that Cranmer still had his freedom because, as Archbishop of Canterbury, he was required to summon the Convocation of the Church, but he also received his usual summons to attend the parliament called for October.[10] He was, moreover, required for one last great public ceremony for, as Mary had been persuaded (however reluctantly) that her brother should be buried with the religious ceremonies introduced in his reign, Cranmer presided at his funeral.

Perhaps one reason Mary allowed her brother a funeral in the religion in which he died was that, as monarch, she would follow the longstanding precedent that rulers did not attend their predecessor's funeral. Edward's funeral was celebrated with much of the customary ceremonials and pomp for a king on 8 August, and attended by those of his household and Council still at liberty. It was conducted according to the *Book of Common Prayer*, in both rites and vestments. The only sign of an imminent change in the service was the tenor of the sermon preached by the newly reinstated Bishop Day of Chichester. No foreign representatives felt free to attend the evangelical rites, and Mary's conviction that her brother had been misled in his religion by evil men continued to the end. She quieted her own conscience by having separate services celebrated for Edward: the Latin service for the dead the night before the funeral, and later a requiem mass, with Gardiner officiating and the queen and all her ladies in attendance.

Cranmer was only one of a significant number of evangelical clergy still at large, but his freedom ended after he wrote – and a self-declared 'friend' published – an attack on the Latin mass re-emerging in many London churches. Cranmer described that mass as a device of the devil, hardly a politic move. Within days he refused the chance to repudiate his writing, just as he had ignored the opportunities to flee abroad. Brought before Mary's Privy Council, he was found guilty of sedition – his hesitation about endorsing Queen Jane did not protect him – by a group which included many of his recent colleagues on Edward's Council. Within days he was in the Tower of London, initially for sedition until he was later charged with heresy, as Mary had always intended he would be.

By the end of August, moves were under way to reinstate the five Henrician bishops in prison at the end of Edward's reign, and to remove insistently evangelical bishops from their dioceses. Recently disgraced bishops who had broken with the Edwardian changes at different points – Edmund Bonner (London), Cuthbert Tunstall (Durham), George Day (Chichester) and Nicholas Heath (Worcester) – were set at liberty and reinstated in their dioceses as evangelical bishops were removed. At the same time Mary's long-term friend the Duchess of Somerset was also set free, having been in the Tower since her husband's second and final arrest.

As another instance of Mary's early clemency, which Renard repeatedly found so dismaying, only three men, Northumberland and two of his close associates, died for their part in the Janeite adventure. By any standards, but especially those of her father, Mary showed remarkable clemency in that. She showed mercy again (to Renard's despair) in her early insistence that Jane Grey was innocent of any part in the plot to put her on the throne, and that it would be against her conscience to have Jane put to death. Northumberland's fate, however, was always clear. His defence – that he had always acted only with the agreement of the Council, and that the judges at his trial included men who had been his partners in those actions – were simply brushed aside by those he was trying to implicate.

Northumberland's trial was presided over by the Duke of Norfolk, now freed from the Tower and restored to all his old eminence if not to all his landed estates. Without consulting his fellow judges, the duke sentenced Northumberland to a traitor's death – hanging, drawing and quartering, a most dishonourable end. It was almost certainly the remarkable reconversion of Northumberland back to Catholicism that ensured the success of his plea to Mary for the more honourable death by beheading. He declared himself restored to the 'true Catholic faith' being among those who had 'erred from the faith these past sixteen years'. That is, he was returning not to the religion of Henry's later years but to a version closer to the time the English regime had broken with the papacy.

Bishop Gardiner had spent many hours with Northumberland after his sentence, and the duke's choice of 16 years as the time of his error most likely reflected those conversations. Gardiner, like Mary, had – during the Edwardian years of what they saw of egregious errors and heresy – come to the view that the papacy was, after all, crucial to the maintenance of orthodox Christianity, but few were prepared to support publicly the restoration of papal authority at this early stage of the new regime. Probably, for example, no member of her Council knew that Mary had already expressed to one visitor with connections to Rome her wish to restore papal authority when her reign was more secure, though she emphasised that for the moment such matters could not be spoken of publicly.

THE CORONATION OF THE QUEEN REGNANT

As Mary became a focal point of public interest, more reports of her behaviour and personality have survived. One of the most quoted sources is Renard, the new Imperial ambassador in England. As with any other ambassador, his reports were designed to convey many messages – especially how well he was coping with difficult circumstances – but he sometimes included fascinating and plausible glimpses of Mary. One example is his report that, two days before she was due to leave the Tower for the round of public ceremonies which marked her coronation, Mary had summoned all her Council and:

> sinking on her knees before them spoke at length of her coming to the throne, the duties of kings and queens, her intention to acquit herself of the task God had been pleased to lay upon her. ... She had entrusted her affairs and person, she said, to them, and wished to adjure them to do their duty as they were bound by their oaths.

He had presumably heard the story from one of her Council for, he added, they were all deeply moved, and at a loss how to answer this 'humble and lowly discourse, so unlike anything ever heard before... and by the Queen's great goodness and integrity'.[11] Certainly it was not the manner in which Somerset or Northumberland, let alone Henry VIII, spoke to their councillors.

What is most telling about that anecdote is the strong suggestion that Mary was pleading with them for the disinterested and dispassionate advice she knew she needed. According to the Imperial ambassador, she had already told him that she could not trust her Council. That anxiety about trusting her early Council and seeking advice from the Imperial representative has often been criticised, but it is worth remembering that many of her Council had been fully complicit in the attempted installation of Queen Jane and the exclusion of Mary. Moreover Mary had an acute awareness of the religious problems she faced in her realm, many of them promoted by the government of those same men. Their reputation for the self-aggrandisement and self-interest, which had so often played a role in the previous administration, was in no way diminished by their recent readiness to turn on erstwhile colleagues like Cranmer – or Northumberland.

But now it was time to turn to the celebration of the queen's coronation. Traditionally, English coronation ceremonies were spread over four days, with the procedures each day clearly defined. Mary maintained the customary practices, with again the few modifications essential for the accession of a female monarch. The first day (28 September 1553) required little alteration. Mary, previously at St James, moved to the royal apartments in the Tower by barge, and, as was also customary, the mayor and aldermen in their decorated barges and with many musicians accompanied her along the Thames. Once again her sister Elizabeth travelled with her, with many other women. The music, as ever, had to compete with 'much shooting of guns'; one object was always to produce the loudest possible 'sounds of joy' on this as on other great occasions.

The next day the queen created 15 new Knights of the Bath, including Edward Courtenay, already Earl of Devon; the young Earl of Surrey, Norfolk's grandson and heir; William Dormer, who had been among the first to come to her aid in July, and father of a favourite attendant, Jane; Sir Henry Parker, who had several times dedicated writings to Mary; and Rochester and Jerningham of her former household. Some who had suffered in or supported her cause were reaping their early rewards.

The third day was conventionally the day the monarch rode through the city of London, to receive both the homage and the welcome of its citizens. Some aspects of this repeated greetings given the new monarch on her first entry into London, but there were also significant differences. Preparations for London's coronation welcome were under way by 12 September, as streets were again hung with streamers, banners and colourful fabrics, but this time pageants were built along the route the new monarch traditionally followed. Fountains, which would run with wine on the day the monarch passed through, were refurbished and statues regilded. All the streets were freshly gravelled 'that the horses should not slide on the pavement'. New railings and stands were placed along one side where members of all the city's crafts and guilds would line the streets as their formal welcome to their new monarch. As well as those devised by the City of London, the Genoese, the Hanseatic merchants, and the Florentines all set up pageants, a reminder of the importance of international trade for London. The Florentines compared Mary with Judith, the Israelite heroine, and by implication, Northumberland with Holofernes, the Assyrian leader sent to destroy her people and beheaded by Judith.

In the afternoon of the third day, the queen rode through the elaborately prepared London streets, from the Tower to Temple Bar, past the assembled crowds and past the pageants praising and acclaiming her. This occasion was traditionally the formal greeting of the City to the new monarch, with a lengthy procession. The procession began with the queen's messengers and the ambassadors' servants. They were followed by the carefully ordered hierarchy of clergy, officers, judges in their ranks, the ambassadors of Spain and France, and the representative Hanseatic merchants. That part of the social hierarchy culminated in the mayor of London, then the three great officers of the day: the Earl of Arundel, carrying the sword of state; the earl marshal, the Duke of Norfolk; and the lord great chamberlain, the Earl of Oxford. Then came the monarch.

But the appearance of this monarch was different. Where a male monarch was dressed in bright colours and rode a horse, Mary was dressed in white cloth of gold, her skirt and mantle furred with miniver and powdered ermine; she sat in a litter lined with the same cloth of gold. Over it a canopy of white cloth of gold was held by four knights. Even more curiously, she travelled with her hair hanging loose over her shoulders. Modest Tudor women kept their hair neatly bound in public. The one exception was as a king's wife went to her coronation, when it was worn loose. That had been the custom for centuries, and probably denoted the wife was fertile and would bear the monarch's children – always the first duty of any queen consort. So that day Mary presented herself as if a queen consort. The descriptions of her on that occasion were unusually varied, and although some described her attire and litter accurately enough, none explicitly reported any analogy with the traditional dress of a queen consort. When, some five years later, Elizabeth went to her coronation in exactly the same way, she was described as going 'according to the ancient precedents' – that is, the precedents for a queen regnant as created by Mary. And so another tradition was invented, as Mary's response to her unprecedented role.

Another innovation was that whereas the king's womenfolk had usually watched that procession from a window, again the important women rode with Mary, not just those who had been with her on her first entry into London but more beside. Immediately behind her was another litter, lined with cloth of silver, and in it sat Elizabeth and Anne of Cleves. Accounts vary as to whether they wore cloth of silver or crimson velvet, but they clearly occupied the pre-eminent place of honour among the women. They were followed by an unspecified number of other ladies and gentlewomen – once again estimates of numbers varied considerably, but they were headed by the Duchess of Norfolk, the Marchionesses of Exeter and Winchester, and countesses, all wearing crimson velvet. The French ambassador thought there were perhaps 70 ladies there; another observer more cautiously recorded 'a flock of peeresses, gentlewomen and ladies in waiting never before seen in such numbers, who accompanied the queen in all her glory'.

After them, the procession worked its way down the social order again, ending with noblemen's servants. In general, there was agreement that it was all a splendid show, but observers contradicted each other on such matters as what the queen wore on her head, and even such matters as whether she was wearing white cloth of gold or, as one contemporary had it, blue velvet, seated in a litter decorated with red velvet – which suggests a lot of colour, if not elegance. The striking contradictions in what was reported that day owed something to what people expected to see and confusion about what, if anything, to expect of a queen regnant, that previously unknown phenomenon.[12] Whatever the details of those matters, there was no doubt that great numbers attended the occasion: 'such a multitude of people resorted out of all parts of the realm, to see the same, that the like had not been seen before.'[13]

The next day was the day of the coronation ceremony itself. There was another spectacular but briefer procession, this time on foot from Westminster Hall to the abbey. Because the coronation of Edward had introduced some innovations to incorporate the new ideology of imperial kingship, and because the actual coronation of a queen regnant was unprecedented in England, Mary's coronation service probably differed again, but little is known about the terms of her coronation oath, or other central features of the ceremony. It is known, however, Mary had sent to Flanders for the coronation chrism (sacramental oil), fearing that the oil held at Westminster had been polluted by 'heretics' in the previous years.

For her actual coronation, Mary was dressed much as kings were dressed, in scarlet garments echoing episcopal dress, and she again wore her hair loose. She was anointed as kings were anointed, she was given a coronation ring as kings were given, and used it to argue, well before Elizabeth did the same, that she was now married to her kingdom. She was given all the markers of royal power that kings were given with the exception that where the ceremonial spurs were put on kings, Mary simply touched them as a gesture of acknowledgement. She was crowned as kings were crowned. Gardiner, not only Bishop of Winchester but now also Lord Chancellor, presided at the ceremony, issuing the challenge to any who would deny her claim, evoking shouts of endorsement from all sides.

The ceremonies had begun in the morning, and concluded late in the afternoon with a magnificent feast, again according to tradition, except that again an unusual number of peeresses were in attendance. Elizabeth and Anne of Cleves sat together, in places of honour at the foot of Mary's table. The whole occasion was, as such events always were, a mixture of extraordinary pomp and splendour, and rank disorderliness. As Mary left Westminster Abbey, there had been the usual scramble for pieces of the cloth she had walked on – but at least there is no report of anyone dying in the crush, as had happened at the coronation of Elizabeth of York. And after the banquet for Mary, conducted on the most splendid lines, there was a wild scramble for the food being thrown out of the kitchen, followed by 'no less scrambling for the kitchen itself, every man that would plucking down the boards thereof, and carrying them away, that it might well be called a waste indeed'.[14] The line between order and disorder was fragile indeed in many facets of Tudor society.

The early portraits of Queen Mary on charters and other official documents which her royal portrait validated often show her wearing the closed imperial crown with her hair flowing loose. The way Mary went to her coronation was adopted as the standard way for denoting a powerful queen regnant, at least on the most formal occasions. It also became the style adopted in the early reign of Elizabeth. The surviving version of Elizabeth's coronation portrait shows her wearing the imperial crown, holding the symbols of her office, and with her hair flowing loose, as we know she wore it for her coronation procession.

An even more striking practice, followed by Mary and continued by Elizabeth, was the practical expression that a consecrated female monarch was the equivalent of a male monarch, even in the exercise of the healing touch. When the French justified their Salic law, they had argued that monarchy was a quasi-priestly function, as demonstrated by the power to cure certain conditions. Being therefore a quasi-priestly office, they concluded, it was obviously one that no woman could occupy. Mary, however, exercised that healing power for her subjects throughout her reign, presumably with as much efficacy as any of her male forebears. It was thought to work particularly well for scrofula, more commonly known then as 'the king's evil' (a medical condition characterised by swelling of the lymph glands, and one in which the sufferer can have long periods of remission).

Mary also revived the royal practice of touching cramp rings, understood to relieve various forms of cramping pains. In March 1554 she sent off 150 such rings to her ailing cousin, Charles V, and later more to the Queens Dowager of France and Hungary, and to the Duchess of Lorraine. The thanks she received included a hope they would prove more effective that those of some of her predecessors, a snide remark possibly directed at her father's fall from Catholic grace. The point being emphasised here is that Mary, consecrated with all the customary rites as monarch, demonstrated repeatedly as she exercised her healing powers that female monarchy was quite as sacred and potent as male.

MARY'S FIRST PARLIAMENT

As Mary was establishing herself as queen, there was some discussion about whether her first parliament should meet even before her coronation. Such a suggestion was without known precedent, and quickly rejected by her on the grounds it would imply that she needed to be confirmed queen by parliamentary act. Mary much preferred to rely on her known right by birth and statute, confirmed by the traditional coronation ceremonies. As Wingfield wrote, when completing his account of Mary's coronation ceremonies: 'To finish this triumph came the opening of Queen Mary's first parliament.' That had always been the relationship between coronation and parliament. The essential business for that parliament, which began 3 October, included the reaffirmation of Mary's title to the throne and the repeal of all Edward's religious legislation. To move the official religion back further than the religious settlement at the time of Henry's death proved politically impossible so soon after the new monarch came to the throne.

As it transpired, the first bill discussed by the Lords was one addressing definitions of treason, an offence which had been significantly redefined by Mary's Tudor predecessors. The effect of the new legislation was to take the basic definitions of treason back to an act of 1352. Among other consequences, the new act expunged all Henry's legislation defining as treason any refusal to accept him as supreme head of the church. It passed the Lords without significant delay; it presumably helped that by then most of the more committed Edwardian bishops were in some form of detention. But the bill ran into problems in the House of Commons, which Mary explained to Reginald Pole, by now deeply embroiled in English politics from his base in Rome. The resistance was because the abolition of 'the title of the supremacy of the church in the realm of the crown [was thought] to be an introduction of the pope's authority into the realm, which they cannot gladly hear of'.[15] The Commons did however finally agree to it.

Of particular importance for Mary was a bill reaffirming the validity of Henry's marriage to Katherine of Aragon. That act ensured that Mary's legitimacy and claim to the throne rested not simply on a papal edict, but also on English law. Mary was insistent on that, though Pole resisted strongly the implication that anything more than a papal decision was ever required. The act removing the Edwardian religious changes, thereby restoring the religious settlement in place at the death of Henry VIII, proved much more contentious. In the Commons there was heated and acrimonious debate over four days before the act was finally passed on the fifth. No division was recorded, but as an indicator of how hard it had been fought, Gardiner thought that of some 350 votes 'only' 80 had gone against the bill. Noailles, the French ambassador, claimed it had been debated eight days amid much disputation, and Mary agreed about the prolonged debates, if not the exaggerated number of days.

The Commons debates made it clear that although there was a majority who accepted Mary's restoration of an older order, there was a significant minority who did not. In the following days various acts of defiance served as a reminder of that; one of the more memorable occurred on the day parliament ended, when a dead dog, tonsured like a Catholic priest, was thrown into Mary's presence chamber. But in many ways the most contentious issue, which went right to the heart of the problems faced by England's first queen regnant, was that of whom Mary should marry. That issue was to generate much more heat even than the abolition of all the Edwardian religious changes. Englishmen were well versed in the belief that it was a wife's God-given duty to obey her husband. Moreover, by English common law, a wife's property usually passed to her husband's control after marriage. It is understandable then that, although many were anxious for the queen to marry so as to secure the dynasty, they were also apprehensive about all that was thought to be at stake when a queen regnant married and became a wife. But that was not a topic any parliament would be permitted to discuss, if Mary could possibly help it.

8

PROBLEMS FOR A MARRYING QUEEN REGNANT

EARLY MODERN IDEAS OF MARRIAGE

It has long been a historical orthodoxy that one of Mary's greatest mistakes as queen was to marry Philip of Spain. But rather than simply repeating that enduring judgment, it is informative to reconsider just what alternatives she had, given the general consensus that she *should* marry. Charles V spoke for many, both English and foreign, when he said she must marry because: 'it is important that she have heirs, and still more important that some one may be at her side to assist her in the conduct of her affairs.'[1] Only Reginald Pole – himself named by some as a possible marriage partner – is known to have questioned whether Mary should marry. His view was that given her age and medical history she was unlikely to bear an heir. Therefore, the question of her heir, he argued, should be left in the hands of God. But all the evidence suggests that for everyone else it was self-evident that the queen *should* be married; only the matter of a suitable husband was one for debate.

It was well understood that the choice of Mary's husband was critical, for, as the story of Adam and Eve made clear, husbands had God-given authority to rule over their wives. The punishment God prescribed for Eve for her part in man's Fall and expulsion from the Garden of Eden was read as applying to all women: 'in sorrow thou shalt bring forth children; and thy desire shall be to thy husband, and he shall rule over thee.'[2] In England, the general subordination of wives meant that usually not only a wife and her children but also her property fell under her husband's control.

There were no established historical precedents to establish whether, in the case of a female monarch, that included control of her realm, although Henry I had gone to considerable lengths to establish that in Matilda's case it did not. Edward's assumption of the comprehensive subordination of wives to husbands was part of his public justification for excluding both his (unmarried) sisters from the throne. His preferred heir, Jane Grey was already safely married to an Englishman, thereby removing any danger of a foreign husband taking control of the English realm, introducing foreign customs and, above all, imposing foreign (i.e. Catholic) religion.

But now Mary reigned. After her accession and coronation in 1553, she resisted early suggestions that she should marry by showing her coronation ring, and declaring herself married to her kingdom. Indeed, her personal preference may well have been to remain unmarried, but for Mary there was the knowledge that, as matters stood, her next heir was her half-sister, Elizabeth. Not only was she the daughter of the deplorable Anne Boleyn, but also her repeated strategic delays in fully accepting Catholic rites could only reinforce Mary's desire to produce a soundly Catholic heir of her own.

As monarch, Mary believed she could follow her predecessors' examples and exercise the same freedom of choice as her father had so often enjoyed. As an aging maiden, however, she was conventionally modest enough to look for guidance in the matter and turned 'naturally' to her familiar adviser and relative, Charles V, ignoring her subjects' belief that they had a strong political interest in whom she married. Above all, her councillors – all male – believed she should be guided by their opinions, precisely because of the inevitable political consequences of her marriage.

THE CASE AGAINST AN ENGLISH MARRIAGE

Mary had been Henry VIII's bargaining-piece of many marriage negotiations but the question of her marrying within the realm had never been a serious possibility. Nor was it in her brother's reign. Although Edward once joked about marrying Mary to his Uncle Thomas Seymour 'to turn her opinions' on religion, everyone understood that any English husband for her could become a dangerous leader of resistance to the regime she so frequently defied. That was one reason some English families had been suspected of scheming to win her in marriage. As far as is known, Mary herself had never contemplated, and still did not seriously consider, marrying an Englishman.

Criticisms of Mary for taking a foreign husband have long ignored the arguments against her marrying within the realm. The most persuasive was that Mary's marrying a husband from an English family could easily upset the balance of affinities and clientage networks in the realm. Mary had, after all, had in her father's time the chance to see first-hand on four occasions the extent to which the family and affinity of an English queen consort could accumulate an impressive amount of power, influence and wealth. If even Henry VIII as monarch/husband did not completely control his English in-laws and connections, Mary had strong grounds for avoiding the problems a monarch/wife might face.

It was not only that she was reluctant to marry a subject, although she always was. There was also no obvious suitable partner for her. The popular English candidate for her hand was Edward Courtenay, restored as Earl of Devon by Mary's first parliament. Ten years younger than Mary, his royal blood, through his Yorkist grandmother, was never enough to outweigh the disadvantage that he had been isolated as a prisoner in the Tower for some 15 years. Well educated in the classics by his fellow prisoner Stephen Gardiner, he had little else to recommend him. Despite her longstanding friendship with his mother Gertrude, Marchioness of Exeter, Mary insisted that little was known of his personality or qualities. Indeed, events to be described later in this chapter fully justified her reservations about Courtenay's character.

THE CASE AGAINST A FOREIGN MATCH

The hostility of Mary's councillors to a foreign match reflected their own private concerns – such as anxiety that a foreign husband would displace English men of affairs from their offices and profits by installing his preferred foreign advisers, but they also had in mind important foreign policy considerations. There was little doubt that any foreign husband

Mary chose would inevitably alter the balance of English foreign policy. The choice of a Hapsburg ally would provoke French interests. However improbable it might seem, if Mary *did* choose a French ally as husband, then the Hapsburgs would face much greater dangers travelling between their possessions, for the English Channel, which provided the Hapsburgs with the easiest route between their realms, would be much more hazardous with potential enemies on both coastlines.

Following her accession, the anxiety about Mary marrying outside the realm was so widespread that Charles V hesitated to suggest his son, Philip of Spain, as her husband. It was only after Mary indicated her own preference for him that Charles did so. She had already told her Hapsburg confidante, Simon Renard, that, when she married she would, of course, love and obey her new husband as any wife should, 'but if he wished to encroach in the government of the kingdom, she would be unable to permit it.' Renard immediately reported to Charles Mary's clear distinction between herself as 'public' monarch and as 'private' wife.[3] However unfamiliar such a distinction was to most Englishmen, Mary's own family history provided an impressive model for it. As previously discussed, her maternal grandmother, Isabella of Castile, had been queen regnant of Castile before she married, and remained queen with full authority in her own realm after she married Ferdinand of Aragon. That was, indeed, a classic example of a situation where status and office could transcend conventional gendered limitations.

Through her mother Katharine of Aragon, therefore, Mary was well-versed in the distinctions between public and private authority possible within a royal marriage, and meant to retain that distinction in her own marriage. Renard, in all his subsequent negotiations, understood this to be the case. Her councillors also came to understand it as demonstrated by a Council letter of December 1553 to Nicholas Wotton, Mary's ambassador in France. Henry II of France had scoffed at the idea that England could be independent after Mary's marriage, stating that once Philip was married to Mary 'he shall be King himself, and then what councillors will or dare counsel against his King's pleasure and will?'[4] For Henry, as for so many the word 'king' carried a strong resonance of authority in the way 'queen' could never do. Wotton, however, was instructed to repeat Mary's determination that 'if the marriage took place the government of the realm should always remain in her Majesty and not in the prince.'[5]

THE ELIGIBILITY OF PHILIP OF SPAIN

If Mary could indeed maintain England as an independent realm, then Philip was a highly suitable partner for her, although 11 years younger. He had already been married once, to Maria of Portugal, who died in 1545, following the birth of their son Don Carlos. In the years that followed, Philip was in no hurry to remarry; he enjoyed a very active social life, which included hunting and the company of women. He was, however, well placed to understand the political advantages of such a match for the Hapsburg interests across Europe.

Since 1546, Philip had gradually assumed control of Spanish affairs as his father's regent. Before he came to England to marry Mary he had completed an extensive tour of the Netherlands, another important part of his inheritance. It was, however, precisely because he was heir to so large a part of the Hapsburg realms that so many Englishmen feared he would inevitably embroil England in the great rivalry between the expanding French empire and the even greater Hapsburg territories. On the other hand, proponents of the marriage argued that Philip would bring political experience to support the queen, while being too concerned with the unstable territories his ailing father ruled to intervene much in English affairs.

As early as September 1553, London gossip claimed that Mary would marry Philip or not at all. The hostile rumour mill went to work, elaborating Edward's fears that English laws, customs and administration would give way to foreign practices. In the following months – and years – secretly published pamphlets offered graphic and disturbing details of the Hapsburg family tactics, expanding its territories by strategic marriages and the gradual absorption of their hapless wives' possessions. This concern fed into a more familiar xenophobia and resentment of foreigners. Above all, since the devoutly Catholic Mary was marrying the devoutly Catholic Philip, the pamphlets made clear, that marked the end of all the hopes – both religious and political – of Edwardian Protestants, let alone their dreams of an Anglo-Scottish union of two peoples, to share and spread evangelical religion and a common language, against a Europe still mainly ruled by Catholics.

OPPOSITION TO MARY'S MARRIAGE: FROM PARLIAMENTARY PROTEST TO REBELLION

For many reasons, then, the idea that Mary would marry Philip caused considerable alarm and dismay. Her Privy Council, with the possible exception of Sir William Paget, opposed any foreign marriage; Paget was quicker than most to realise how firmly Mary was set on marriage to Philip, and therefore where his own political future lay. Gardiner, by way of contrast, still hoped for a match with Courtenay and was deeply implicated in encouraging an unusual deputation to Mary to warn her against any foreign match. Mary postponed the meeting for three weeks, using her familiar excuse of ill health, so that by the time the parliamentary deputation did meet her, she had secretly committed herself to Philip, through Renard. The only other person present on that occasion was Susan Clarencius, who had been with Mary for some 20 years, and was probably closer to Mary than anyone since her mother's death.

Mary finally met the deputation to persuade her to marry within England on 16 November. It was an impressive delegation, made up of many of her most senior nobles, including the Duke of Norfolk, the Earls of Arundel, Shrewsbury and Derby, several (restored) senior bishops, Lord Chancellor Gardiner, and other important dignitaries. On their behalf, the Speaker of the House of Commons spoke at length, using historical instances and rhetorical art, to advise Mary against marrying outside the realm. Such a marriage, he warned with unusual bluntness would anger the people, be a financial drain on the realm and quite possibly lead to a disputed succession after Mary's death.

It is hardly surprising that Mary found the speech deeply offensive, and despite all those years of training in passivity and self-control, she showed it. She replied herself, instead of following convention and leaving it to the Lord Chancellor, to answer for her. She knew that Gardiner was still promoting Courtenay as her husband, and she strongly suspected that he was also the inspiration behind the parliamentary deputation. Instead Mary made clear her view that the delegation's attempt to dictate whom she should marry was offensive and violated all precedents. Pointing out that kings, even minors, had always had freedom in deciding their marriage, she added 'wherefore they ought always to enjoy the same';[6] for she was a female king.

Despite that confrontation, some still intrigued on Courtenay's behalf, but Mary had no intention of changing her mind. Within days Paget, at least, was loyalty and obedience personified, working on the treaty for the forthcoming marriage. Negotiations were conducted entirely between representatives of Mary and Charles V; Philip knew little if anything of them. The process went so well that Renard reported to Charles that when the full Council saw a draft, the only condition they added was that her prospective husband would not be able to take the queen out of the country against her will. That clause was easily accepted, but is a telling comment on the enduring English problems in coming to terms with the full implications of Mary's future status as woman, queen regnant and now wife.

Because of continuing widespread unease about it, the terms of the final marriage treaty were published in January 1554, and ratified by Parliament in April. The final text made very clear that Philip's role was to assist and advise his wife, not rule her; he could have the title of king, but not the authority of one. He could not introduce foreign office holders, nor could he embroil England in his foreign wars. Should Mary die childless before Philip, he would have no further claims on England. Instead, the English succession would fall where it belonged according to English practice. Should a child be born to the pair, however, it would inherit a new expanded kingdom of England and the Low Countries.

Philip's immediate reaction, when he first saw the terms of the marriage treaty, was to make a solemn vow that he was in no way bound by them. This vow remained a well-kept secret but many Englishmen were also incredulous that a husband could have so little control over his wife's affairs. Hard as Mary's subjects found it to comprehend 'queen' as a term for ultimate power, Philip had as much difficulty in accepting the title 'king' as defining the subordinate status of a monarch's spouse. Divine, natural and English law surely all prescribed that a husband's authority was pre-eminent; Philip found the idea of any marriage as a relationship between two equals, let alone two rulers, most unusual – which suggests that he knew rather less about his Spanish forbears than did Mary.

Once Mary's marriage to Philip was formally agreed, her leading subjects, including the Lord Mayor of London, the nobility, gentry and 'sundry persons of credit' were all informed individually of the queen's decision. The news was then announced more generally. Her subjects were reminded that they should 'like obedient subjects accept ... her pleasure, and be content and quiet themselves'.[7] That was what 'good' subjects were always expected to do, suppressing any doubts they harboured for the greater good of obedience to a properly ordained monarch. Unease, however, continued, especially – but not only – among those who had adopted the Edwardian religious changes and disliked the whole tenor of the new regime.

THE WYATT REBELLION

Some of those opposed to Mary's marriage believed (as it turned out, accurately) that it would lead to the full restoration of Catholicism, complete with papal authority. Others believed England had to be saved from a foreign takeover. The French were offering particular fearsome forecasts about the likely results of the marriage. Philip would come, they warned, with a huge army to impose his will upon a conquered land, and inevitably embroil it in the Hapsburgs' European wars, in which France was the main enemy. Immediately after Mary refused to accept the parliamentary petition against a foreign marriage, there was some talk of resisting Mary's marriage plans by force. There were even rumours of a plan to assassinate the queen before she could marry.

It was not surprising, therefore, that some began to plan raising a rebellion against the queen and/or her marriage. Precisely what the objective was – or even if there was an agreed objective – has never been entirely clear. The steadfastly evangelical Jane Grey was still alive and in the Tower, and there was some talk of restoring her to the throne, but there was always more talk that Elizabeth should marry the rejected and resentful Courtenay. Presumably the pair were then to assume the English throne. It is likely the conspirators were united less by a shared religious position than by fear of imminent Spanish domination. Such domination would involve much more than just the loss of all the most attractive – and lucrative – public offices, although that was one consideration. After the collapse of the uprising, however, the victors preferred to paint all the conspirators as heretics, yet another warning against the evils of false religion and an argument for Catholic loyalty.

From late November still rather sketchy plans were under way for co-ordinated uprisings, headed in Kent by Sir Thomas Wyatt, in the

South West by Edward Courtenay and Sir Peter Carew, and in Leicestershire by the Duke of Suffolk, father to Lady Jane Grey. French support was limited, in part because of their scepticism about whether such a rising would succeed; however there was sufficient support and money from the French to encourage the plotting. The English government also soon knew the outlines of the plot, and was well aware of the involvement of the French ambassador. It seems to have been widely agreed that Elizabeth and Courtenay were key personnel for the conspirators, but the extent of the complicity of either was less clear.

Courtenay, who had been actively involved to some extent, lost his nerve under questioning from Gardiner and told him something of the plot in late January, but Gardiner, still anxious to protect his protégé, was reluctant to make a move for fear of implicating him. As the information spread further, Carew was the first to be summoned to court. He ignored the order and continued recruiting, but even though he repeatedly reminded people that the arrival of the 'King' of Spain with vast numbers of troops would inevitably mean that English wives and daughters would be raped and Englishmen robbed and ruined, he won little support. He finally fled to France, where he took refuge at the French court. Then the Duke of Suffolk, pardoned only weeks before for his support of Northumberland's attempted coup, fled from his country residence, trying to raise more forces as he went. He was soon arrested, and taken as prisoner to London.

Of the leading conspirators, only Wyatt remained to offer any serious threat. He raised enough Kentish forces to set out for London. At Maidstone, however, he invited the townspeople to join him, promising that 'before God … we seek no harm to the Queen but better counsel and Councillors',[8] but still had disappointingly little response to his recruiting. In the meantime, London raised some 500 troops from its citizen militia, and Mary put the aged Duke of Norfolk in command. What neither the Duke nor any other London officials knew was that some leaders of the Whitecoats, as the London trained bands were known, had already agreed to join Wyatt.

Norfolk subsequently ignored a warning about the Londoners' unreliability (he thought it a trick on Wyatt's part) and made a stand against the rebel forces at Rochester. He was completely unprepared when many of the Whitecoats deserted and joined Wyatt, leading to a rout of Mary's forces. Those London bands which had not joined Wyatt straggled back into the city, bedraggled and beaten, their coats turned inside out, their arrows, their swords and even the strings for their bows, surrendered.[9] The aged Norfolk, utterly humiliated, ignominiously retired to his estates and to a private life until he died in August of that year.

THE FINAL STAGES AND AFTERMATH OF WYATT'S REBELLION

After the disaster at Rochester, London was left almost defenceless against the approaching rebels. Mary's Council had little choice but to offer generous terms to Wyatt, including a proposal for a committee to discuss any outstanding problems Wyatt and his sympathisers had with the conditions of the marriage treaty, and even a free pardon to all those who returned quietly to their homes. But when Wyatt was invited to name his securities against the peace negotiations being a trap, he wanted both the Tower of London, and the queen herself in his keeping. Such unrealistic demands ensured there was no further attempt to negotiate with him, and on 31 January Wyatt and all those with him were proclaimed traitors.

With Wyatt's triumphant forces halted on the south bank of the Thames, there was panic in London and at Mary's court. After some weeks of indecisiveness, during the crisis of early February Mary became much more assertive. She flatly rejected well-intentioned suggestions that she should join the ambassadors and others in leaving her capital for the relative safety of Windsor. Instead, accompanied by the great men of her realm and with an impressive display of well-armed guards, she rode through the streets of London to Guildhall. Just as some six months before, she had rallied her supporters at Framlingham, she now rallied the citizens of London with another rousing speech.

She reminded them that she was queen by the consent of them all (declared by their representatives at the coronation ceremony and in the first parliament). She declared she grieved at the thought of bloodshed of her people as much any mother would grieve to see her own son die. She promised that she would not marry without the assent of her commons and would shortly call parliament to hear their advice. She outlined the negotiations with Wyatt, and declared his purpose was to depose her (although queen by their consent), to destroy her nobility and finally 'the robbing and despoiling of you my faithful subjects'. She called the Londoners to arms, announcing that the Earl of Pembroke and Lord William Howard would lead their defence of the city.[10] Even Foxe recorded the enthusiastic reception of her speech. It obviously had a considerable impact and Machyn, for one, noted Mary's promises in his *Diary*, in unusual detail.

Inexplicably, Wyatt and his forces did not arrive at Southwark until 3 February, and then stayed on the south bank of the Thames. That allowed the city authorities time to better organise some resistance, but there was still uncertainty about just how many Londoners might defect to Wyatt's cause. Suddenly there were reports – at 4 a.m. on 7 February – that Wyatt and his troops were across the river and almost in the city. Almost certainly Mary was again advised to flee, and again refused.

Quarrels broke out among her nobility, including one when Courtenay claimed that his social precedence gave him the right to command the queen's forces rather than Pembroke. Courtenay finally withdrew and Pembroke led, ultimately successfully. There was more general panic at court, but eyewitness accounts agree that Mary herself remained quite calm and steadfast throughout that confused day. No coherent account of the day's events has survived, but Wyatt's men approached the city gates crying 'God save the Queen. We are her friends,' which may help explain the confusion which followed. But in it all, someone recognised Wyatt as his group approached Ludgate, and shut the gates before they could enter the city itself. The rebels surrendered soon after, having achieved nothing beyond some 40 deaths and an uncertain number of other casualties.

The reaction of Mary's Council and Mary was more conventional than the unusual clemency shown to those implicated in Northumberland's attempt to install Jane Grey as queen; there were, however, still complaints about Mary being too clement. Machyn records the hanging – and often quartering – of 51 men at major sites throughout London after the fighting. A few days later, however, he also recorded the very public theatre of royal clemency, when several hundred Kentish prisoners were paraded through the streets, with halters (for their hanging) around their neck. In the tiltyard at Westminster they all kneeled before the queen who pardoned them all and sent them home. They at least had good reason to cry 'God save the Queen'.

Others more politically significant were less fortunate. The most innocent victim was Lady Jane herself. Inadvertently compromised by the actions of her father the Duke of Suffolk, she and her husband Guilford Dudley died because of the potential threat to Mary's regime their continuing existence represented. Courtenay, who had plotted with the conspirators, betrayed their plans, and then squabbled with the Earl of Pembroke over who should lead the defence of London, escaped trial. He was held as a prisoner for some months, then given permission to travel. His requests to return to England were all refused and he died abroad in 1556. Some said that the reason he was kept abroad and never fully examined about the conspiracy was fear of what he might reveal under questioning about the role of Elizabeth in those months.

What lay behind the plotting did not become any clearer amid the deaths. Wyatt for example, insisted in his final statement that he rebelled because he believed Mary's marriage would bring his country 'bondage and servitude by aliens and strangers'.[11] But despite his silence on any religious issue, anxiety about the consequences of foreign rule was not the only concern; another significant development was suggested by the numbers of strongly committed Protestants who joined this rebellion, including some who had supported Mary's accession six months before. But by the time a contemporary report was written by John Proctor, a Marian supporter, the revolt was presented as the work of heretics and foreigners, a conclusion which suited the victors but may well have mis-represented the range of anxieties caused by Mary's proposal to marry Philip.

MARY'S TROUBLESOME SISTER

Elizabeth's relations with her half-sister Mary had always been ambiva-lent, particularly in Edward's reign. After Edward's death, the sisters had necessarily maintained a carefully close relationship, in public at least. After all, they had a shared interest in ensuring that the 'Queen Jane' enterprise did not succeed, since they would both have been excluded from ever assuming the crown. At Mary's first entry into London, as at all the ceremonial occasions surrounding her coronation, appropriate precedence was carefully accorded to and maintained by Elizabeth. But Mary was probably never persuaded of Elizabeth's sincerity in her adoption of Catholic practices, and by late 1553 the relationship was becoming more fraught.

The Venetian ambassador thought the tension began after the October parliament confirmed Mary's legitimacy, which necessarily denied the legitimacy of the daughter of Henry's second wife, born while his (now legitimate) first wife still lived. In November there was some discussion at court of excluding her from the succession because of her illegitimacy and probable heretical inclinations, but Mary was advised, then and later, that parliament would not endorse Elizabeth's exclusion.

There were occasions at court when Elizabeth was publicly required to give precedence to her cousin Margaret Douglas, the daughter of Henry VIII's elder sister Margaret and Archibald Douglas, and long a companion of Mary. Mary's grounds for believing Margaret had a stronger claim to the throne than Elizabeth included that their cousin was the child of an indisputably legitimate and Catholic marriage. There were even suggestions that Mary suspected that Elizabeth was the daughter not of the king, but of Anne's musician, executed as one of the several men with whom Anne was said to have committed adultery.

By December 1553, Elizabeth's position at court was increasingly uncomfortable and she requested permission to retire to her house at Ashbridge. The theatre of mutual good will was enacted publicly by Mary's parting gifts of pearls and a very costly sable hood, and Elizabeth's plea to her sister to believe no evil reports of her without giving her the chance to answer them. That request is a telling comment on how many suspicions surrounded Elizabeth, even in the earliest stages of what became the Wyatt conspiracy. Shortly after Elizabeth set out for Ashbridge, she sent a messenger back to Mary's court to request the copes, crosses and chalices necessary for Catholic forms of worship in her chapel, but that did not persuade Mary of her religious orthodoxy.

Once the Wyatt conspirators had begun to talk of Elizabeth as a marriage partner for Courtenay and his partner on the throne, her position became much more perilous. There is now no conclusive evidence of Elizabeth's implication in those activities, but when pressed, she admitted receiving at least one message from Wyatt. It counted against her that she had not reported that to anyone in authority. More damningly, a copy of one of Elizabeth's letters to Mary was found in a French diplomatic pouch; at the very least it could hardly had got there without the connivance of someone in Elizabeth's household. That someone needed to be sufficiently in Elizabeth's confidence to know the letter existed. It gave further grounds for suspecting her involvement, however inadvertent, with some conspirators.

Before Wyatt attacked London, there had been enough concern about Elizabeth's activities, for her to be 'requested' to come to court, a request she ignored. To ignore such a command from the monarch was at best disobedience, potentially much worse. A more peremptory demand for her presence followed. In a move reminiscent of Mary's own strategies in similar circumstances, she replied that she was too ill to travel. Mary sent her own physicians to Elizabeth, and they decided she could make the journey, but slowly.

Elizabeth did not reach London until after Wyatt had been defeated, and when she arrived she travelled through London with the curtains of her litter drawn back. All, both sympathisers and critics, could see how ill she looked – 'pale' and 'bloated' were two adjectives often used to describe her appearance. Her reception at Mary's court this time was remarkably like those Mary had received at Edward's court when her fortunes were lowest, with almost all her retinue excluded from court, and no ceremony to greet her, least of all from her sister the queen.

For the next three weeks Elizabeth was confined to her quarters at court, without visitors and with little sense of what would become of her. There were many, including Renard, who pressed for Elizabeth's death. So did Gardiner, but cautiously since any evidence that existed against her would probably be stronger against Courtenay. Mary resisted all such demands; Elizabeth's survival was undoubtedly partly due to her being legally the queen's heir, making any action against her politically hazardous. But what to do with her was a real problem. No noble was prepared to accept the responsibility of safeguarding her, itself an eloquent indicator of the general anxiety that Elizabeth was already generating, despite the absence of conclusive evidence against her.

The first solution found was to place her in the Tower, the usual place for royal prisoners. Before she was taken there Elizabeth, denied a personal interview with her sister, wrote a her letter which illustrated again the problems of naming a queen regnant. Reminding the queen of Elizabeth's parting request the previous December – that she should not be found guilty of any offence without being permitted to defend herself before Mary – Elizabeth reminded her of the 'old saying that a king's word was more than an other man's oath'.[12] The unsolicited letter from her disgraced sister infuriated rather than swayed Mary, and Elizabeth remained in the Tower for some weeks, without any interview with the queen or any sense of what might become of her.

She was finally released into the custody of Sir Henry Bedingfield, governor of the Tower and a reliable Catholic magnate who escorted the princess to Woodstock. There she led a circumscribed but pleasant enough existence. Stories of Elizabeth's hardships during her time in the Tower and at Woodstock owe much to the sympathetic account written by John Foxe during Elizabeth's reign, when his concern was to establish Elizabeth among those who had suffered at the hands of the Catholic queen. But it might well be argued – given the general consensus that Elizabeth knew beforehand something of the Wyatt conspiracy, that her name was constantly raised by conspirators in relation to it, and that she admitted to having contact with the conspirators – that her imprisonment in the Tower and confinement at Woodstock was hardly an unduly harsh response.

THE PARLIAMENT OF APRIL 1554

Mary kept her promise made in February that she would call a parliament to endorse her marriage. Originally it was to meet at Oxford, probably as a sign of royal displeasure with those Londoners who had accepted Lady Jane Grey and then supported the Wyatt uprising. But the lack of accommodation in Oxford and the Londoners' vociferous laments for the trade they would lose saw the venue shifted back to Westminster. The important legislation all dealt with ramifications of Mary's forthcoming marriage. One was the parliamentary endorsement of the proposed marriage treaty, proclaimed in January. Ratification by parliament, always deemed to represent the whole of England, was effectively the people's consent to the marriage. Despite the amount of hostility shown earlier, the treaty easily went through both Houses, thereby, as Renard happily wrote, discomforting those he called the 'heretics', and the French.

Other issues raised by Mary's forthcoming marriage were also addressed. One adjustment extended the treason act to protect Philip as royal consort, since the 1352 statute protected only a female consort. New legislation confirmed that the authority of a queen regnant was precisely equivalent to that of a king; even more significantly it was also enacted that Mary now 'sole and solely queen' would retain entirely that status – and sole royal authority – after she was married. The message thereby being reiterated was clearly the one that Mary had given to Renard before any serious marriage negotiations got under way: As a wife, she would of course love and obey her husband, 'but if he wished to encroach in the government of the kingdom, she would be unable to permit it.'

THE COMING OF PHILIP

By May 1554, the leaders of the Wyatt rebellion were dead, in prison or fled abroad, often to the French court, Elizabeth was under close supervision, and the marriage treaty ratified by parliament. Still Philip showed no interest in rushing to England to marry Europe's matrimonial prize. It was a political match, and Philip had taken no active part in the negotiations; like an exemplary son, he had been entirely at his father's disposal. A widower for eight years, Philip's enjoyment of female company was well known. Mary acknowledged that his time as widower had not been chaste, but she was misinformed if she really believed, as she said, that he was ' free of the love of any other woman'. He had a much-loved mistress, a Spaniard who remained unmarried (there are some reports Philip had secretly married her) and who was to die extremely wealthy in 1590.[13]

For many months after the marriage was mooted, Philip made no gesture to Mary, leaving all gifts and expressions of pleasure to his father. It was June 1554 before he finally sent Mary a superb jewel; in return Mary ordered a particularly elaborate Garter insignia for his arrival. First expected in England in February, Philip's departure was repeatedly delayed by political issues in Spain and by his plan to assemble what he saw as a relatively small company – somewhere between 3,000 and 5,000 as his personal retinue and some 6,000 soldiers and mariners to protect them from French attack. Plans for such a company gave strength to the rumours the French had so assiduously spread in January that Philip was coming to England as king, to conquer the realm. He was persuaded to reduce the numbers but he still brought so many lords and ladies (and 4,000 troops to go on to the Netherlands) that it took 70 large ships and a number of smaller ones to transport them.

Philip finally landed at Southampton on 20 July 1554, in pouring rain, after a very rough sea voyage. He was welcomed to England by the leading men of the realm, and presented with the Order of the Garter, always a particularly distinguished honour. After resting in Southampton, on 23 July the prince rode a white horse gloriously caparisoned, through a heavy rainstorm into Winchester. There he finally met Mary, to whom he spoke in Spanish. She replied in French, and as he left, half an hour later, he spoke his first and only known English words 'Good night, my lords all' to small group of courtiers.

His Spanish companions were not flattering about the appearance of Philip's new bride. One remarked that Mary was older than they had expected, though it was no secret that she was then 38. Another of Philip's entourage wrote that Philip's sister had sent Mary a 'fine present of [Spanish style] dresses and coifs. ... I believe that if she dressed in our fashions she would not look so old and flabby.'[14] As ever, it would seem, clothes did much to make the man – or woman. English women more generally did not please the newcomers, at least initially, for another complained that Mary's companions at her wedding were either elderly, or if young 'not lovely'. In general, English first impressions of the new-comers were hardly more enthusiastic, but that was often the case in such dynastic marriages. Political unions were expected to transcend such minor problems for the greater good, and for some 18 months the marriage of Philip and Mary was much less disastrous than other such unions in sixteenth-century Europe.

THE MARRIAGE OF A QUEEN REGNANT

English kings seldom made great public occasions of their marriages, but Mary always intended that her marriage should be spectacular, partly to counter the hostility it had first generated. Although the proc-lamation summoning those nobility, gentry, their ladies and 'others appointed' was not issued until 21 July, they all obviously had forewarning, and were given time to prepare suitably sumptuous cloth-ing. In London, well away from the chosen marriage site of Winchester, bonfires and feasting in the streets and ringing church bells – the mark-ers of officially sponsored public rejoicing – duly expressed that pleasure, as did church processions and celebrations. It is not known whether the citizens of London found this compensation enough for missing both the great spectacles of the marriage and the financial benefits of having so many of the great in the land gathered in London for such an occasion.

At Winchester, there must have been considerable problems in accommodating all the participants and guests, let alone their retinues. Spectacular preparations had been made within the cathedral. The hangings were of cloth of gold, and a special structure had been built within the church for the wedding ceremonies. Both Philip and Mary walked the short distance, with their separate processions, to the church. Philip wore his Order of the Garter and the bejewelled suit of white brocade Mary had sent him the previous evening. Mary was equally richly dressed. He had a great company of nobles and gentlemen with him, but Mary had more, and of greater eminence. She also had a sword carried before her, to signify she was the monarch. In the midst of the sumptuous pomp and splendour, Mary insisted on her wedding ring being a plain band of gold without any jewels for, as she said, she wanted be married as maidens were in olden times. In the exchange of vows between the couple, Philip endowed his wife with all his goods, but only the moveable ones. His realms remained his own. Hers were not mentioned.

Once they were married, a sword was presented to Philip, so as they left the church they each had sword carried before them.[15] He was a king not in his own right but, the ritual signified, by virtue of being married to the queen. In many ways Philip's subordinate status was reiterated throughout all the ceremonies, not least that he was always placed on Mary's left hand, so Mary was on his right. Gardiner, who officiated as Bishop of Winchester as well as Lord Chancellor, had begun the service itself by announcing that the Emperor had transferred the kingship of Naples to Philip. Charles's reported purpose was so that all men could see that the queen was marrying not just a prince, but also a king.[16] If that elevation of his son was to gratify the people, it was not very successful, since little note is taken of his promotion in surviving reports. Nor did it alter his official status. At the wedding feast, to the baffled fury of his entourage, the pre-eminence of the queen over her husband was again reiterated. Philip, for example, was served on silver dishes, gold ones being reserved for the queen. Thereafter when they were in a royal residence, the queen used the rooms known as the king's quarters, and Philip the queen's.

None of those assertions of Mary's pre-eminence could have occurred without her approval, but they all took place within the relatively closed world of the royal courts, which may explain why they seem to have attracted little contemporary comment. The new titles for the royal pair received much more attention, perhaps because they fitted with popular fears and expectations. During the treaty negotiations, the Hapsburg representatives always insisted that Philip's name had to precede Mary in the form of titles agreed. To arrange them otherwise would be, Renard argued, against human law, divine law, and Philip's prestige and good name, especially since 'the treaties and Acts of Parliament gave him the title of King of England.'[17]

The treaties, as later confirmed in parliament, did give him the title but made it equally clear that, as king, he was not to rule, but to advise. That proviso is what some in Philip's entourage and many English either lost sight of or disregarded, as both groups attributed to him the right to more power in England than ever he sought, or was able, to exercise. But whatever the limits on his authority, the titles suggested otherwise. First proclaimed at the wedding, they were then published and ordered to be read in every parish church. The form was:

> Philip and Mary by the grace of God King and Queen of England, France, Naples, Jerusalem, and Ireland; Defenders of the Faith; Princes of Spain and Sicily; Archdukes of Austria; Dukes of Milan, Burgundy and Brabant; Counts of Hapsburg, Flanders and Tyrol.

That was the sole indicator that Philip took precedence over Mary, but it was also the one most widely disseminated across the land. If people managed to miss the implications of that ordering, it was brought to their attention by Philip's name thereafter taking precedence over Mary's in all legislation and all proclamations. Whatever the practice within the court, the most publicly available forms all reiterated that Philip was king, and Mary (just) a queen.

This apparent return to the divinely ordained ordering of the household was widely noted and commented on in a way that no markers of Mary's pre-eminence were. The next grist for the mills of those who argued that Philip would naturally dominate the English queen came when the royal couple first entered the City of London. The customary genealogical pageant was included in the welcoming ceremonial for

Philip. It reiterated a point made when Katharine of Aragon first arrived in England to marry Prince Arthur, and repeated when Charles V had visited his aunt and her husband Henry VIII in the 1520s. The relevant pageants noted that each of the three, Katherine, Charles and Philip, shared with the English royal house an English ancestor, Edward III, through John of Gaunt. English sensitivity to this genealogy had first appeared when John Christopherson, a chaplain to Queen Mary, published it some months before the wedding. He did it, he explained, to show that Philip was no stranger to the realm, but descended from royal English blood. On both occasions, Philip's published genealogy led to many rumours that it was paving the way for Philip to claim the English throne as his own, by descent as well as by marriage.

Such issues recurred for the remainder of Mary's reign. Mary may have been a crowned queen regnant, but she was a wife. No treaties declaring his circumscribed role, no legislation declaring that after her marriage as before Mary was sole and solely queen, no public placing of Philip on the queen's left side and installing him in the queen's quarters while Mary occupied the king's, nothing could silence the widespread insistence that husbands ruled their wives, and that, to the extent Mary ruled England, she did so in the interests of her husband.

And, it might be added, for Mary, it was particularly difficult to separate her interests as queen from those of her husband, when they had so much in common, including opponents among the Protestants in England and the Netherlands, and in the French monarchy. Those problems arising from that marriage continued to be a potent tool for her critics for the rest of the reign but, it will be argued, often for reasons – and misunderstandings – well beyond Mary's control. It is hard to see what else she could have done to protect herself from the charge that she had rendered herself simply her husband's instrument.

9

THE PROSPEROUS YEAR OF PHILIP AND MARY, JULY 1554 TO AUGUST 1555?

BEGINNING MARRIED LIFE

Mary's married life, from July 1554, began more easily than for many royal brides. As a queen regnant she retained all her familiar household around her and she created another household for her husband, an opportunity to reward appropriate men by granting them good access to the new king. Most important for her was that in those early days Philip proved a caring and attentive husband, giving Mary both gifts and his time, neither of which he had bestowed on his first wife. Mary soon assured her father-in-law that she was delighted with her husband, and just weeks after her marriage the new Venetian ambassador reported on Mary's appearance in (almost) flattering terms. Although he found Mary very thin (itself a frequent enough comment about her), she had large eyes and reddish hair and 'were not her age [38½] on the decline she might be called handsome'.[1]

After the marriage, Mary followed the usual custom of remaining in seclusion for some days, but before that Winchester was the scene of yet more feasting and public celebrations. The round of displays had begun with the marriage feast itself. Just what a lavish affair it was is suggested by the comment by one of Mary's gentlemen who, at the end of the feast, was given an unused 'great pasty [pie] ... very delicately baked which ... I sent unto London, to my wife and her brother, who cheered therewith many of their friends'. He also commented on the feast's entertainments, suggesting that the Spanish, especially the king himself, were quite dismayed when they saw how superior the English dancing was to their own.[2] In exchange, the Spanish gave the English their first sight of cane fighting, an exercise the English simply found baffling. Mary's response to either display was not recorded.

The marriage was dutifully celebrated across the country, for sung *Te Deums,* bell-ringings, bonfires and public feasting were ordered in London and across the realm. But the joy at their queen's new husband was tinged with anxiety, for close attention was paid to the new royal titles as they were proclaimed across the land, and read out in parish churches. The form of those titles, naming Philip first and as king, was noted in an unusual number of contemporary diaries and journals, an indication of just how seriously the titles were taken. Mary's subjects had understood that Philip would be 'rather as a subject than otherwise', but that was not what the titles suggested. Only one person, Sir Robert Wingfield, wrote an explicit defence of Mary's apparent subordination of herself to her husband, as 'most renowned token of obedience which such a princess might show her husband'. Many more fretted that the apparent reversal of titles redefined the queen's status, worrying that the king's precedence there foreshadowed his precedence in other matters as well.

PHILIP'S EMERGING ROLE IN ENGLAND

Even in the midst of the early pleasant diversions, political and religious matters were never far from the couple's minds. Mary quickly resumed her habitual many hours with state documents each day. As the Emperor's heir, and gradually assuming more responsibilities in his realms, Philip always had many political matters of his own to attend to. He was, for example, again at work at seven o'clock the morning after his wedding, writing letters to Flanders and Italy; Hapsburg business occupied much of his time for the 13 months he was to spend in England. Given those commitments it is less surprising that he apparently accepted his advisory role in England, despite his original secret repudiation of the marriage treaties even as he signed them.

Two days after his marriage, Philip assured Mary's Council that he was there to help, 'but not to introduce changes. As for what was to be done in the future, they must consult the Queen, and he would do his best to assist.'[3] To help her, however, Philip needed to be informed about the business at hand. As he arrived in England Mary instructed her councillors always to inform him of their discussions by making a note of them in Spanish or Latin. Moreover she honoured her husband – but increased the ambiguity of his role in England – by issuing instructions that all Council papers were to be signed by Philip as well as herself. A stamp with both names was made for the lesser documents, and in each case Philip's name preceded hers.

Historians have often ascribed the many clashes on London streets between Philip's followers and the English to political resentment of the marriage. But the English, who resented most foreigners, were infuriated by Spanish attempts to set up trading stalls in London against the city's regulations. That mutual antagonism may have been fed by resentment about the marriage, but it was more commonly expressed by insults about the eating and drinking habits of the English, and the perceived arrogance of the Spaniards.

There was thieving, fighting and some killing on both sides, and an even-handed proclamation issued just six weeks after the marriage required all 'vagabonds and idle persons, as well English as strangers' preying on the unwary, to depart the court and the city forthwith.[4] It is now impossible to know how much of such repeated hostility arose from specific antagonism to the foreign king, and how much was just another expression of a more generalised hostility to all foreigners and outsiders.

At the higher social levels, Philip worked steadily to develop his relations with English gentry. His attention and gifts for some, political interventions for others, and fondness for such exclusively masculine pastimes as tournaments, frequently proved mutually beneficial. Men like Ambrose and Robert Dudley, sons of the late Duke of Northumberland and both deeply implicated in the attempted coup for Lady Jane, were still in the Tower when Philip arrived. They were out before the end of October and in mid-December reconciliation was apparently complete when they both took part in a spectacular court tournament organised by Philip, in which English and Spanish courtiers had joined in a mutual and lavish celebration.

The event was apparently very public, for Machyn (always an indicator of what the London citizenry might have known) described that 'great triumph'. He was probably present since he described it all in some detail, including the colours the men wore and that the teams 'fought' with both spears and sword. Both Dudleys, along with others similarly 'redeemed' for the regime by the new king, were to fight for Philip and Mary against the French later in their reign. Such mutually satisfactory reconciliations were a significant part of Philip's contribution to the relative stability of Mary's England, a contribution that went some way to countering the early hostility to his presence.

THE ROYAL ENTRY INTO LONDON

When the married couple set out for London, they travelled by easy stages, pausing first at Basing House, the residence of the Marquis of Winchester, now Mary's Lord Treasurer, who had been one of the five nobles who gave Mary away at her marriage. Along the way, they often engaged in that traditional royal pastime, the hunt. At Windsor, Philip was installed as a knight of the Garter; Mary placed the collar of the order around his neck, and thereafter he presided over the order's chapter meetings, since Mary felt such chivalric business was properly a masculine responsibility. They also killed an unusually large number of deer in their appropriately royal pleasures.

As they reached Richmond, news came of a French siege of Hapsburg forces at Renty, prompting many of Philip's entourage to depart for the wars. The Spaniards had arrived with high expectations of the land where King Arthur had reigned and so many chivalric deeds been performed. Instead, they had found the wet summer and the open hostility unlike anything promised by the Arthurian stories, although the Round Table at Winchester was much admired. Elsewhere in England the newcomers saw numbers of beautiful women, but they generally decided that the ladies of Mary's court were 'quite ugly',[5] perhaps another complaint about the unfamiliar court fashions. Whatever the reason, many were ready to leave Arthur's homeland.

As the remaining entourage moved on to London, the city's officials had spent a great deal of money to welcome their queen's husband to her capital; they were also anxious about security for the royal couple, but the great public occasion passed off safely. The entry procession followed traditional lines, with privy councillors, ambassadors, English and Spanish nobility and many others preceding the royal couple along the usual route, as ever lined with crowds, and punctuated with pageants and newly re-gilded fountains. The royal couple, welcomed by the firing of cannon at the Tower of London, received the traditional welcome from the Lord Mayor before they inspected the pageants and acknowledged the considerable crowds.

It was indeed all well done, but not with any strikingly innovative flair, if we accept Wriothesley's laconic note that the king and queen were 'with great provision received [by] the citizens, pageants in places accustomed, the Cross in Cheap[side] new gilt, etc.'[6] The pageants had been designed primarily to praise Philip; he was welcomed as 'sole hope' of the modern Caesar, Charles V, compared favourably with other great Philips in history, including Philip of Macedonia, and reminded that the royal couple shared a common descent from John of Gaunt, reiterating the genealogy which had already been seen by some as suggesting Philip had a better right to reign than Mary.

That pageant, on the hostile reaction to which so many historians have since focussed, received high praise at the time, as 'a very pretty pageant, being but slight, but marvellous fair, made in the manner of a ... tree', with the royal couple together at the top.[7] Later historical comments have focussed on Mary's evangelical critics, who saw the pageant as yet another sign the realm was about to be handed over to papal Catholics and cruel Spaniards. It was, however, a conventional enough comment on the longstanding links between the royal families, and the great majority of London's citizens saw it as precisely that.

The displays were undoubtedly sumptuous, and the reception splendid enough. Philip wrote contentedly to his sister back in Spain that he had been warmly and well received. He probably did not know that the English were already commenting darkly on the sheer numbers of his countrymen. As one wrote, 'At this time there were so many Spaniards in London that a man should have met in the streets for one Englishman, above four Spaniards, to the great discomfort of the English nation.'[8]

Mary, as very few commentators noted, rode throughout the progress on Philip's right hand, reminding all who cared to observe it that she, not he, was the monarch of England. Two swords of state were carried before them, but that symbolism was easily lost to the onlookers. When the practice was repeated at the opening of the next parliament, there was a report that: 'Many persons were of the opinion that one of these swords would have been enough, as husband and wife are one and the same thing.'[9]

Enacting the supremacy of the queen was and remained a matter many found it difficult to comprehend. One published account did note that when they reached Whitehall, 'the queen's majesty entered that part of the court commonly called the king's side, and the king's high-ness entered the other part called the queen's', a practice followed all the time Philip was in England. The issue of who actually reigned soon flared up again, when in September a newly minted coin, commonly called the double crown, was issued. As the name suggests, it departed from usual practice by having the image of not just the monarch but also her consort on the coin. To add to the possible ambiguity, the royal pair faced each other at the same height, with a single crown floating over their heads. The coin caused much comment among their subjects in England and more among the Protestant exiles who had fled abroad. It was widely taken as further evidence that Philip had been given as much authority as if he were indeed king of England, and some darkly foresaw that his coronation as king would soon follow.

On the other hand, the constant ceremonial reminders of his wife's superior authority gave rise to many dark rumblings among Philip's ret-inue that he was not being treated by Mary's court with due deference. His followers had noted immediately that his plates were of silver while hers were of gold, and were much more observant than Mary's English subjects of the many ways in which she took precedence. Philip's entou-rage produced recurrent rumblings that he should leave England on account of the constant slights he received, although there is no decisive evidence that Philip ever shared this view.

He did, however, share his retinue's view that he should indeed be crowned. It seems unlikely Mary supported a coronation for him. She was content to accept her councillors' advice that her subjects would not accept his coronation, and showed no wish to confuse the existing situa-tion further. As it was, the effect of the mixed messages of precedence in titles and ceremonial was to give Mary's critics evidence enough to argue, with apparent plausibility, that Philip was indeed *de facto* ruler. As will be discussed later, even when he was out of the realm, the rumour that he would be crowned proved a fruitful way of promoting unease among Mary's subjects at home and in exile.

Initially there was some confusion and more resentment in Philip's households over how duties – and honours – were to be shared between the two groups, the one he had brought and the one Mary had provided. Unlike any female consort Philip was never granted any English lands or revenues with which to support his English household, so he could only reward his English friends and advance his English interests by drawing on his Spanish revenues. At first, this lack of any funding may have been because Mary, like everyone else, expected Philip's stay in England to be very brief (there was talk of his staying only days, rather than weeks) but the financial situation was never changed, even though he stayed for more than a year.

Philip resolved some of the problems of his two established households by retaining his own household for more personal matters – he could at least speak their language – and giving the more public roles to his English household. Thereafter, members of both households could – and did – complain that their reduced roles dishonoured them. And at the emerging court, there were many well-wishers and opportunists at all social levels flocking to seek any advantage for themselves available. There were, however, also genuinely warm letters of congratulations like a particularly affectionate one from Anne of Cleves, wishing them well and hoping to visit the court soon. Widely seen by contemporaries as one of Henry's more acceptable wives, she always retained her good standing with his immediate family and many of his subjects.

In the early months of the royal marriage, there was a marked increase in court festivities. The Spaniards repeated their performance of cane-fights, and perhaps the English came to appreciate them more. There were tournaments, masques, and more dancing than in the earliest months of Mary's reign, when she had had less time – or occasion – for such pleasures. She had always been very fond of dancing (indeed her brother, when king, had gravely rebuked her pleasure in such frivolity) and enjoyed opportunities to do so.

One masque, on 12 October, was reported in enough detail for readers to be impressed by the lavish displays they presented. The masquers, dressed as mariners, wore cloth of gold and cloth of silver – fabrics quite as expensive as their names suggest – and were led by Lord William Howard, Mary's Lord Admiral, and loyal adherent from the earliest days of her reign. Philip and Mary joined in the more general dancing which followed, to the gratification of the onlookers, and there were several reports that they were both in good health, and merry. The marriage was looking promising, and the queen was manifestly enjoying her married state.

THE RESTORATION OF THE PAPACY

When Philip advised his father that he would be remaining in England longer than the few days or, at the most, weeks originally envisaged, he gave as one major reason his concern to help with the full restoration of Catholicism. For him that would always meant England's complete acceptance of papal authority, at least in religious matters. As already discussed, Mary's experience of the ease with which traditional religious teachings had been abandoned in Edward's reign had persuaded her that the Papacy was crucial as a protection for true doctrine. From the earliest days of her reign, Mary had secretly told papal representatives that she hoped soon to see the restoration of the Pope to his traditional position as supreme head of the Catholic Church in England.

Mary had always made plain her distaste for her title as supreme head of the English Church. Nevertheless she had been willing enough to use the authority that went with the title to enforce the changes her first parliament had made to English religious practice. Early efforts, however, to have parliament remove her religious supremacy from her titles had foundered on the widespread suspicions of any weakening of the crown's authority. A major anxiety was that the restoration of papal authority would lead to the Catholic Church's recovery of all the ecclesiastical lands it had lost since the beginning of Henry VIII's attacks on the monasteries.

The proposed reconciliation with Rome was a matter in which Reginald Pole, Margaret of Salisbury's sole surviving son, was always much involved. Since his attacks on Henry's 'divorce' from Katharine of Aragon, Pole had been based in Italy, following scholarly pursuits and, in the late 1530s, becoming part of a group called the *spirituali,* which still hoped for reconciliation between the Lutherans and the Catholic Church. By the 1550s, his views about Catholic teachings had probably hardened (a matter under current debate); he was particularly resolute about the need for full restoration of church property.

He also argued that papal authority took precedence over all other law, so that he found it offensive for a parliament to endorse any papal decisions in English statute law. Such ideas, an understandable anxiety about how the English would react to them, and Charles V's more general suspicion of Pole's intentions, kept him from England until November 1554. Meanwhile, Pole was ostensibly required as a mediator for the Franco-Hapsburg wars, but he soon realised that neither side was yet prepared to commit to any serious peace proposals. He may well have suspected (correctly) that the real reason he was being kept from England was his insistence that what had been ecclesiastical property before Henry VIII's assaults on the monasteries must revert to the church.

Whatever her own preferences, Mary had always understood how cautiously she needed to proceed in restoring a fully Catholic church, including the authority of the Pope. One of her earliest actions was to have the legal invalidity of her mother's marriage overturned by another statute, even though the Papacy had always insisted on its validity. And even as she insisted that she had always been (inwardly) most obedient to the Papal See, in early September 1553 she was sending messages to the Catholic hierarchy that Pole should not be allowed to return to England in his private capacity, let alone as papal legate. The main reason she wanted him kept away was clear enough in the correspondence between them, in which Pole demanded the immediate restoration of papal supremacy, and the restoration of all property of which the Church had been deprived. All this, he insisted, should be done as soon as the first parliament met.

Mary understood that was an impossible condition. The comprehensive return of properties which were once church possessions was well beyond any reversal, not least because the process had enriched many of the great of the land, as well as creating many new wealthy families. But there was also a broader principle at stake, the issue of whether anyone, even the Pope, had any jurisdiction over the distribution of land within the realm of England. Pole was most reluctant to concede any ground on what he saw as mere 'worldly' considerations. Mary however understood the political realities Pole so easily discounted, and on the matter of land ownership she was as resolute as any of her councillors.

Finally, in November 1554, after being prevented from doing so for a year, Pole was allowed to return to England as papal legate. Mary advised him, however, that she and Philip still thought it advisable that he should travel in England without any display of the insignia and ceremonies appropriate to his papal role. His official identity should be publicly displayed only after the realm was fully reconciled with the Church. Matters were, however, so far advanced that when the new parliament, expected to confirm the reconciliation with Rome, first met on 12 November, a prayer for the Pope was included in the opening ceremonies.

As was now customary, parliament began with a mass, attended by both king and queen, both resplendent in their velvet and ermine. The sermon had called for the parliament to enact laws supporting the 'true catholic religion', as well as the strength of the realm. Gardiner, speaking in his capacity as Lord Chancellor, and in the presence of both king and queen, delivered an opening address to both houses that lasted for two hours, reiterating the need to restore 'true religion'. The first bill, which reversed Henry VIII's attainder against Pole, a cardinal since 1536, passed rapidly through both houses. Both Mary and Philip attended parliament ten days later, to give their assent to the bill. Two days after that, Pole entered the kingdom and took up his residence at Lambeth, traditionally a residence of the Archbishop of Canterbury.

The main celebration to mark the confirmation of a new religious era was held at court on 28 November. Parliament was summoned to attend, and Pole, in the regalia of a papal legate, sat with the king and queen, before delivering a speech of comprehensive praise for Philip, a king of 'great might, armour and force' who had come to England in a spirit of pure friendship. He also praised Charles V who had struggled so hard to restore the English church to Roman obedience. Mary was also commended, albeit in markedly less heroic metaphors. She had, he pronounced, survived the worst efforts of her enemies to keep her from her rightful throne:

> And see how miraculously God of his goodness preserved her highness, contrary to the expectation of men, [so] that when numbers conspired against her, and policies were devised to disinherit her, and armed power prepared to destroy her, yet she being a virgin, helpless, naked and unarmed, prevailed.[10]

Pole described his own position as representing the Papacy and coming to rebuild true religion again in the land which was the first to receive Christ's message – a reference presumably to the tradition that Jesus visited England in the years before he began teaching in Palestine. Pole promised that all things past should be 'cast into the sea of forgetfulness' just as soon as parliament repealed the legislation separating England from the Holy See. Two days later a parliamentary supplication for reunion with Rome was presented to Philip and Mary and then, with all on their knees, it was presented to Pole who gave his blessing to the assembled multitude. They, it was reported, with one voice cried 'Amen'. There was almost no parliamentary resistance to those changes.

But all the problems associated with the reunion with Rome could not be made to disappear so easily. Above all, the anxieties of property holders had not been put to rest. Pole had been effectively silenced on the question, but John Feckenham, the Dean of St Paul's, now preached that the owners of what had once been monastic and church lands were under a moral obligation to restore it. This was also Mary's position, but she did not proclaim her belief so insistently, and indeed returned to the church only some of her own property from that source.

There was a fraught meeting on November 28 to discuss the terms in which the legislation should deal with that contested issue. Present were Pole, Mary, Gardiner and other councillors. At one stage an appeal was made to precedents during Edward's reign, and Mary threatened to withdraw if it was to be argued that Edward's reign provided any proper precedents in such a matter. Pole made a long and unhelpfully sarcastic speech reiterating that the Papacy had such comprehensive authority that secular/statute law could not constrain it. Mary apparently agreed with Pole, thereby reversing all her previous public positions on property and indeed her previous confirmation of her own legitimacy. Her councillors were astonished, and the meeting was abruptly adjourned.

When it met again the next day, Mary had reverted to her previous position. Pole won one concession, that the bill should include a supplication to the Pope that church property now in lay hands should be allowed to remain there. But in the statute's final form, the requested dispensation was part of the text, with another statement that land titles in England were always based on statute law. The clear implication was that no other authority could override it. Pole was dismayed, but the new law passed in mid-December without further dispute. For good measure, the medieval heresy laws, which had previously raised considerable anxiety about the implications for those who owned church lands, were also revived without further problems.

The old religious order was now restored, with the acquiescence of almost all parliamentarians, but despite his residence at Lambeth, Pole was yet not officially installed as Archbishop of Canterbury. That could not occur until after the death by burning of Cranmer in March 1556, a matter to be discussed in the next chapter. Pole was, however, as papal legate already the *de facto* leader of the church in England. The governors of England had every reason to be pleased with the November 1554 parliament for, as it has been neatly summarised, 'the queen had her spiritual satisfaction and her subjects their secularised property.'[11]

MARY'S FIRST PUTATIVE PREGNANCY

Mary's two fruitless 'pregnancies' have long been regarded as further grounds for deriding her as delusional or 'hysterical'. But, surrounded as we are by all the benefits and resources of modern medicine, it is particularly difficult to appreciate just how hard it could be in early modern times to determine whether a woman was indeed pregnant. Many factors could influence that problem, but one well-known medical phenomenon may be particularly relevant to considering Mary's experience.

Ever since in the fifth century BC Hippocrates recorded the first accounts of 'phantom pregnancy' – also known as *pseudocyesis* – many more have been noted up to the present day. Modern medical knowledge has not completely ended the phenomenon, as an article in the *British Medical Journal* in 1985 recorded patients recently presenting with many recognised signs of pregnancy even though they were, in fact, not pregnant.[12] Another discussion of the condition appeared the *New York Times* on 5 December 2005; the jury, it reported, is still out on what causes the recurring condition, but since it also appears in some animals, the weight of evidence points to a hormonal rather than psychological origin. So there are other explanations for Mary's experience, without resorting to her alleged 'hysterical' nature.

In the sixteenth century, all signs of pregnancy were understood to be so ambiguous that, it has been said, nothing was certain until a child was born. In Mary's case her fertility was always a matter of much public debate; even before she married, the question of whether she was likely to have children became an important issue of high politics. After her marriage it was even more so. Rumours that Mary had been told by her doctors that she was pregnant were circulating by September but, significantly, Mary herself was uncertain whether she was with child well after that. As late as 9 November 1554 Sir John Mason, Mary's ambassador to Charles V, reported a conversation about the rumours with the Emperor:

> How goes my daughter's belly forward? quoth he. Sir, quoth I, I have from herself nothing to say therein, for she will not confess the matter until it is proved to her face, but by others I understand, to my great joy and comfort, that her garments are very strait [tight].[13]

Given that Mary was always described as somewhere between slight and thin, it is understandable that any visible tightening of her garments would have been read as a promising sign of pregnancy – but not a sufficient one. Mary's scepticism was apparently overcome some two weeks after Mason reported his conversation about it, for when, in late November, Mary met Pole again after two decades, she reported that she then felt a quickening in her womb. She had finally accepted that what her doctors had been diagnosing as a pregnancy was indeed just that.

28 November 1554 must have seemed a truly blissful day for Mary. The restoration of papal authority had been confirmed in the afternoon. In the morning, however, there had been another important announcement. High mass was celebrated at St Pauls, with the Lord Mayor and aldermen in their scarlet gowns and cloaks, the Commons in their liveries and at least ten bishops. After the service, a letter was read out to the assembled notables, publicly announcing that the queen had conceived and was 'quick with child'. A *Te Deum* was then sung. Given all the circumstances, this did indeed seem to Mary's Catholic subjects to be a miraculous occasion.

The apparently miraculous nature of Mary's pregnancy was consciously reinforced by the frequent reiteration of her much praised virtue and chastity. As one published prayer put it, the Lord knew that she 'took a husband, not for carnal pleasure, but only for the desire and love of posterity, wherein thy name might be blessed for ever and ever'.[14] Her modesty, her virtue, her chastity, combined with her sense of duty, were repeatedly presented as the epitome of a Tudor ideal woman. A much more partisan note was evident in a prayer offered by the Dean of Westminster, reflecting the intensity of responses to her announced pregnancy. Appropriately enough, he prayed for Mary's safe delivery of a healthy child, but added an exhortation to his God not to disappoint the hopes of all good Catholics: 'Let not the enemies of thy Faith, and of thy church, say "Where is their God?".'

Such a royal pregnancy was always going to be an extraordinarily public affair. The Council sent reports of it to the bishops of the land, instructing them to spread the news. *Te Deums* were ordered in churches throughout the land as well as special prayers for the queen's good health and for 'this good hope of certain succession'. Ballads were published, rejoicing at the dismay of the Protestants on the same grounds:

> Now sing, now spring, our care is exiled
> Our virtuous Queen is quickened with child
> Our doubts be dissolved, our fancies contented
> The marriage is joyful that many lamented
> And such as envied like fools have repented
> The errors and terrors which they have invented.[15]

As both the ballad and the Dean's prayer suggest, many committed English Protestants had been confident that she would never conceive; those who remained in England, like those who fled and/or plotted abroad, looked most often to Elizabeth as Mary's legal successor, to take her place. The news of Mary's pregnancy was greeted by them with considerable suspicion and deep dismay, and Catholics were well aware of Protestant doubts about the queen's fertility, and their 'heretical' confidence that their God would never allow this pregnancy to result in an heir. There were some who went further and prayed that if Mary would not renounce her religion, she should soon die. Both sides of the great religious divide accepted that the future religious well-being of England hung upon the outcome of this pregnancy.

PREGNANCY IMPLICATIONS FOR PHILIP'S STATUS

Once Mary's pregnancy was publicly confirmed, Philip's formal status needed some redefinition. By the marriage treaty, any child of this marriage would inherit not only England but also the Hapsburg territories in the Netherlands. Much more significantly, he was now not only consort to England's Queen, but father to the prospective heir. This would become much more of an issue should the queen not survive childbirth, a possibility which all understood. As the whole history of the Tudor dynasty, and the childbirth statistics set out in the opening discussion remind us, childbirth was dangerous for any woman, and manifestly more likely to be so for any woman facing her first delivery as she neared her fortieth year.

The implications of Philip's future standing were extensively debated and finally agreed by the November 1554 parliament. As father to a prospective heir, his prospective position needed careful redefinition. But because of the dark suspicions many Englishmen still retained about Philip's longer-term aims, there were several attempts to impose unusual limits on Philip's powers as regent to his child.[16] In brief, the original draft limited Philip's powers by providing a council of six peers to assist him, and defining a range of decisions he could not make about the child's future. Any such limitation was resisted by Hapsburg interests, which argued strongly that the king should have the right allowed any father, to administer his child's property during its minority. In this case, however, the property would be the realm of England.

Mary supported the more conservative argument against the unusual limitations proposed for Philip's paternal authority. The official argument for this outcome was that it ensured stability of government; potential opponents were reminded of the many changes and disputes which had resulted from power struggles between rivals within the Council of Edward VI. Ultimately, whatever the reasons, the final act ensured that should a child be born to Mary, and should her own death follow, sixteenth-century understandings of God's law and English law about paternal rights ensured that Philip would become *de facto* ruler of England.

The failure of Mary's pregnancy was to become one more ground for her critics, then and for centuries, mocking her. In the early months she had seemed in radiant health and happier than she had ever been. As the months passed, and further indicators of pregnancy failed to develop, Mary's doctors continued to assure her that she was indeed pregnant. Perhaps the date for her delivery had been miscalculated, they said, and suggested she would be delivered of her child in April.

Philip, who was anxious to join the dynastic wars on the continent, where he hoped to make his military reputation, nevertheless decided to remain in England until the child was born. Much of his time he still spent working on Hapsburg issues. Some of his time he passed in fencing lessons, some in tournaments, in which he played such an enthusiastic part that Mary often feared for him. Machyn the diarist, for one, was particularly impressed by the great tournament held on Lady Day (25 March). That day, he recorded not only the colourful details and styles of the dress of combatants, but also that 'there was broken two hundred staves and above'. A great spectacle indeed!

The royal couple withdrew to Hampton Court at Easter 1555, in preparation for the queen's delivery. All the appropriate preparations for that, and provision for the anticipated infant, had been made. There was some debate among her advisers about whether there should be an announcement confirming Elizabeth as next heir, should the infant as well as the queen die in childbirth. That would minimise the chances of civil strife, but Gardiner tried (again) to have her excluded from the succession. He may by then have shared Mary's frequently stated preference for Lady Margaret Douglas as next heir, but the discussion ended with no decisions made, leaving Elizabeth as next heir by default.

By late May some rumours were circulating that the queen was not, after all, pregnant. Or perhaps, as her doctors insisted, she was, but the baby was not due until June. Some who saw her thought that she walked with such a light step she could not be pregnant at all. There were more whispers circulating, attributed to such close associates as Susan Clarencius, that Mary now showed few if any signs of pregnancy. But still officially expectations of an imminent birth were maintained. Draft letters were prepared announcing the delivery of a child (with a space for the sex to be inserted) and a richly decorated cradle stood in the queen's bedroom.

In early June one of Philip's companions explained to a friend that the further deferment of the expected delivery was because those round her were misled when they first saw her with a great girth. As late as 29 June, there were still some who believed in the queen's pregnancy, but more were increasingly of the view that nothing would come of it after all. There were even tales of an attempt to find a substitute baby, from a woman in the queen's kitchen perhaps; the tale foreshadows the seventeenth-century tale of the baby born to James II, and circulated when his critics were incredulous a male infant was so opportunely born to him. Such is also the stuff of numerous folk tales.

In July the queen emerged from her semi-seclusion. No public announcement was made about the end of her retirement, and some reports claimed that privately Mary was still insisting she was with child. Publicly she still said nothing; privately she raged to sympathetic ears against the flattery and falsehoods by which she had been surrounded, and by which she had allowed herself to be persuaded. Whatever the reasons, the swelling of her body had subsided, and it was clear there would be no child. She progressively resumed her public duties; once again her training in royal inscrutability stood her in good stead, and apart from reports of her fury with her doctors and midwives, we know nothing of what she felt about it all. We may, however speculate that her chagrin and disappointment both ran deep.

The French ambassador Noailles, the same who had earlier conspired with Wyatt in his attempted rebellion, had insisted throughout that there never had been a pregnancy and that at most Mary had had a tumour. It seems unlikely that that is a satisfactory account of what had taken place, but no sufficient medical diagnosis can be confidently asserted at this distance from the events, though many have been suggested. Occasionally historians still dismiss the event as a 'hysterical pregnancy' but, in Mary's case, that seems less plausible because for such a long time she remained doubtful about her pregnancy; in the final stages her attitude may seem irrational, but hardly in the early months.

It may be relevant to note that if Mary Tudor's apparent pregnancy *was* a case of pseudocyesis she was by no means the only élite Tudor woman to experience it. Another well-known case is that of Lady Lisle, wife of Arthur Plantagenet, then governor of Calais. Unlike Mary, she already had several children by a previous marriage, but still believed she was probably pregnant between November 1536 and August 1537. Her case is particularly well documented because of the many letters in which she discussed both her likely pregnancy and her reservations about it. A surprising number of her female friends at court had apparently undergone or knew of similar experiences.[17]

So the most that can confidently be said about Mary is that she undoubtedly accepted her doctors' assurances that she was pregnant for a surprisingly long time, and well after others were increasingly sceptical. Those who were well disposed to her probably understood Mary's case, but of course disaffected Protestants at home or in exile had many reasons to rejoice at her probable embarrassment, and certain disappointment. As so often happened, it was probably the disaffected whose responses have survived disproportionately in the historical records.

PHILIP'S DEPARTURE FROM ENGLAND

Once it was clear that Mary would not be producing an heir, Philip had little reason to remain in England, and many pressing reasons to go. When Pole had been delayed on the continent for a year before re-entering England, one ground had been that he was required to mediate between the Imperial and French forces, which were again at war. The main lesson Pole learned then was that neither side was seriously interested in a peace, but Philip, detained in England, was becoming increasingly fretful that he would miss his chance at true military glory if he stayed away from the wars any longer. He was soon preparing to depart.

There is a longstanding historical debate about just how much influence Philip actually exercised during his time in England, and what became of Mary's resolve that she would not permit him to 'encroach in the government of the kingdom.' This is a difficult issue to assess, partly because, as already noted, she insisted he should be fully informed of state matters, to enable him to offer her sound comments and advice. It is the more difficult to determine since his name appeared before hers on every public statement or signature issued by the queen. On the other hand, as long as he remained in England he was at the queen's left side on all great public occasions. His own retinue often felt he was being slighted; there was always resentment among them that he had not been crowned, and a suspicion that Mary's explanation that parliament would not allow it was merely a transparent device.

If one looks beyond the most immediate court circles, and the Protestant minority always anxious to believe the worst of both king and queen, there is curiously little evidence that Philip was seen as an independent source of power. One plausible indicator of his limited standing is that, although there had been a steady stream of works published with dedications to Mary both before and after she came to the throne, after his arrival in England there were none for Philip. There were just four jointly dedicated to both king and queen. One is a poem in praise of their marriage, and another hailed Spanish colonial expansion as a great opportunity for Christian conversions. At most, Philip was occasionally mentioned in dedications to Mary. The absence of any dedications to him, in Latin or English, in works published in England suggests that most English subjects did not view him as a source of independent power or patronage, even during his long year in England.

Whatever direct or indirect authority he could command in England, Philip had primarily stayed to see his wife through her pregnancy but was anxious to leave as soon as was seemly thereafter. As well as his general wish to achieve military glory on the battlefield, he was under pressure from his ailing father, Charles V. The emperor was ageing, subject to gout, and ready to retire to a more contemplative life in Spain, but his abdication could not take place until his son had joined him and prepared to assume much greater responsibilities.

On 26 August 1555, the royal couple passed through London on their way to Greenwich. Philip rode his horse, Mary travelled in a litter beside him. In his several farewells Philip had, quite unusually, instructed the Council as if he were indeed the monarch. In his absence, they should obey Pole in all things, and his farewell address to them did not mention Mary at all. He may, however, have been reminded by the rapturous acclaim with which Mary was received by the assembled crowds, as she travelled beside him through London, that actually *she* was monarch of England. The Venetian ambassador reported that when her people heard she was there (for the first time since her seclusion) they ran from one place to another, to assure themselves that despite her recent experiences she was indeed well.

Two days later, the Privy Council sent messages to all sheriffs and Justices of the Peace, advising them of Philip's imminent departure for Flanders, and warning them to be alert that 'spreaders of false rumours' should be punished. Unfortunately, no hint of the import of such rumours has survived. One day after that, Mary bade Philip her final farewell at Greenwich. As he sailed away, he stood where he would be most visible, waving his hat to his wife until he was out of view. Mary, again according to the Venetian ambassador, controlled her grief so regally and so well that no one could have guessed its extent. Once she was alone however, he reported, she collapsed into deep sobbing, gazing after Philip's ship long after it was out of sight. That is the usual image of Mary, grief-stricken at the loss of her husband, but her self-control in public was agreed to be impressive, and by the ambassador's account there were no witnesses to her weeping. One might wonder how he knew.

It would indeed have been surprising if she was not despondent at the departure of the one person in whom she could confide fully and on whom she relied for more disinterested advice than she expected from her councillors, concerned to protect their interests as well as hers. Still, it is worth remembering that there are other persuasive accounts, exemplified by a report from one courtier to Courtenay in September, that the queen was well and merry. A letter between friends is at least as reliable as any report from any ambassador, whose first concern was always to demonstrate to his masters how well informed he was. The balance of probabilities then, is that she coped with Philip's departure rather better than the Venetian ambassador believed.

10

RELIGIOUS TRIALS AND OTHER TRIBULATIONS

MARY WITHOUT PHILIP

Despite the enduring tradition that Mary was inconsolable after Philip's departure, court life went on very much as before; nor did she give any sign that she knew of the affairs Philip reportedly began as soon as he was back on the continent. The most obvious change at court was a sharp decline in the number of tournaments and the other chivalric pursuits Philip so enjoyed. The court, however, still had such diversions as masques, plays and other courtly entertainments. Mary continued her interest in current fashions, and was responsible for setting some new ones. Her close attention to richness in both dress and jewellery remained an important means of maintaining the high standards of magnificence expected of any Tudor monarch.

We do not know to what extent Mary continued her classical studies after she was queen, but the presence of the learned Lady Anne Bacon in her household provides one indication of an ongoing interest. She still received works by writers, including Henry Parker, Lord Morley, whose studies had been presented to her since the 1530s, until his death in 1556. Indeed, his final work, *Miracles of the Sacrament,* which incorporated his unique account of service at Margaret Beaufort's court, was almost certainly a New Year's gift for that year.

Mary maintained her long-standing interest in painting, particularly portraits, and still enjoyed music (in which she also instructed some of her court ladies). She was active as promoter of such influential musicians as Thomas Tallis, encouraging a range of sophisticated and innovative musical activities. Mary's most enduring musical legacy was undoubtedly the restoration of church music, in forms which are still important in the modern Anglican tradition. Her actions reversed the decisions of the Edwardian regime, which had previously expunged all music from church services. The Chapel Royal provided one avenue for its restoration, being at least as important in promoting these developments as it had been in Edward's reign for enacting his religious changes.

Above all, Mary always took what she understood to be her God-given role as the monarch of England very seriously. Theoretically her responsibilities were vast; as Sir Thomas Smith wrote a few years later, the monarch of England was indeed 'the life, the head and the authority of all things that be done in England'.[1] That was the constitutional ideal, but actual practice varied considerably between rulers. As for any monarch then, matters of government kept her as busy as she would allow them; Mary allowed them to occupy a great deal of her time. As her predecessors had discovered – and her half-sister was to discover – mid-sixteenth-century England was, for a variety of reasons, a difficult realm to rule.

This was the more stressful for her since she never entirely trusted advice from her Council, given the intensity of competing interests within it. Again, the question of how far Philip was ever a major force in her government is still a matter of debate. One biographer doubts he ever strayed from a literal reading of the marriage treaty: 'Philip's detachment from English affairs was exemplary. If asked for an opinion he always referred matters to the queen.' But others dissent from that.[2] Even how far Philip shared Mary's responsibilities during his stay is hard to assess. He fulfilled all expectations in his ceremonial roles, and was closely involved in the restoration of papal authority, a policy to which he was particularly committed. Surviving records do not indicate what impact he had more generally on the government. His was always formally an advisory role, and he necessarily devoted more time and effort to the affairs of the troublesome Hapsburg holdings than to English affairs. After he had left England, Mary may well have felt she had lost a confidant and companion, but it is difficult to conclude much more than that about how he was missed.

The most striking aspect of Philip's behaviour once he left the realm was that the very regal tone which he first adopted to Mary's councillors just before leaving the country was retained in his subsequent communications. But although he set out his opinions so authoritatively, surviving documents suggest strongly that, while Philip was kept informed of Council decisions, that was after they had been made, so that his comments were endorsements of decisions already taken rather than interventions in their formation. The most notable exception was his instruction, in October 1555, to both houses of parliament, regretting his absence but insisting upon his continuing importance: 'For your respect to us and the queen, consider us present, as we are in spirit.'[3]

That Philip was more explicit about his authority from abroad than he had been in England may indicate his increasing determination, once out of the realm, to return to it only to be crowned as the king he nominally was – should, indeed, he return at all. There were, after all, many rumours circulating that such was the advice his entourage gave him; he may well have found the idea very attractive, given the general belief that a king, once crowned, had much more authority than a (mere) male royal consort.

MARY'S VOICE IN ENGLISH GOVERNMENT

The queen always had her Council, court officers and, after the first year, her husband to advise her on policy decisions, but her own judgement can be seen in formal announcements of royal policy throughout her reign. There is, for instance, little doubt that when, against all available advice, she cancelled the subsidy granted by Edward's last parliament, her decision was more benign than prudent. It did however provide an immediate boost to her already high popular standing. A more permanent result of the difficult financial situation she had inherited (discussed in Chapter 7) was the resumption of the dubious practices of the two previous Tudors, selling off crown lands to augment her annual revenue. On the other hand, she worked to end the devaluation of the coinage, a result of practices adopted by her father from 1542 and continued in Edwardian times. In that her regime was relatively successful.

Something is also known of Mary's response to the increasing numbers of indigent poor, and to growing concerns to distinguish between the 'deserving' poor and those deemed 'wilfully idle'. The Edwardian regime had founded new institutions, like Christ's Hospital, designed to rescue very poor children from the corruption of the 'dunghills of iniquity' in which it was thought they were raised, and Bridewell, designed to 'reform' (more accurately, to punish?) the resolutely idle. Mary did accept those existing Edwardian institutions, but only after some hesitation. So they continued in the new reign, but there were few fresh initiatives in that direction under Mary. The familiar and long-lasting system of parish relief for the very poor was finally put in place in the reign of Elizabeth.

One reason for Mary's hesitations was that those new institutions had all been established on what had been mendicant or monastic property, and she was under pressure to restore such institutions to their previous purposes. But it also mattered to her that her personal response to dealing with the poor was to distribute charity without that Edwardian concern to discriminate between 'deserving' and 'undeserving' recipients. That was her preferred practice at both the individual and the policy level. A favoured companion, Jane Dormer, recalled many years later that, when she was in the countryside, Queen Mary liked to visit the poor in their cottages, presenting herself as just another lady of the court and distributing alms and redressing such grievances against royal officials as she learned about from them. For her, charity was primarily about the virtue of the giver, rather than the virtue of the recipient. She demonstrated this in institutional form when she restored Henry VIII's foundation, the Savoy Hospital, which provided food, alms and a night's lodging to any poor who came to its doors.[4]

PROBLEMS OF RELIGIOUS DIFFERENCE

Well before Mary came to the throne, religious differences in England were well enough established for the conflicting groups to have offensive labels for each other. Their opponents called religious conservatives 'papists' – although many had abandoned their loyalty to the Pope up to 20 years before. The conservatives in turn named adherents to the newer forms of worship 'heretics' – though theirs was the religion sanctioned by the prevailing laws. One indicator of the impact of the unstable and changing religious situation was a marked decline in church attendance in both Edward's and Mary's reigns. One scholar suggests that those declining congregations reflected, 'not so much [religious] indifference as trauma ... a polarisation of religious attitudes, not an abandonment of religion'.[5] Whatever the reasons, the result was that many no longer attended their parish church, long a focal point for community life.

Before 1553, 'Protestants' looked to foreign, usually German, reformers; English reformers still called themselves 'evangelical'. In the first decades of Henry's reign that term reflected the concern of many humanist-trained people, including some who remained within the Catholic tradition, to recover what they considered the original nature of the Christian church. But after Mary's accession, 'Protestant' became a term more commonly applied to all those committed to Edwardian rather than Marian church practices.

After July 1553, Protestants faced the choice of either going into exile, or staying in England and challenging the Marian religious laws, or accommodating themselves to the new religious order. The best-known Marian Protestants were those who stayed in England and paid the ultimate price of dying a traditional heretic's death by fire. Given the prominence their deaths have always had in Marian historiography those deaths will be discussed at greater length further on. But, despite the considerable historical attention to them, that actively Protestant party was very much a minority group in Marian England.

PROTESTANT OPPOSITION

There was always a sub-culture of criticism and, frequently, libel of early modern monarchs. But Mary's reign was remarkable not only for the usual verbal slanders, but also for the rapid growth in the numbers of hostile pamphlets, sometimes published abroad but circulated within England with up to 1,000 copies at a time. That was one marker of the rapid growth in the new medium of print that facilitated and transformed religious debate, as well as other forms of communication. Mary was seldom directly attacked, for her critics wanted to avoid any direct association of Protestantism with treason, but the distinction they drew was often a very fine one. The pamphlets often warned against the dangers of false clergy, foreign royal marriages (especially to Spaniards and/or Catholics) and of Mary's pro-Spanish bias, inherited from her mother.

The authorities' standard response to subversive activities was reiterated in an early Marian proclamation, 28 July 1553: anyone who overheard such 'light, seditious or naughty talk' and failed to report it to the authorities would be treated as the author of it. But the increasing use of print to disseminate what the rulers regarded as 'heretical' matter posed new problems. The relatively new Stationers Company, anxious to protect the interests of its publisher members, suggested a process to control both who was allowed to produce books, and the places where they could be produced and sold. As a result, the Stationers Company not only began to control and license what books were printed, but also acquired the power to search premises for any illegal books, and seize them.

This basic structure for the control of book production and sale endured for centuries, but there is little sign that it was particularly effective in the days of Queen Mary. Her last proclamation against 'many and sundry most horrible, false and seditious tales, rumours and lies against the king and queen' was issued late in Mary's reign. History has, perhaps, shown how justified she was in fearing the potency of print, for the publications of a small group of dissidents (figures for those who went into exile vary between 800 and 2,000) have survived to be the most readily available evidence of what all her subjects thought on religious matters and her marriage.

The political weakness of the more radically evangelical minority in 1553 had been demonstrated the swift collapse of the attempt to entrench their religion by crowning Lady Jane Grey. Even some of the leading Edwardian clergy had resisted that enterprise, preferring to uphold the succession established by law. But although evangelicals remained a minority of the population, they were a significant minority, concentrated in the wealthiest and most influential part of the country, from East Anglia to Dover and the Bristol Channel. Their locations gave them easy access to major trading routes, which in turn allowed books and pamphlets hostile to Mary to be smuggled more freely into England, as they were throughout her reign.

PROTESTANT ACQUIESCENCE

By far the larger group of Edwardian 'evangelicals' remained in England during Mary's reign, conforming to her religious laws enough to survive, and re-emerging as Protestants when Elizabeth assumed the throne. Their choice to conform was deplored by those Protestants who, following such writers as John Calvin, attacked those 'evangelicals' now accommodating themselves to the Catholic regime, as 'Nicodemites'. The reference was to the New Testament Nicodemus, a Pharisee who came to Jesus for instruction only under cover of night. 'Nicodemites', however, sometimes in positions of some authority, were frequently able to protect the interests, above all the property, of exiles during Mary's reign. Many of them also went on to play important roles in the establishment of the Elizabethan regime and of the Elizabethan church.

The so-called Nicodemites accepted the view, strongly promoted by each of the Tudor monarchs, that obedience to the ruler was a God-given duty, to be observed by all for the good of the whole community. William Cecil for example, private secretary to Somerset and close adviser to Northumberland, began Mary's reign in her favour, and became pre-eminent in the government of Elizabeth. An anonymous writer described Cecil's attitude to the monarch in Mary's reign: 'he would ever serve and pray for [Mary] in his heart and, with his body and goods, be as ready to serve in her defence as any her loyal subjects, so she would grant him leave to use his conscience to himself and serve her at large as a private man.'[6]

Just what Cecil meant by that, however, is not immediately clear. The law required Cecil to attend Catholic services and he did; it required him to hear mass from time to time, and he did that too. He was one of the welcoming entourage for Cardinal Pole, and played a significant part in the 1555 parliament. But after his injudicious support of the property rights of some exiles (who included his father-in-law) against a law proposed by Mary's Council, Cecil was to slip into relative obscurity for the remainder of Mary's reign. Perhaps ironically, in 1572 he supported a similar bill, then directed against Catholic exiles.

Because the preferred Protestant narrative from Marian times until recently was one of their persecution and martyrdom, English historiography has conventionally downplayed just how many Protestants were active in Mary's regime and at her court. Their return to Protestant orthodoxy under Elizabeth meant their conformity under Mary was glossed over. There is, however, also some evidence that, far from being intrusive about her preferred religion, Mary took an accommodating attitude to those around her. Her own religious practice was always very devout, but it could be that Mary, like her sister after her, was prepared to accept the service and support of any who publicly conformed to the official religion. The crucial test was one of obedience to the law.

It is certain that many formerly Protestant Edwardians prospered under Mary. The Sidney family offers one such example. In 1552 Northumberland had granted Penshurst in Kent to Sir William Sidney in perpetuity. Married to Northumberland's daughter, Mary, William's son Henry Sidney had signed Edward's will naming Jane Grey as heir, but survived the change of regimes well enough to be part of the Earl of Bedford's deputation to escort Philip to England in 1554. Thereafter he remained on sufficiently good terms with both king and queen to name his first son Philip, after his royal godfather, and he became Lord Deputy of Ireland, a post he held well into the reign of Elizabeth.

Some women celebrated in modern historiography as lifelong Protestants were also familiar presences in Mary's household. Lady Anne Bacon, mother of the famous Sir Francis Bacon, was one of the five daughters of Sir Anthony Cooke (and the one most widely celebrated for her scholarship). She may already have been a member of Mary's household during Edward's reign, perhaps because of a shared interest in scholarship and translation. They certainly met at the court of Queen Katherine Parr who shared the same interests, and was surrounded by a group of humanists that included Cooke himself.

Married to Nicholas Bacon in February 1553, Anne was in attendance on Mary in July, when Cecil was sent to Mary to plead the case of himself and several Edwardian councillors for having supported Jane Grey. Anne, also Cecil's sister-in-law, was able to assure him that Mary 'thought very well of [Anne's] brother Cecil'.[7] (Cecil was married to one of Anne's sisters.) The companionship of the two women appears to have been quite unaffected even by the fact that Anne's father had joined the evangelical exiles at Strasbourg, and Anne was still in attendance on the queen in 1558.

This Marian policy of relative and selective leniency was not restricted to members or potential members of Mary's court. Clergy brought before the Privy Council for 'naughty' and 'seditious' words, usually directed against the restored Latin mass, were frequently held only until they recanted of those naughty words, and then set free. Almost everyone who had the opportunity did recant, albeit sometimes in very equivocal terms. Such equivocation was a conventional enough practice, first of the Lollards and then of errant clergy brought before Henry's courts. Dr Edward Crome is one famous exemplar; he seems to have perfected the art of recantation in terms which could be read as remarkably close to a reformulation of his allegedly heretical views. Apparent submission to authority was all that was required, but it might well bring the charge of being a Nicodemite from less accommodating co-religionists.

Catholic authorities also tried to avoid confrontation where they felt it was appropriate. Stephen Gardiner, restored to his episcopal status as Bishop of Winchester, boasted of his success in frightening those he deemed appropriate out of the realm. His preferred tactic was to request his targets to call on him at his official residence as soon as possible, and he noted with satisfaction how many of them retired abroad in response to that invitation.[8] But his use of that option can be exaggerated, for there are also examples of Gardiner having Protestants arrested even as they tried to flee the country. Cranmer himself, however, never seriously considered flight, though he strongly advised others to do so. Exile, after all, was not always a satisfactory outcome for the regime, since the co-operation of exiles with dissidents in England led to plots and attempted rebellions throughout Mary's reign.

RESTORING THE CATHOLIC CHURCH

Mary was the only Tudor monarch after Henry VII not to plunder the church; indeed she actually directed more resources to it. This included the 1555 restoration to church authorities of First Fruits (equivalent to the first year's income of any benefice), revenue which Henry had diverted from papal revenue to his own treasury from 1534 to mark his royal supremacy. Although this was known to be Mary's own initiative, there was strong resistance to it in the Commons before it was accepted. One argument was that the act reduced royal revenues by some £15,000 a year, a very significant sum given the crown's recurrent financial crises. The more usual Tudor practice of diverting church revenues to the crown was restored on Elizabeth's accession. The explanation offered then reiterated that Mary's decision had discounted the crown's financial needs.

When Mary began her reign, both universities were also in serious financial straits. As the good humanist and sometime scholar she was, she was personally generous to both universities, and shared the view that a sympathetic approach to them was more likely to win their co-operation for her religious restorations. She presented Oxford with three ex-monastic rectories; she renewed her father's establishment of Trinity College Cambridge as a mainstay of Catholicism in that once significantly Protestant place, complete with its new chapel and choral foundation. In her will, she bequeathed £500 to each university for the relief of poor students, particularly those planning 'to be religious persons and priests'.

Neither Mary's early abandonment of the title 'Supreme Head of the Church', nor her respect for the orthodox clergy progressively restored to the church hierarchy, prevented her from playing an important part in the restoration of the Catholic Church. The course she pursued reflected her own humanist training and her commitment to restoring both music and ritual to what she saw as their proper place in religious practice. Little is known of her own position on the great doctrinal issues of the day, but her practice, always centred on the mass, was consistent and her piety never doubted. The one thing that can be said with confidence is that she was never a simply reactionary restorer of a medieval past. Recent writers who differ about the significance of many nuances in Catholic theology in Mary's reign still agree in using 'Catholic Reform' as a covering term to describe the changes made when Mary was monarch.

Latin services were quickly restored as standard church practice. Although many Catholic clergy, including perhaps Pole himself, were sometimes ambivalent about the saving qualities of preaching, teaching and exemplary behaviour as compared with the transformative power of religious ceremonial, Mary frequently reiterated her support for all those strategies. As she wrote to her Council in December 1554: 'There is much want of good preachers to overcome the evil diligence of preachers in the schism, not only by preaching but by example, without which, in my opinion, their sermons shall not so much profit.'[9]

Her own printer, Wayland, was granted sole right to publish all 'authorised' primers. More generally, as Jennifer Loach noted, the use of printing presses in Mary's reign was comparable to that of Edward's; printing presses were a preferred weapon for both sides in the religious wars being waged in mid-sixteenth-century England. Marian popular publications ranged from a children's catechism, prepared by Bishop Bonner and printed in red and black for the easier studying of question and answer, to adult manuals with titles like *A Profitable and Necessary Doctrine for every Christian Man*. At the time of Mary's death, with her active encouragement, and despite Pole's hesitation, the initial steps had been taken towards producing a new 'orthodox' English translation of the New Testament. If the point needs repeating, that stance surely confirms Mary's claim to be judged as more than a simply reactionary Catholic.

We have already seen how active she was in the restoration of papal authority. She also encouraged the restoration of familiar and spectacular forms of religious practice in processions, music and visual splendour, and she actively endorsed the restoration of many holy days and fasts. The cult of the Virgin Mary was also restored, not by Mary, but by others, and partly to enhance the queen's own standing. As Bill Wizeman put it, as 'one Mary possessed an essential role in salvation, so the other possessed an essential role in England's participation in salvation. Both Marys were intercessors, acting on behalf of others' redemption.'[10] There is little evidence that Mary ever sought to promote herself by such associations, despite her personal piety being so frequently acclaimed.

THE MARIAN BURNINGS REVISITED

Mary I is still popularly known as 'Bloody Mary' for the deaths of some 300 Protestants burned as heretics in her reign. Those deaths have always overshadowed any positive consideration of the achievements of England's first queen regnant. Since Mary is traditionally so closely identified with those burnings, it is desirable to look again at these events in the light of recent scholarship, for most judgements have long been clouded by the confessional commitments which first shaped discussions of these painful matters. The following sections first revisit sixteenth-century rationales for such burnings and then reconsider the extent to which Mary was personally responsible.

In the sixteenth century, as in preceding ones, burning was a mode of execution traditionally reserved for the most heinous crimes. Like all punitive deaths, it was an exemplary occasion, conducted in public precisely to instruct onlookers and potential offenders about the dangers of such offences. Heresy, sometimes referred to as 'soul killing', was widely agreed to be the worst of all crimes. Any person's time on this earth was fleeting; but an individual's soul was eternal, its condition of eternal bliss in heaven or eternal torment in hell being decided by the transitory mortal life. Heresy, therefore, was:

> a perilous weed ... the seed of the devil, the inspiration of the wicked spirits, the corruption of our hearts, the blinding of our sight, the quenching of our faith, the destruction of all good fruit, and finally the murder of our souls.

When the Henrician Catholic bishop, John Fisher, spoke these words, he was expressing a view which Calvin, Melancthon, Latimer and almost all other evangelical reformers shared. Sometimes, most famously in the case of Servetus, they could even agree that a particular victim should be burned, but they more usually divided along confessional lines. Almost all the Edwardian prominent clergy, including a majority of those who were to face that fate themselves, agreed that obdurate heretics should be burned. Cranmer, for example, had been actively involved in the burning of at least one heretic, and wrote the standard penalty for heresy into his draft canon law, although Edward died before it could be ratified.

What follows from the widespread agreement that obdurate heretics should be burned is that Mary, who shared that view, was thereby a thoroughly conventional person. Very few church activists, other than John Foxe, thought obdurate heretics should live. Two heretics were burned in Edward's reign, and two more in Elizabeth's reign. The last English burning for heresy took place in 1612 during the reign of James VI & I. Such considerations should shift the focus in Mary's reign from the principle of burnings, to concentrate on the extraordinary number of them, precisely because that is what was so extraordinary.

However they are reckoned, the numbers burned in Mary's reign were exceptional in English history, even before the very short time over which they occurred is taken into account. It was always expected that some heretics would die for their offences after Mary came to the throne. As one example, Cranmer was judged a traitor for his involvement in Northumberland's plot, but he was always destined for death as a heretic. (Death for treason was not noticeably preferable, being either by hanging, drawing and quartering – the victim being alive still as his entrails were removed – or, as a privilege reserved for a few, by beheading.) Cranmer's 'offences' as heretic were taken to include all the religious 'corruptions' he had visited on England and, indeed, on Mary's own family over 20 years, a litany of offences much more heinous than treason.

The Marian burnings of heretics began 1 February 1555, the first victim being a clergyman, John Rogers (who supported burning heretics in principle), condemned by Gardiner. The last five, condemned by Cardinal Pole, were burned at Canterbury on 10 November 1558, just seven days before Mary died. The total of all those burned was, on the best evidence available, some 285. Of those, 74 men were burned in 1555, 85 in 1556, 82 in 1557 and 44 in 1558. Although the initial expectation had been that a few, probably leading clergy, would be heresy victims, it came about that at least 54 women were also burned, and many males of much lower social status and education than the first victims.[11]

From one perspective, all their deaths might be seen as part of what Brad Gregory called the 'Christian martyrdom in the Reformation era'. Across Europe, the struggles between the Catholic (by far the more powerful group at the time) and the Reformed traditions meant that neither could endure the teachings of the other, unless sheer lack of power forced the protagonists into a toleration that almost everyone believed was fatal for true religion – and therefore to salvation. In the 50 years of that martyrdom era, from the burning of two Augustinian friars in 1523, some 7,000 Protestants died as heretics across Europe.[12]

In England, those figures include Protestants of varying degrees of radicalism under Henry, but by far the greatest number occurred during Mary's reign. It is likely that, as elsewhere, a high proportion of those interrogated recanted, however temporarily. But a striking number did not. In France under Henry II, the surviving records from the Parlement of Paris, which handled perhaps one-third of all French cases, indicate that in 17 months from 1548–50, 37 heretics were sentenced to death. But that is essentially to repeat the point that elsewhere – including in the Netherlands – many other Protestants died painfully for their beliefs. The point remains that, however the deaths at Smithfield and in Kent (sites of numerous burnings) measure on the European scale, the Marian burnings were uniquely intense in the English experience. In the

Netherlands, Vigilius, President of the Council of State in Brussels esti-
mated that in 1556 alone, some 1,300 heretics had been 'burned, hanged
or drowned'. Those are the only statistics which clearly surpass the
English deaths, and were sufficiently striking for Vigilius at least to recognise the inevitability of some degree of toleration.[13] Philip, however,
proved very reluctant to allow toleration even there.

The hostility shown to these burnings by following generations, usually reared in the Church of England restored by Elizabeth in 1559, is
not surprising. The victims nearly all died as good Protestants, testify-
ing to their faith. To that confessional sympathy should be added the
consideration that nearly all of those burned as Marian heretics were
identified and celebrated in John Foxe's massive work, familiarly known
as his *Book of Martyrs*. His detailed account of the sufferings of the Marian
martyrs has ensured that all subsequent generations have known in
detail about the horrors of their deaths. Foxe also includes reports of
some of the often equally horrible deaths of Henry VIII's victims, but
within traditional Protestant historiography Henry's victims received
less attention. There was no comparably detailed account of the some
200 Catholic priests and sympathisers hanged for treason under Elizabeth
(at a time when hanging meant death by slow – sometimes very slow –
strangulation), nor of those Catholic adherents who died in her reign
while being questioned or in prison.

Catholic officials, however, should have been, and may well have
been, as dismayed by the numbers being burned as was John Foxe. His
view that all burnings for religious views were deeply offensive to God
and man was indeed exceptional, but in theory the Church (in whatever
confessional manifestation) officially regarded every burned heretic as
failure on its part to reclaim an errant soul. As Foxe sometimes
complained, the prosecuting clergy often laboured long and hard to
achieve a last-minute conversion. The justification for both that effort
and the final punishment remained. If the victim refused to recant his or
her error (both sexes were subject to the same punishment for this
offence) then the accused was obviously an obdurate heretic. It followed
than any leniency towards such heresy would imperil not only the offender's own soul, but that of countless others.

It has been conventional to describe what happened to the Marian
protestant victims as 'persecution'. So it was, but it was also 'prosecution', since accusations of heresy followed a carefully defined legal form,

and there was a way to survive. In England, the process was first set in place by parliamentary statute. The relevant heresy laws were re-enacted, without any recorded protest, by parliament in the session that returned the realm to papal obedience. There followed edicts from the monarch and Council setting the machinery in place. Thereafter, however, any prosecution required assistance. As Gina Alexander pointed out, that meant 'the active co-operation of the respectable and responsible members of society carrying out government decisions. [Ecclesiastical] courts were filled with suspected [accused] heretics because the Council, the commissioners, the justices and the jurors placed them there.'[14]

Charges of heresy could be raised by church authorities but also arose from within the local communities, including those against people from the lower social levels. There were, therefore, opportunities for a variety of revenge strategies, and occasional indications that it took place. In a time of social stress and growing trade in estates described in Chapter 7, with subsequent tensions over customary rights and privileges, neighbourhood rivalries and antipathies burgeoned. Anyone was free to report a suspect heretic to the authorities for further investigation, and the social level of some victims suggests they did.

Whatever the initial expectation that at most a handful of leading clerics would suffer the penalty, the heresy trials soon reached much further and wider. Thanks to Foxe's prodigious work, an extraordinary amount of detail about the victims is still recoverable. The first four to die in England were all clergymen, which seems predictable enough, but the fifth was a fisherman and the sixth a weaver. Husbands and wives were burned, sometimes together, and at least once a married couple and a daughter were burned together. One woman was apparently burned because, at an early stage of her process, her husband had refused to post a bond for her release while awaiting trial. Some seem actively to have sought martyrdom, like the stranger in Norwich who first drew attention to himself by asking a group leaving mass for directions to a Protestant meeting.

One new factor in these developments may have been the attacks by some Protestant writers on the traditional practice of evasive and ambiguous denial. The attacks on Nicodemism, already discussed, had been a response to the more desperate spirit generated by the intensity of that era of 'Christian martyrdom'. It was also a response to an emerging international debate which specifically attacked that older practice of equivocation. Between 1537 and 1544, John Calvin was one who published several works attacking any prevarication, so frequently practised by English accused.

Calvin for one argued strongly for the much sterner alternative of open and insistent witness to the faith, with its inevitable consequences. Some historians have accepted his 'Nicodemite' criterion for defining true Protestant behaviour, but Calvin was bitterly attacked at the time as merciless. As one friend wrote to him, 'they say that it is easy for you to preach and threaten over there, but that if you were here you would perhaps feel differently.'[15] Whatever the reason, in the context of the surge of Protestant martyrdoms across Europe, many believers accepted a heightened commitment to manifesting their faith by their own deaths. Correspondence has survived between Protestant English clergy safely abroad and their parishioners – both male and female – who were contemplating accepting martyrdom by openly confronting Marian authorities and persevering in that until burned. Some were encouraged to do so, if they felt strong enough to confront and endure all that was involved. The battle for Christian truth in mid-sixteenth-century Europe made very high demands on many participants, and an understanding of the Marian martyrs must be set in that context.

MARY'S ROLE IN THE BURNINGS

For at least one historian deeply versed in mid-Tudor England, the Protestant tradition still prevails. David Loades has written, presumably sardonically, of Mary's 'crowning achievement' in burning so many in so short a time. For him, hers was indeed the primary responsibility for the whole process. At one level, since Mary was monarch of the realm, that is an indisputable proposition. But he then argues that Mary increasingly drove the processes on as others found it increasingly distasteful.[16] It is important to reassess this judgement, since until quite recent times it has stood substantially unchallenged since the sixteenth century. Foxe's characterisation of Mary's as a 'horrible and bloody' reign has long set the tone of discussion, but the focus here is more directly on the extent to which Mary's personal responsibility for those events can be established.

Mary shared the widespread, indeed orthodox, belief that heretics could be burned if they remained obdurate, and endorsed the proposal of her chaplain, John Christopherson, that Protestant preachers had killed more souls in one day than all the 'naughty' physicians had killed bodies in 20 years. She also, however, shared the general view that the most desirable outcome was to persuade 'heretics' to recant, repent and then return to the true church. If they refused to do so, their deaths should be exemplary for the edification of the wider public. Her initial instructions to the Privy Council for conducting the burnings required that they should be done 'without rashness', punishing those who, by abusing their own learning, 'seem to deceive the simple; the rest to be used [so] that the people perceive them to be justly condemned' and thereby be warned against imitating such errors.[17] The first targets for trial, apparently, were to be some of the leading Edwardian Protestant clerics

What challenged the whole regime, including Mary, was the unexpected number and social range of such obdurate heretics as were repeatedly exposed by accusation and legal process. The impact of the anti-Nicodemite response may well have taken the regime unawares, since the older tradition of equivocation and evasion was a much more familiar response. The failure to find another response to such unprecedented persistence in profound error, as the regime saw it, has frequently been criticised. But once embarked on its course, it is difficult to see how the regime could abandon that punitive policy without apparently conceding its own defeat. Conversely, to a modern mind, the chilling rider to such persistence is that the declining numbers of those burned towards the end of the regime may suggest the campaign was having some effect.

There were always secular as well as religious reasons to justify punitive investigations of religiously suspect subjects. By definition, heretics were refusing to obey secular as well as divine laws. In a society where religious and political were tightly intertwined, religious dissent always at least potentially indicated political dissent as well. Mary, moreover, had every reason to be particularly anxious about such matters. She could hardly forget Edward's attempt to replace her as next heir by their cousin, a move justified as defending Edward's true (against Mary's false) religion. Similarly the Wyatt rebellion was ostensibly about Mary's imminent marriage to Philip, but many sympathisers were driven by resistance to anything which might further entrench the Catholic restoration. Such schemes and plots were a recurrent feature of her reign. At that time the nexus between religious and political obedience was tight.

Mary was actively involved in the restoration of the heresy laws for the pursuit of active and obdurate 'heretics'. As monarch, she had ultimate responsibility for and indeed was 'the fount of' all the central legislative and judicial processes by which the realm was governed. But, like even her father, she was never an absolute monarch, and in most matters – the most noted exception being her marriage – she needed to achieve some form of consensus for any policy she pursued. Of course Mary carried responsibility for the burnings, but so, in varying degrees, did many others in her regime, including her Council, many clergy and even those who restored the legislation without obvious demur in 1554. Local officials who raised and tried cases, and those laity who accused their neighbours of heresy also carried some responsibility for the prosecutions which followed, and were successful. There are no figures for those who were set free after investigation, but Loades has suggested there were thousands.

Previous attempts to allocate responsibility for the Marian burnings have often proceeded by discussion of who was *not* responsible; biographers of eminent individuals from this era have often sought to downplay their subject's involvement in such a distressing activity. Discussion of Philip's involvement provides one example. His exculpation rested largely on his association with his confessor, Alfonso de Castro. Foxe's work includes a report of a sermon by Castro, who said that heretics should not be burned, 'but they should live and be converted.' Since the sermon was followed by about a month free of burnings, Foxe drew the inference that by mid-1555 Philip, then still in England, was uneasy about more burnings. But elsewhere Castro had made clear his view that when all efforts to save failed, 'anyone who thinks the punishment of heresy should be left to God is crazy.'[18]

Philip himself, five months after the burnings started, and just before he left England, noted his instructions that members of Parliament 'should take great care in their districts to punish offences against religion, from now on', despite their own sense they were already doing enough.[19] His own policies of intolerance towards heretics in his realms gave force to his 1566 declaration, that he would prefer to lose all his states and his own life many times over than become 'the sovereign of heretics'.[20] Accommodation, let alone toleration, was not part of Philip's preferred agenda, but Foxe's selective use of a chaplain's sermon has been repeatedly invoked on his behalf.

Similarly biographers have exempted Cardinal Pole from too close identification with the burnings – despite his condemnation of a number of victims. Rather, he was deemed to be uneasy about the process. But in a sermon Pole had delivered to Londoners in 1557, when there had been demonstrations against the burning of an eminent Londoner, he insisted that the ostensibly heroic 'martyrs' of London, who drew such sympathy from many onlookers, were displaying not 'holy courage' but 'devilish pertinacity.' It was, Pole pointed out, the wicked thief on Calvary who showed no fear, 'and so do these heretics at their death like the blasphemer, whatsoever their words be in honour of Christ'.[21] Like so many of his contemporaries, he knew where the truth resided and had no interest in defending those who persisted in error, even to their end.

The salvation of souls was almost always a primary imperative for death by burning, but not universally. The most famous exception for which Mary and *perhaps* her closest advisers bore responsibility was that of Thomas Cranmer, Archbishop of Canterbury under both Henry and Edward. As most powerfully and extensively described in a recent biography,[22] Cranmer did recant but his several recantations – while a great propaganda victory for the regime – were not enough to save him. At the last, he recovered his evangelical faith, and this gave rise to the famous scene where he thrust into the fire his right hand, as a final gesture of repudiation of the hand which had signed the recantations. Cranmer could accurately be described as a victim of Mary's revenge for the humiliations he had visited on her mother and, more indirectly, herself. But his was always an unusual case.

There were always some 'sound' Catholic men like Renard, still ambassador for Charles V, who took a more politic view, and repeatedly warned against the public burnings in London, which often attracted large and sometimes vocally disapproving crowds. That, however, was exactly the situation which Pole, for one, confronted by reiterating just how dangerous such pseudo-martyrs were, seeking to win followers for their errors, even as they were dying. For it was always an important part of the ritual of such admonitory deaths that they should be public. These events all occurred at a time when a 'private' execution, without official witnesses and onlookers, was almost unthinkable; indeed such a 'secret' would defeat the whole point of death by execution.

A final point to bear in mind, when considering the respective roles of the various actors in this painful drama, is that every person brought before the ecclesiastical authorities had some form of a trial. Charges were sometimes brought by clergy, but also by neighbours in the local community. Given the social tensions endemic in mid-Tudor society, it would be astonishing if some of the charges did not arise as much from local rivalries and tensions as confessional differences. (Witchcraft charges in the same period offer some fruitful analogies.) There was a careful process of examination, which often led to recantation. Payment of a fine could suffice, in some cases, if the offender was found guilty at all.

Other lesser penalties were also available. Local authorities sometimes simply refused to proceed with particular charges. Those who were condemned were those who had asserted their beliefs in the face of all attempts to dissuade them. By the legal and doctrinal criteria of the times, they were indeed 'heretics'. This is not to blame the victims, but to acknowledge the logic of their choice to witness to their faith by dying for and in it. Their choices were often heroic in their own terms. But to expect the orthodox authorities to overlook such dangerous threats to the souls of others was, at the time, made only more difficult by the numbers being examined. And, given the trial processes through which each 'heretic' passed and the numbers of adjudicators involved, it seems a less than dispassionate judgement to hold Mary peculiarly responsible for the whole tragedy. There are many others who willingly took part in the processes, and sixteenth-century England would have been a most unusual society if there were not some in local communities who were pleased to take advantage of such processes for their own purposes.

In short, Mary carried the same responsibility for enabling the burnings as she did for the consequences of any legislation she sanctioned, for that was an integral part of being a personal monarch. It is however worth recalling that, as previously remarked, Cranmer had also planned to restore death by burning as the ultimate penalty for heresy before Edward's death intervened. It could be worth considering whether the charges against Mary through the centuries would have been modified if she had simply been invoking Edwardian legislation. There are certainly a number of identifiable occasions where she actively intervened – certainly with Cranmer, and almost certainly with Ridley, for example.

But the vast majority of the more than 250 cases were initiated and prosecuted by others; officials as lowly as constables presented charges and private individuals could also do so. One has only to look at the extraordinary social range of the victims, including lowly villagers, to realise the need for a more nuanced account of who was responsible for invoking the legislation, This is particularly in the areas where Protestantism had been strong, for there the social and economic tensions so endemic in mid-Tudor England were only compounded by the ascendancy of the new religion.

11

THE ROAD TO WAR AND THE LOSS OF CALAIS

As 1554 ended, Mary had every reason for high optimism about the future. After 18 months, she sat as securely on the English throne as any monarch. She had established herself as England's first female sovereign, however problematic many within and beyond England still found a woman's rule. She had restored papal supremacy in England to secure 'true doctrine', especially the traditional mass. On the other hand, the endorsement by English statute of such papal decisions as the legitimacy of her mother's marriage, and her refusal to accede to papal (and Pole's) wishes that ecclesiastical land be restored to the Catholic church, indicated her reservations about how far papal supremacy extended beyond religious matters or took precedence over English statute law.

As well as restoring the Catholic faith, Mary's achievements had included marrying probably the most eligible man in Europe, the heir to the most extensive territories within Europe and beyond. The once vehement anti-Spanish feelings so frequently, and violently, expressed on the streets of London, were fading as many of Philip's entourage departed to take part in the continental wars. As the (old-style) year ended in March, some burning of heretics had taken place, but there was as yet no reason to anticipate just how many would defy the new religious order and die for their beliefs. Above all, and most wonderfully for Mary, her doctors assured her that she was pregnant. A Catholic heir to the throne, to displace her much-mistrusted half-sister, would ensure the continuance of true religion, and much more.

By the end of 1556, however, many of Mary's hopes were crumbling around her and continued to fade in the next two years. Her pregnancy had failed, and her husband had left England some 18 months previously. There was no sign of when he was planning to return, and her legal heir was widely believed to be a particularly nominal Catholic. The situation was made more difficult by matters well beyond her control. Among the most problematic was the election of a new pope in early 1555; Paul IV loathed all Hapsburgs and increasingly mistrusted both Philip's wife and her cardinal, who was also the papal legate, Reginald Pole. And relations between England and France or, more properly perhaps, between Henry II and Mary I were deteriorating further. As Mary was so frequently reminded, England might lie offshore, but it could never stand apart from wider European issues.

MARY'S EARLY RELATIONS WITH FRANCE

During the reign of Edward, Mary's only potent protector was the Emperor Charles V. Consequently Henry II of France always believed that her accession would be antithetical to his interests, entrenching the Hapsburg camp not only across the Channel but also at Calais. English control of Calais was a constant irritant to the French, for the same reasons that it was important for England. It not only ensured English control of the sea passage through the Channel, but provided a secure base from which English forces could launch attacks on the French. It is widely accepted that its possession was very important for English policy-makers, but there is also a suggestion that two weeks before Edward's death, when Northumberland was planning to install Jane Grey on the throne, he offered Henry II the return of Calais as a mark of gratitude for French support in that project. One particularly unreliable rumour had him offering Ireland as well. No conclusive evidence of the reported Calais offer has survived, but there are circumstantial grounds for suspecting Northumberland did so.[1] At whatever price, Northumberland had been given promises of military support, probably through Antoine de Noailles, and sent a relative to the French court to secure it when Mary first challenged Jane Grey as queen. Mary's rapid success quickly rendered that request redundant, and the proposed *quid pro quo* was never tested.

In the 1520s there had been discussions about the possible marriage of Mary Tudor and Henry Valois, but only the most superficial traces of Anglo-French amity survived by the time Mary emerged as monarch of England in 1553. Noailles, French ambassador after Mary's accession, had previously supported the attempt to crown Jane Grey. He was similarly embroiled in the abortive Wyatt rebellion of early 1554, and both times he was acting with the approval of Henry II. English hostility to any foreigners was strong enough for the earlier Wyatt conspirators all to agree that from Henry II they wanted weapons, munitions and money, but *no* French soldiers. The appearance in England of any French soldiers, they believed, would create an English reaction at least as hostile as that towards any Spaniard. There were also rumours that, to support Wyatt, the French were preparing for a diversionary attack on Calais.

As previously discussed, Wyatt's rising ended as a fiasco in the streets of London. Many of the leading conspirators fled to France, and for a time it seemed possible that comprehensive French support for the rebels would bring about open warfare between England and France. Henry II was more convinced than ever that war with England would be inevitable after Mary had married Philip. Mary's advisers, anxious to avoid war – as she was herself – recommended that the marriage treaty should include a clause that: 'England by occasion of this matrimony shall not directly or indirectly be entangled with the war that now is betwixt the most victorious [Lord the] Emperor the said Lord Prince's father and Henry [the] French King.'[2]

That was probably always a forlorn hope, because Henry, having failed to thwart her accession, continued to do whatever he could, short of outright war, to thwart Mary's interests and the stability of her regime. He was totally dismissive of the proposition that as monarch she was an independent power, even more so after she had married Philip. In 1554 the Venetian ambassador to Henry's court noted that his 'virulence [to Charles V] is so deep that death alone or the total ruin of his enemy can cure it.'[3] The origins of that deeply personal hatred lay in the years he had spent as a young prince in the hands of Charles V as a hostage for his father Francis I. His attitude to Philip was only marginally less hostile, and was easily extended to include his English wife.

By 1556, Mary's sense of grievance against Henry may have been equally well developed, since the French king continued to fan English discontents and entertain English conspirators at his court. Like every other Tudor monarch's, Mary's reign was characterised by rumours of sedition and incipient rebellion, at a level comparable to that of her predecessors. There were intermittent rumours that Edward VI was still alive, echoing the many pretenders that Henry VII – and, indeed, Henry VIII – had to deal with. Into the next century, local disorders, always endemic, could easily grow to something larger and more dangerous; loose words, carelessly spoken, could be, and sometimes were, reported to the Council and construed as a potential national threat. But what was distinctive about unrest under Mary was that Henry consistently provided shelter, succour and resources to those who plotted against her. Generally, the English exiles at the French court were an irritant rather than a potent threat to the English regime, backing piratical raids on the English coast rather than plotting an invasion, but occasionally, as with the two to be discussed later, they showed a capacity to be more dangerous.

MARY AS ASPIRING PEACEMAKER

Despite Henry's hostility to her accession, within weeks of it Mary had offered herself as potential mediator for peace between French and Hapsburg interests. Very much her mother's daughter, Mary shared Katherine's enthusiasm for the Erasmian dream of a 'Universal Peace' to be established throughout European Christendom, an idea widely but briefly popular in European courts three decades before. Humanist scholars and women, subsequent events suggested, were more attracted to the idea of peace than kings, who in the sixteenth century still aspired to demonstrate their legitimacy – and glory – by leading their troops into battle, as medieval and mythical kings of old had done. The Arthurian legends were still familiar tales in sixteenth-century European courts.

Despite the derision with which Noailles (privately) and Henry (more publicly) responded to her attempts, Mary tried her hand as peacemaker again in mid-1554, after the frustration of Pole's efforts at mediation. When Noailles paid his courtesy visit to the newly wed Philip and Mary on 21 August 1554, he recalled Mary's earlier argument that her marriage was far more likely to promote peace rather than war between French and Hapsburg interests. Six weeks later, as their fortunes on the battlefield waned, the French returned o the possibility of a peace agreement, understanding that at least Mary and her Chancellor Gardiner were sympathetic. But Mary's efforts at mediation were defeated, this time by mutual mistrust between the main protagonists. Philip and his advisers were convinced that Henry was playing for time, and Noailles believed the same of Philip.

The prospect for peace negotiations improved again in early 1555, to the point that Noailles even reported Mary's health notably improved by her hopes for European peace.[4] (It should be remembered that at the time Mary believed herself to be pregnant.) There were further negotiations for a fortnight in May and June. By then not only were Henry II's own fortunes improving, he was increasingly confident that Mary would never bear a child, so curtailing Hapsburg influence in England. English attempts at mediation proved to be such a failure that when the truce of Vaucelles was finally agreed between France and the Hapsburgs in February 1556, Mary had played no part whatever in the negotiations. And soon, more evidence of French support for Marian rebels came to light, driving Mary further towards war.

THE DUDLEY CONSPIRACY

Sir Henry Dudley, a relative of Northumberland, headed the new plot. He was sufficiently well known at the French court to have been sent to Henry II by the duke for the promised urgent assistance for Jane Grey. By November 1555 Dudley was hatching a plot to replace Mary by Elizabeth, less because of her religion and more from personal grievances that he nursed against Mary. He gathered around him a diverse group of discontents, including lesser gentry making such living as they could by their swords, and some with specific hopes disappointed by Mary. The plot, however, did include men in England sufficiently well placed and trusted by the Marian regime for it to become potentially very dangerous.

When the plot was betrayed, and interrogations began in March 1556, the informants once more insisted, as the Wyatt conspirators had done, that although they had asked for 'munitions, arms and money' from the French king, they had never asked for French soldiers. A major propaganda platform had been their insistence that the coronation of Philip was imminent. Once he had been crowned, they argued, he would become an irresistible power. Beyond that, however, much of the detail was confused, as exemplified by a bricklayer's account that 'the earl of Pembroke should go to fetch the crown from the earl of Shrewsbury to crown the king ... but [the speaker] and 500 men would spend their lives in keeping the crown in Englishmen's hands; strangers should never have it.'[5]

The same informant repeated another, and more far-fetched, rumour that the queen was so uneasy on her throne that she 'watched in harness every night till 3 o'clock, and was watched by her guard in harness for fear'. Such reports are only worth mentioning now because Noailles fed them back to Paris where they were picked up by, among others, the Venetian ambassador. Those reports have since been used by some historians, without much other information, to construct an image of a frightened, even hysterical queen, unable to sleep and restlessly pacing through her palaces, desperately pleading with her husband to return. Substantiating evidence has not survived from those who were more likely to know.

The Dudley conspiracy was always intended to take two parts, the actual rising, which was to come later, and a more unusual and ambitious plot to steal some £50,000 worth of silver bullion from the English treasury. To cover conspiracy expenses, that bullion was to be made into forged coinage at a mint already established in France. That part of the plan might well have succeeded.[6] Once French arms and support had been secured, the troops were to be raised in the conspirators' own areas. As the plot unravelled, it became dismayingly clear that some men of real significance – like the Governor of the fortress at Yarmouth and the Vice Admiral of the Severn, Sir Anthony Kingston – were deeply involved. The landing of English exiles in France would be the signal for other west-country men to raise their own followers, and the conspirators were soon talking of the thousands they could raise. One conspiratorial report claimed Kingston alone could raise 10,000 men.

Just how dangerous this conspiracy could have proved is now a matter for academic debate. As news of the latest plot spread, members of Elizabeth's household were questioned, but not Elizabeth herself. Kat Ashley, the mistress of Elizabeth's household, admitted to having heard rumours of a scheme to steal the queen's silver to fund the enterprise, but comprehensively denied any involvement. Elizabeth's Italian tutor, Giovanni Battista, was questioned about his foreign contacts when he visited London, including contacts with both the French and Venetian ambassadors, but the questioning produced nothing more sinister than the information that while there he bought some new strings for Elizabeth's lute. Elizabeth herself was not questioned about this conspiracy.

As well as alarm about the eminence of some of those found to be privy to Dudley's conspiracy, the other concern for the Marian regime was that once again Henry had harboured English rebels and even allowed an exile mint, producing forged English coins, to be established in his realm. Also, the conspirators later reported, Henry had promised them 'a hundred thousand pounds'. Henry baulked at that when it was raised with him, and prevaricated further when Dudley himself arrived at his court; then Henry's precondition was that he would provide Dudley with 'men, money and other things necessary' only if Philip were to send his troops against the Turks. It should have been impossible for anyone to believe that Philip, confronting many problems across his European territories, could have considered such a diversion. But still the conspirators kept crossing the Channel!

One victim of the failed conspiracy was Antoine de Noailles. The French ambassador had survived the suspicions – and sometimes certain knowledge – that he had been complicit in almost every anti-Marian move since before her accession. But after the Dudley affair was uncovered, there were sufficiently strong rumours that he would be charged with conspiracy against Mary, to whom he was accredited, for him to be seriously alarmed. He wrote urgently to his king begging for his recall. Finally, he was allowed to depart, being temporarily replaced by a more discreet brother, Gilles, until the third Noailles brother, François, could return from his very awkward mission to the Pope. It had been his task to explain why Henry II had signed the truce of Vaucelles with Philip without any discussion with Paul IV, leaving the Papacy facing Philip's forces in Italy alone. Meanwhile, Dudley remained safely abroad and Henry II gave him authority to grant or withdraw pensions from fugitive English in France. Clearly nothing of the tensions on either side of the Channel had been resolved.

RUMOURS OF PHILIP'S ENGLISH CORONATION

One issue the Dudley conspiracy exemplified was the extent to which, by 1556, rumours of Philip's imminent coronation had become a politically useful tactic for anti-Marian conspirators. When Philip was crowned, the claim went, the nobility and gentry would be 'brought to confusion' and the commoners 'made slaves'. The case of Naples, of which he was made king just before his marriage to Mary, and which he had never visited (and about which very few Englishmen knew *anything*) was cited as evidence for this likely outcome.

It has been a truism among historians that Mary, deeply in love with Philip, wanted to have her husband crowned, and was only prevented from doing so by widespread English resistance. That belief has served well as a further example of the extent to which Mary was probably irrational and certainly out of touch with the wishes of her people. At the time, the most potent aspect of rumours of Philip's imminent coronation was that, once crowned, then he would indeed be king of England. The underlying but little remarked implication was that Philip had previously *not* exercised regal power in England.

That view of his hitherto very circumscribed status was shared – and deplored – by many of Philip's own entourage, who were repeatedly dismayed by the subordinate role which public ceremonial routinely conferred on the queen's husband. For them, therefore, the way to assert his proper pre-eminence was indeed for him to be formally crowned in England. The early advice from Renard to Charles V had been that 'in England, the coronation stands for a true and lawful confirmation of title, and means much more here than in other realms'.[7] Renard thereby confirmed the Emperor's own belief in the importance of an English coronation for his son. In practice, a crowned Philip would still legally have been a king consort, not a king regnant, and still constrained by the terms of the marriage treaty, but somehow, it was believed, his status would be redefined to something more befitting his European stature.

There was, therefore, discussion of Philip's possible and/or feared coronation coming from his entourage, from his father's court, and from those English subjects who argued that the consequences of such a coronation would be to threaten the very integrity of the English realm, the latter usually making that case to promote subversive propaganda purposes. The issue has been further confused in recent years, since it has been suggested that discussions Philip had with the Council about his royal titles after he returned to Europe also referred to his wish to be crowned king. Those discussions, however, actually addressed a quite separate issue, of Philip's wish to reorder his many titles when in Europe: that is, simply changing their order so his English title no longer took precedence over all his European ones.[8] Once that material is read in its correct context, then there is very little if any evidence of any informed or official English discussions about any coronation for him.

What remains of the 'coronation' issue, as historians have understood it, is that Mary's response, as described in ambassadorial reports, was that her people would not allow it. That may or may not have been her assessment of the case; Mary was quite enough of a Tudor to dissemble, and hide her own will behind the imputed opposition of others. She *may* have been willing to consider a coronation for her spouse in the early days of his rule, when she did feel some affection for him, but as his prolonged absence from England left her feeling more isolated, the probability that she would support his coronation became increasingly remote. By 1556, the surviving correspondence between them has a very business-like tone. We know nothing of how much she knew of his several romantic liaisons in Europe in those years, but by then the references to a coronation for Philip are gossip either to promote a conspiracy, or, only marginally more persuasively, in ambassadorial reports.

Noailles provides a good example of this point. As early as 1554, he reported to the French court that no coronation had been agreed for Philip. There is, however, no evidence that the question was ever raised in the parliaments. In the sixteenth century, the most important questions to be asked of any ambassadorial report was: 'who was feeding him his information, to what end, and who benefited from his believing it?'[9] Mary's early declaration that she would love her husband but could allow him no part in the government of her realm suggests another reason for her ever refusing to countenance Philip's coronation, whatever the wishes of his family or entourage. The real interest in the ongoing rumours about Philip's coronation, and its likely consequences, is the light the whole matters throws on the difficulty in accepting that a woman could be a queen regnant, particularly if she was also a wife.

PHILIP'S WARS AND ENGLISH INTERVENTIONS

The Neapolitan Giovanni Carafa had been elected as Pope Paul IV in May 1555. He was always fiercely anti-Spanish, and had negotiated a secret treaty with France in October of that year, by which the French were committed to joining the papacy in driving the Hapsburgs from the Papal States and other parts of Italy, presumably including Naples. In September 1556, responding to activities which he saw as papal provocation, the Duke of Alba, Philip's viceroy of Naples, invaded the Papal States. By January 1557, France had invaded Italy to support the papacy, and another French army attacked the Hapsburg Netherlands. Most of Europe was, it seemed, now at war. For a time, England remained aloof, but in March Philip, desperate for money, ships and soldiers sailed from Calais to England to seek English support.

He arrived at Greenwich on 19 March 1557, to a 32-gun salute and, as the indefatigable Machyn reported, many cries of 'God save the king and queen'. *Te Deums* and bell-ringing greeted him, and a ceremonial ride through London completed the formal welcomes. He resumed his ceremonial duties, including presiding at a splendid ceremony of the Order of the Garter on St George's Day. But above all, he had come to persuade his wife and her Council to join his war against France, an outcome the French had already accepted was a likely result of their fresh alliance with the papacy.

Philip was in the awkward position of understanding that his wars were a serious drain on his already strained economic resources, and confrontations from which he could expect to win little. This was particularly true of his wars in Italy since, if he lost, he lost the kingdom of Naples; if he won, he could hardly take over the Papal States. A negotiated peace with the papacy was the best he could hope for, but the hostility of Paul IV to all things Hapsburg made an acceptable settlement seem improbable. France was an even more difficult case for him, and Philip may well have believed his best hope was a powerful push against Henry by his forces and those of England to force a peace. Although his primary needs were money and shipping, usually well-informed observers believed England could put up to 100,000 men on the battlefield, an appealing (if unlikely) proposition for Philip.

If the case he laid before his wife was for a final strong push against France to force a comprehensive peace, it is easier to understand her decision to join his war. She had pursued the idea of peace in the face of widespread French derision for some years. On a more pragmatic level, she had also endured a series of attempted rebellions against her by men whom Henry had publicly entertained at his court. But Mary's Council still resisted any declaration of war, offering several compelling arguments. They pointed out that, because of the recent appalling harvests, the English were enduring endemic famine. As a consequence France was too important as a source of grain in England for the realm to go to war against Henry. (In fact, France like the rest of northern Europe was suffering similar food shortages, but the French were making a particular effort to supply England, precisely to keep that country out of Philip's wars.) The marriage treaty specifically forbade Philip dragging England into his European wars. There was no money in the treasury. The nobility had no extra resources to help fund such a policy and merchants would suffer from the inevitable disruptions of trade.

The force of those arguments might have seemed compelling, but Mary insisted the councillors, collectively and individually, reconsider their stance against the war. Philip remained in England – and therefore away from the battlefield – for nearly four months, a telling comment on how much he needed English support. He spent some time hunting, some time in the usual courtly pastimes such as masques, and a great deal of time urging the case for English support. Once that was finally won, he left England on 6 July 1557, having spent his last night in England with his queen at Dover. There were no reports this time of her inconsolable grief at his departure, but that was to be the last time Mary saw her husband, or that he stood on English soil. But he left knowing that well before his departure, Henry II had finally provided the rationale for England to enter the war against France.

STAFFORD'S RAID ON SCARBOROUGH CASTLE

The most bizarre and, as it transpired, most badly timed of the conspiracies against Mary launched from France was that headed by Thomas Stafford. Describing himself as child of the rightful Duke of Buckingham, he was the second son of Margaret of Salisbury's daughter Ursula and the grandson of the last Duke of Buckingham (executed in 1521). His hopes of his family's restoration on Mary's accession had not been realised and, like other disappointed men, he turned to plotting against her. After some association with both the Wyatt and Dudley plots, he was at the French court in November 1556, presenting himself as 'next heir to the crown' and using the full arms of England on his seal to prove it, apparently with Henry II's approval.

In April 1557, with some 100 men on two small ships, Stafford seized the decaying Scarborough Castle. He proclaimed himself 'protector of the realm', come to rescue England from the 'naughty nation of Spaniards' and from England's 'unrightful and unworthy queen'. In that last point, Stafford picked up a theme which had been previously invoked by Dudley's co-conspirators, that Mary had broken Henry VIII's will by marrying without the express consent of the councillors her father had provided for Edward. The main interest in this astonishing charge is the extent to which it underlines the difficulty some of Mary's subjects had in coming to terms with the concept of a female monarch. No male monarch would ever have been subjected to such a restriction, even if it still made any sense given the passage of time and the uncertainty as to which councillors Henry VIII might have intended to make such a decision. But in the context of a female monarch, it appeared to be an argument of some polemical value.

Stafford's attempt failed abysmally. The main importance of that otherwise bizarre episode was its timing and, above all, that it manifestly had support from the French. It confirmed Mary's decision that she should join in the Hapsburg struggles against French interests. Before she could declare war there were even more reports from her ambassador at Henry's court that Mary's fugitives and rebels in France, 'persisting in devilish imagination', were still plotting to seize some English ports – Poole and/or Weymouth – or Portland Castle, and still hoped to involve Henry II in their schemes. The French backing for such plots seemed as endless as the supply of potential discontented English rebels.

THE WAR AGAINST FRANCE

The timing of Stafford's attack was so fortuitous that David Loades has suggested that he was actually the victim of a convoluted English plot, perhaps overseen by Mary's most pro-war councillor, Paget.[10] There is no firm evidence to support the hypothesis, but the raid certainly made it much easier for Mary to persuade her Council to war. Philip was still In England and the combined efforts of the royal pair finally prevailed. The decision to go to war against France was taken in early May, and preparations for war set in train immediately thereafter. It was, however, at least a month before Mary finally issued her declaration of war against Henry II.

Mary issued her proclamation to her own people declaring war against France on 7 June 1557. Unlike any other comparable document of her reign after her marriage, it was issued in Mary's name alone, that is, without Philip's. There was to be no doubt that it was the queen of England who was declaring war. She listed for her subjects her many grievances against Henry II, beginning with his known support for 'the notable and heinous treason' of Northumberland, and his secret support for the 'conspiracy moved against God and us by Wyatt'. As long as possible, she claimed, Mary had preferred to hold his ministers rather than the king himself responsible and had made many attempts to broker a peace between Charles V and Henry II. His response had been to receive at his court and support more English rebels, implicated in the Dudley and Stafford conspiracies. He had supported 'notorious pirates ... spoilers of our subjects', particularly merchants. He had repeatedly 'condoned forgers of false money' and 'counterfeiters of our coin', and finally he had 'with all hostility invaded the Low countries to the defence and preservation whereof we are bound by special treaty'. She was now, therefore, urging her own subjects to treat 'the French King and his subjects as open enemies, annoying them by all such means as men may and are wont to do their enemies'. This conventional form, which followed any declaration of war, was an invitation for her subjects to harass and rob any Frenchmen they could find. That command most subjects were only too happy to obey.

The English herald arrived at Henry's court on the same day as the English proclamation was published, but Henry postponed hearing his message until he had completed another two days of hunting. On his return, he summoned all the ambassadors at his court to hear the herald. Once it was clear the traditional form of defiance to war came in the name of the Queen of England alone, Henry silenced the herald, refusing to hear any of her reasons for her declaration. He explained to the assembled ambassadors that 'as the herald came in the name of a woman it was unnecessary for him to listen to anything further, as he would have done had he come in the name of a man, to whom he would have replied in detail', adding derisively: 'Consider how I stand when a woman sends to defy me to war.' Throughout Mary's reign indeed, he consistently demonstrated at least as much difficulty in coming to terms with the idea of a female exercising full royal authority as did any of Mary's subjects.

MARY'S PROBLEMS WITH THE PAPACY

Whatever Mary's reasons for declaring war, she made her decision without consulting her usually close adviser Cardinal Pole. Since declaring war against France necessarily meant waging war against Henry II's ally Pope Paul IV, Pole had resolved all possible tensions between his allegiance to his Pope and his allegiance to his queen by remaining in Canterbury throughout the relevant discussions. This did nothing to assuage the marked antipathy of Paul IV (elected 1555) towards Hapsburgs in general, and Mary by association. Moreover, the new Pope had also long had deep suspicions about Reginald Pole's religious opinions.

The antipathy was first publicly expressed during the papal elections of 1549, from which Julius III had emerged as victor. Pole had earlier emerged as favoured candidate in that election, and had been vehemently attacked by Carafa, now Paul IV. In the 1530s, moreover, Pole had belonged to a group, the *spirituali,* which then hoped for reconciliation with the Lutherans and sought an accommodation with them on the issue of salvation by faith. However high-minded that might have been in the 1530s, by the 1550s, with hardening divisions within Christianity, more conservative Catholics, of whom Carafa was unarguably one, scented heresy in such doctrinal compromises. He nursed other suspicions of both Pole and his good friend Morone, both often described as on the more 'liberal' wing of Catholicism.

Pole had arrived in England as papal legate in late 1554, and did not, could not, assume the office of Archbishop of Canterbury until Cranmer had been degraded from the office and died his heretic's death in March 1556. For the next year Pole was both archbishop and papal legate, but in April 1557 Paul IV cancelled his legatine status and recalled him to

Rome. Mary, who soon after her accession had described herself as the pope's most obedient daughter, refused to allow Pole to go, and refused to accept the papal nomination as new papal legate of William Peto, once confessor to her mother, on the grounds he was far too old and in retirement. Peto also declined the position arguing both his advanced age (he may have been in his early seventies) and his lack of suitable experience. In May Mary wrote to the Pope, pointing out the damage which would be done to the ongoing restoration of the Catholic Church in England if Pole were withdrawn. Subsequently both the Council, and Pole himself wrote to the same effect, but without making any impact.

At the end of May, Morone, who was in Rome, was charged with heresy and by June it was very clear that charges were also being prepared against Pole. When a papal nuncio tried to deliver the relevant documents recalling Pole to Rome, Mary refused him admission to her realm. She also forbade Pole from acting on his wish to go to Rome and clear his name, not least because she had received very clear advice from her ambassador there that if Pole went to Rome he would simply disappear into the prison of the Inquisition, as Morone had already done. As David Loades succinctly summarised the position, thereafter 'deadlock had been reached. English business could not be discharged in Rome, and papal directives could not be received in England.'[11] English, and more specifically Mary's, affairs had moved a long way from the apparently widespread acclamation of restored papal authority in late 1554.

From July, diplomatic chatter had it that Philip was anxious to make peace with the Pope. This was finally achieved more by the decision of the French to withdraw from northern Italy than by any wish for peace on the part of Paul IV. On 6 October 1557, Mary commanded the Lord Mayor and aldermen to attend a High Mass at St Paul's to celebrate the 'joyful news of the peace between the Pope's Holiness and the King's Majesty'. She also ordered the customary celebratory bonfires throughout the city,[12] but was soon to learn that Paul IV would not easily change his attitude to England.

Pole continued to discharge his duties as Archbishop of Canterbury; one possible embarrassment was removed when Peto died, and the Pope made no move to appoint another legate, but he also made no move to confirm the various ecclesiastical appointments referred to him by Pole. Rumour has it that Paul IV rejoiced when he heard of the almost simultaneous deaths of the heretical cardinal and Mary, whom he called the

'Hapsburg' queen, in November 1558. Presumably as it became clearer just what the accession of Elizabeth represented for his authority in England, he reflected more ruefully on his initial reaction. Mary's reactions to the papal interventions of the last 18 months of her rule do however suggest that at the end of her reign, as at the beginning, her obedience to the Holy Father was always tempered by a strong sense of the proper limitations of papal authority within her kingdom.

THE ENGLISH AT WAR

Once war against the French had been decided upon, few others shared Pole's scruples about formally going to war against the Pope, however vicariously. Rather, many members of the nobility and upper gentry were only too pleased to undertake what most of them still regarded as their primary role, that of military leadership. In an age of dynastic realms, and when honour and reputation were most firmly established by war (to say nothing of the possible financial benefits from ransoms and plunder), English men flocked to join Philip's forces. They included not just those whom Philip had previously won over, like the sons of the late Duke of Northumberland, but also some who had been in self-imposed exile, such as the Earl of Bedford. Remarkably, early active conspirators in the Wyatt rebellion like Sir Peter Carew and Sir James Croft were among those who went to war for Mary. The regime may well have seen some advantage in sending potential troublemakers to war abroad, but that was only possible once they had volunteered, which they presumably did in part because of career and financial opportunities, but also perhaps because fighting on Mary's behalf against the French was a route to political rehabilitation.

Natural military leaders by virtue of their inherited positions, such as the Earls of Pembroke, Rutland, Shrewsbury and Westmoreland, all assumed their traditional noble responsibilities. Tensions between traditional personal loyalties and emerging proto-nationalist commitments were captured by a telling exchange between Westmoreland and his Scottish equivalent with whom he was seeking to ensure the security of the Scottish border. Westmoreland was concerned about the dominant French interests in a country where Mary of Guise was still regent for her young daughter. Reassuring him that the Scots were not concerned to pursue French interests, the Scottish Earl of Cassilis remarked to the English earl that he was no more French than Westmoreland was Spanish. Westmoreland, however, answered that 'as long as God shall preserve my master and mistress together, I am and shall be a Spaniard to the utmost of my power.'[13] Personal obligations and loyalties were still stronger than a more abstract idea of national identity. In that age of dynastic kingdoms, even the English realm, incorporating Wales and Ireland, Calais and Cornwall (which a few years previously had rebelled against a prayer book in, for them, incomprehensible English) had a more dynastic and less 'national' identity.

If his English followers were fighting for glory and riches, Philip's major problem was his lack of financial resources. He had looked to England for relief in that, but there is little evidence that Mary supplied it in strikingly large amounts. She did not call a parliament to seek a subsidy until January 1558, although the delay may well have been the result of the assessment by her Council that raising more revenue would prove very difficult. They explained to her that rising prices and fixed incomes left all levels of the gentry unable to meet further subsidies, the merchants, especially in the cloth trade, had fallen on hard times and the commoners were suffering too much from the effects of famine and unpaid debts to be able to meet any further taxation demands.

AT WAR WITH FRANCE

One of the many Edwardian policies reversed during the reign of Mary was the treatment of the navy. Northumberland in particular had sold off old ships and not provided any new ones, reversing Somerset's policy but continuing his early steps to establish a safe anchorage for remaining warships. In Mary's reign, however, rebuilding the navy began in earnest. By 1557 there were two new warships, the *Philip and Mary* and the *Mary Rose* (a name which might have seemed ominous, given the fate of the previous *Mary Rose,* which notoriously sank off Portsmouth in July 1545 with the loss of almost the entire crew). In January 1557 it was agreed that an annual allocation of £14,000 would be set aside for expenditure on the navy at the discretion of the lord treasurer and lord admiral; the precedent for a permanent dedicated income for the navy had been set.

As soon as war was declared, the English navy of some 20 ships cleared the Channel of French privateers and, when the initial English army was assembled, escorted it safely to the continent in July. Some troops were left at Calais, others at Guisnes and Hammes, and the great majority pressed on to the siege of St Quentin. They arrived too late to take part in the crucial battle outside the stronghold, but did participate in the final storming of the town. One Spaniard reported that the English had fought the best of all the forces, another that they had failed to distinguish themselves at all. But, however they fought, at least they were there, signifying English support for their king. For Mary, necessarily unable to take any active part in such procedures, it was satisfaction enough that they had been present in time to share the ultimate triumph, however transitory it was to prove.

The way was now clear for the combined forces to march on Paris, but Philip was still chronically short of money, and began to wind down the campaign, moving his remaining forces into winter quarters. The English contingent recrossed the Channel. The Duke of Guise, however, just returned from his unsuccessful campaign with papal forces against the Hapsburg troops, recruited another army and appeared before Calais on New Year's Day, 1558. It was most unusual for any major military initiatives to be undertaken in the depths of winter, but Henry II had been advised that the best time to take the apparently impregnable fortress was in January when the marshes and much of the water surrounding it would be frozen. Most unusually, the preparations for the attack were kept so secret that when a spy placed in the French army warned Lord Thomas Wentworth, Lord Deputy of Calais, of an imminent attack, he simply dismissed it on the grounds that wars were not fought in winter.

Guise arrived in the Pale with over 20,000 foot soldiers, 4,000 cavalry and 30 pieces of artillery, against a garrison of some 2,500. Wentworth issued an urgent call for reinforcements, but the report arrived in England only as the attack on Calais was reaching its final stages. Wentworth also wrote to Philip for help, but again it was too late. By 7 January 1558 Mary had ordered £3,000 sent from her treasury to Dover to pay soldiers raised by Jerningham. The following day she wrote to the Duke of Norfolk and others alerting them to the sudden threat to 'a principal member and chief jewel of our realm'. Wentworth sued for terms on 8 January, but it took some time for the news of that to reach London. The next four days, therefore, were spent trying to get more support to Calais, but by 12 January, the queen had the bad news: 'it had pleased God to suffer Calais to be surprised by the enemies.'

By the next day it was clear that any immediate attempt to rescue the English fortress had been frustrated: 'because of extreme tempest last Monday night [10 January], our ships set out to sea for keeping the passage and convoy of our army have been so shaken and spoiled of tackle, some dispersed, others driven ashore that they cannot serve until mended and furnished.'[14] By 17 January, however, levies were once again being raised – with a special admonition to the Lord Mayor of London to ensure the new recruits were 'better than the last ... thoroughly furnished with sufficient armour and weapons'. But bad weather and inadequately furnished levies continued to plague the attempt to relieve Calais, and by the end of January Mary seems to have given up all hope of an immediate recovery. Such preparations occupied a great deal of Mary's time and effort, as Pole frequently lamented in his reports to Philip about how hard the queen was working. When Philip proposed a joint attempt to reclaim Calais at the end of January, the Council informed his envoy, Feria, that they could not consider it, fearing a French-inspired invasion from Scotland – a long-standing anxiety if not an obviously pressing one – and the possible intervention of Denmark and the Hanseatic League, a matter not previously discussed.

The loss of Calais has traditionally ranked with the Marian burnings of martyrs as grounds for treating Mary's reign as a disaster. Her opponents were quick to seize the propaganda opportunities with pamphlets such as 'A Warning to England to Repente, and to Turne to god from idolatrie and poperie by the terrible example of Calece', published, it is not surprising to see, under a pseudonym. Mary may well have agreed at least with the gravity of the loss of Calais, if not the causal explanation. Foxe tells a story of the dying queen sighing disconsolately, refusing to tell her Council why, but confiding to her trusted Clarencius that she sighed a little for the absence of King Philip, much more for the loss of Calais: 'when I am dead and opened, you shall find Calais lying in my heart.'[15]

An intriguing insight, however, into another English view of Calais prior to its loss is to be found in the comment of the Venetian ambassador, in February 1558, that some members of parliament were resisting a subsidy to help recover Calais, saying that 'if the French have taken

Calais they thus took nothing from the English, but recovered what was their own.' Set beside the probability that Northumberland had been prepared to offer Calais to Henry II in return for his support for Queen Jane Grey, this report suggests that the loss of Calais – certainly deeply regretted by Mary – was not necessarily viewed as a disaster by all Englishmen until it became another part of the Protestant black legends of her reign.

12

THE END OF THE REGIME OF MARY TUDOR

PROVIDING AN HEIR TO THE ENGLISH THRONE

In January 1558 Mary informed Philip that once again she believed herself to be pregnant, explaining that unlike her previous possible pregnancy, this time she had waited seven months to tell him. The delay was, sensibly enough, to ensure beyond doubt that she was indeed pregnant, thereby avoiding any recurrence of the humiliating result of the previous occasion. Her husband, who had left England six months earlier, very properly expressed his great delight, and sent Count Feria to England to congratulate the queen on her condition. Given her past history, and her age, Philip had every reason to treat the news privately with more caution that those formal actions suggested. For her part, however, Mary either believed herself pregnant or still capable of conceiving in late March for her will, written then, began by assuming the existence of her own heir.

By April she knew she had again been mistaken about her pregnancy (as presumably were her medical advisers), but made no alteration to her will. Whatever the true explanation for the new swelling of her stomach, it did not cause her any serious health problems, since in early February Pole reassured Philip that Mary's health 'both in mind and body, continues good'. He added that this was in spite of 'the toil and trouble undergone by her for the public need, together with her constant solicitude about the king's affairs', so she was still working at her usual tasks. Like others, Pole was always impressed by, and concerned about, the long hours Mary spent working at – even drafting – papers. She was indeed unusual among the Tudors, apart from her grandfather Henry VII, in her application to her responsibilities,

The failure of her second 'pregnancy' and the consideration that Mary was now 42 revived serious discussion of who was to be her successor. The displays of sisterly closeness with Elizabeth at the start of Mary's reign had quickly died away, and Mary's preference was always for Margaret Douglas as heir. In the queen's eyes, she was preferable to Elizabeth in being both indisputably legitimate and firmly Catholic. She had been raised in her uncle Henry's court, and was close enough to Mary both to carry the queen's train at her marriage, and to be chief mourner at her funeral. Mary's preference, however, was never grounds enough to make her cousin an acceptable alternative to Elizabeth. Mary had several times been warned that no parliament would alter the line of succession established by Henry VIII.

So Elizabeth was necessarily Mary's heir. Mary's resistance to that outcome was partly due to Elizabeth's ambivalence about the Catholic religion, and partly because, in Mary's eyes, Elizabeth's mother had been so promiscuous that it was extremely unlikely that she was truly a daughter of Henry VIII. Philip, however, was strongly of the view that Elizabeth should succeed to the throne, and renewed his efforts to marry her off to the Duke of Savoy, a reliable client of the Hapsburg interests. Mary, always at best ambivalent about Philip's preference to marry his sister-in-law to the Duke of Savoy, *may* have been slightly better inclined to the proposal of the future Erik XIV of Sweden, although since he was a Lutheran her support seems improbable. Elizabeth's response to Mary's question about her response to Erik's courtship was that, as she had rejected some very honourable proposals in her brother's time, so she hoped still to continue in her (much preferred) unmarried state.

MARY'S FINAL ILLNESS

By the standards of the times, and despite her slight physique, Mary may have been relatively healthy in her early years. Her first known significant illness had occurred in 1531, when she was 14. She was briefly ill again in 1533, but this is only known from doctor's fees listed in Privy Purse expenses. Nothing is known of her symptoms then, or in 1542 when she suffered from what was described as 'a strange fever'. Thereafter, despite some intermittent illness, including colic, there are no clear indications of menstrual problems, despite recurrent references to the impact of her womb on her health. In an era when some 500 conditions, many of which also occurred in males, were attributed to malfunction of a woman's womb, this is not a very helpful analysis. Nothing is known of the illness which forced her earlier, as we have seen, to hand her allocated portions of the translations of Erasmus' *Paraphrases* over to her chaplain Francis Mallet. She was certainly prone to headaches, but then she was also very short-sighted, which may well have been a contributory factor to that problem.

It is not known when Mary's final illness took hold of her, nor is there is any agreed diagnosis of what caused her death. Until May, Mary's health fluctuated but gave no grounds for concern. When the illness began, Feria, for one, thought she was simply suffering her 'usual ailment again', whatever that was. She was first described as suffering her 'usual ailment' in 1535. It may have been a menstrual condition, then always the first explanation for female illness, but we also know that she had other more specifically seasonal health problems, included an allergic condition she described as appearing in autumn. Although Feria thought she was 'worse than usual' in June, she recovered within a few days, and he returned to the continent. Unusually, she developed a fever in August, and again in September, but although worrying that was hardly surprising at a time when a disastrous epidemic was sweeping across England.

In late October there were fresh and serious concerns for her health. When that news reached Philip, he sent Feria to her again, this time sending a highly regarded Portuguese physician with him. The matter which was becoming most pressing, and one of many on which Mary had resolutely resisted her husband's will, was that of naming her heir. Elizabeth's was the only name put forward; for the usual reasons, Mary resisted pressure from her Council as well as from Philip to name her as heir until almost the very last. Then, Philip was told, shortly before she died, she was visited by representatives of the three estates (clergy, lords and commons) with whom she agreed that the line of succession set out in her father's will should be followed. She may not have been explicitly named, but Elizabeth would be the next monarch.

It is impossible to know several centuries later, and in a context of very different medical understandings, just what Mary died of, but that has not stood in the way of considerable speculation. Whether she had that fever killing so many of her subjects, or ovarian cancer, or 'dropsy', or tuberculosis or influenza, has been the source of much debate. The only thing that can be said with any certainty is that she was seriously ill for several weeks. When Feria arrived in London and visited Mary on 9 November, he found her to be so ill there was no hope of her recovery. She was, he reported to Philip, 'happy to see me, since I brought news of your majesty, and to receive the letter though she was unable to read it'.[1] His account of Mary's condition raises doubts about her ability to sign during at least the last week, but apparently documents were still being sent to her for a signature. There is a story that some of them, including some of Thomas Gresham's financial accounts, were used for some of the procedures employed when embalming the corpse. Their disappearance also gave rise to widespread but ill-founded rumours that Mary had sent vast amounts of money out of the kingdom, presumably to her husband, in her final months.

Apart from the story Foxe recounted of Mary's heavy sighs for the loss of Calais, the only direct account of her death comes from her faithful – and much favoured – 'darling' Jane Dormer. Years later, long since married to Feria and settled in Spain, she remembered Mary's distress in the final days of her life that she had caused Jane's marriage to be postponed until Philip could also be in England. The consequence, Mary now realised, was that she could not honour the marriage as she would have wished. As Dormer remembered it, as the queen drifted in and out of consciousness, she told those around her that she had seen little children, like angels, playing and singing before her. On the morning of 17 November, she paid close attention to the mass being celebrated in her room, making all the responses very clearly. The last thing she saw was the host, belief in the religious centrality of which was the matter on which she would – and did – never compromise.

For Philip, November was a difficult month. On the 1st, he heard finally of the death of his father on 21 September. Mary of Hungary, Charles' sister and recent regent of the Netherlands, died very soon after. The peace negotiations over Calais were dragging on fruitlessly. In a letter to his sister begun as these events were taking place he wrote: 'It seems to me that everything is being taken from me at once.' In the midst of reporting all these disasters, of Mary's death Philip wrote: 'May God have received her in His glory! I felt a reasonable regret for her death. I shall miss her.'[2] Given the context in which he was writing, and his restrained remarks about his father's death, Philip's regret therefore *may* even suggest a little warmth towards his late wife, in what had always been a political marriage. But it was not long before new political considerations turned his mind to another marriage.

Following a longstanding tradition, Mary's death was announced in England by the proclamation which announced the accession of Elizabeth because 'it hath pleased Almighty God ... [to call] out of this mortal life, to our great grief, our dearest sister of noble memory, Mary.'[3] That was probably the last official statement to refer to Mary in such complimentary terms. On her deathbed, Mary had instructed Jane Dormer, who had long had charge of her jewels, to take them to Elizabeth with the request that the new queen should maintain the old religion, and honour Mary's will. That will was a summation of many of Mary's main interests in her life. She asked that alms totalling £1,000 be distributed to poor prisoners, and poor men and women, that her mother's body be brought from Peterborough and laid beside hers in her grave, that moneys be given to the religious foundations re-established in her reign and to the two universities. She asked that certain jewels Philip or his father had given her be returned to her husband, and that though he would no longer reign he should be regarded as 'a most assured friend in his power and strength' to her heir and successor. She left £1,000 to Pole, but he died, of the epidemic sweeping through England, in the evening of the day Mary died. In the event, Elizabeth observed none of the provisions of Mary's will.

MARY'S FUNERAL

Sydney Anglo, still the authority on Tudor royal ceremonial, once wrote that 'Coronations and funerals were the most imposing and most symbolically potent of all ceremonies of state.'[4] Indeed, early modern funerals were commonly regarded as the final statement of the social identity of the deceased, but the messages from Mary's funeral were confusing from the outset. Even the usual proclamation calling on those nobles who claimed a right to fulfil specific functions at her funeral (and who thereby qualified for some rich rewards in grants for the necessary fabrics) was apparently ignored on this occasion. There was also some anxiety lest even those whose attendance was formally necessary might be reluctant to be there.

It is not possible to know who actually attended in any detail. The one surviving official account is a retrospective description of the ceremonies which reads more like a general reassurance for the Spanish that Mary had been buried with appropriate ceremony, rather than a detailed account of what took place. It lists, for example, the ranks of people attending – including some ranks which could not have been present. It is very vague about numbers, although numbers in a procession were always an important marker of degree. Members of Mary's household were named, especially at her actual interment, but not many other attendees were specified by name.

The delicate balance between honouring the late monarch and winning favour with the new ruler was always a matter of great delicacy, and the more so on this occasion. Lord Treasurer Winchester, who was now serving his third monarch in that capacity, was in charge of this funeral, as he had been for that of Mary's mother some 20 years previously. He raised the problem of reluctant attendees with Elizabeth's Council, and was assured that the new queen would, if necessary, order any recalcitrants whose office required their presence to attend. Winchester also asked Elizabeth's Council for £3,000 to cover the likely cost of this funeral, a sum more fitted for a noble rather than a royal funeral. After some hesitation, he was given that but his costs proved to be even greater.

As one point of comparison, it has been recently noted that Elizabeth's funeral 'was little different *in form* from those of Elizabeth's brother and sister. ... [But the significant difference setting apart] Elizabeth's funeral from those of her immediate predecessors was its scale.'[5] By now readers should be well aware of just how important the precise degree of royal magnificence could be. The funeral of Henry VIII had been a much more lavish affair and the proceedings extended over a much longer period. Edward VI's funeral, which was postponed by the contested accession of Mary, was modelled on that of their father. The surviving details of Mary's funeral suggest, by comparison a much less sumptuous and less prolonged affair.

Once embalmed, the late queen's body lay in the chapel of St James's Palace, where if customary practice was followed, a requiem mass would be held each day until the public procession on 12 December from St James's Palace to Westminster Abbey. As was customary, the central feature of the procession was the funeral bier with the queen's effigy on top, and her embalmed body within. Her effigy was dressed in crimson velvet; on the wooden, painted head (which is still on show in the museum of Westminster Abbey) was a crown. The effigy carried a scep-tre, and, Machyn noted, had 'many goodly rings on her fingers'. The bier, according to convention for a royal funeral, was covered with a pall of cloth of gold, with a silver cross.

The procession of mourners, all dressed in black, included Philip's English servants as well as Mary's, and gentlemen, knights and lords. The greater followers went on horseback, the lesser on foot. There were, appropriately, many banners, including the great banner with the arms of England embroidered with gold, carried by Winchester himself. After him were the royal heralds carrying Mary's helmet, shield, crown and other customary symbols of her royal office. Yet more heralds carried white satin banners with images of saints worked in gold on them. Then came the choir and officials of the Chapel Royal. The funeral bier fol-lowed, attended by the chief mourners, with the ladies of Mary's court following the funeral chariot on horseback.

After them came more mourners, including the monks of Westminster Abbey and bishops 'in order'. At the Abbey door, four bishops and the Abbot of Westminster, John Feckenham, met the bier with incense before it was carried to the funeral hearse set up to receive both body and effigy in front of the altar. (It is worth noting this was one of the last occasions in England for 300 years that Roman Catholic vestments could legally be worn in public.)

The procession might seem magnificent enough to modern readers but Machyn, who was apparently an eyewitness to the procession, was also a specialist in providing funeral furnishings. The few details he does provide do not compare well with those for the much more carefully documented funeral of Henry VIII. As one example, 100 poor mourners attended Mary's corpse (conventionally they were rewarded for their attendance by gifts of money) whereas Henry had been attended by some 250. Such a variation could very easily be read as a slight on Mary's memory. And there is the recurrent problem of having no surviving records of which nobles and officers were actually in attendance.

The next day a requiem mass was held at Westminster Abbey. In those days, one way of honouring the dead was by the offerings placed on the altar. For Mary the offerings were made by 'all the lords and ladies', again according to their precedence, and among those presented were lengths of cloth of gold and of velvet, and other rich presents. Also offered were her coat of arms, her helmet, sword and shield. Machyn adds that: 'a man of arms and his horse were offered.' That event, which sounds rather alarming, referred to the moment when a representative 'man of arms' rode to the altar carrying a poleaxe with the point downward. The axe, like the other offerings was laid on the altar. Those military offerings are a reminder of to the extent to which monarchy was still normatively male, and how difficult it was to adapt the usual funeral customs for a female monarch. After all, nobody was likely to think of Mary as another Boudicca!

Also a problem was the sermon for Mary delivered by John White, then Bishop of Winchester. He was chosen partly because several of Mary's closest religious associates, including Pole, had recently died or were already detained by the new regime. White was, however, a highly regarded preacher. As discussed previously, he struggled with the proper description of Mary as 'both King and Queen', a struggle also indicated in the ceremonial of the funeral. He praised Mary extensively for her piety, her devotion to her people, her charity, her compassion and, above all, her restoration of the Church.

Her sister he praised moderately, suggesting that his audience should seek comfort for their loss in Mary by wishing Elizabeth a prosperous reign in peace and tranquillity. In the sermon, White warned several times against creating divisions within the church, and particularly against heresy, since: 'the wolves are coming out of Geneva, and hath sent their books before.' Just which part of the sermon gave most offence to the new regime is still disputed, but for his pains White was brought before the Council in January, admonished and set free. Within months he was detained again for resisting Elizabethan religious reform and clapped in the Tower.

Immediately after the service ended Mary's body was buried in the Tudor chapel. Her officials broke their staffs of office, throwing them into the grave with her, to mark the complete end of her authority. No monument was erected in her memory. That she lies now within Elizabeth's imposing tomb, topped by a carefully constructed image of the second queen regnant, is a result of actions taken in the reign of James VI & I. Now a Latin inscription at the base of the tomb reads in English: 'partners in throne and grave, here we sisters lie, Elizabeth and Mary, in hope of the resurrection.' In 1977, in a more ecumenical time, a new tablet was set into the floor near the shared tomb. It reads: 'Remember before God all those who divided at the Reformation by different convictions laid down their lives for Christ and Conscience sake.' But there were no markers for Mary's grave in Elizabeth's time, unless one counts as such the pile of altar stones heaped over it in 1561. That year all the altars in Westminster, pulled down in Edward's time, and replaced in Mary's, were pulled down again and, reportedly the rubble was all stored over Mary's grave. By then much more explicit attacks on the reign of Mary were well established.

But on 13 December 1558, as was usual in early modern times, after Mary's interment all the mourners moved from the Henry VII chapel to the customary funeral feast. As they went, the assembled crowds fell upon the hangings, the coats of arms and escutcheons set round the walls of the abbey. At least the crowd was not as disorderly as it had been after of the coronation of Elizabeth of York, and contrary to some reports Mary's hearse was untouched by the crowd. This is known because on 19 December Winchester, by then organising the obsequies for the late emperor, wrote to Cecil to suggest that the ceremony might be moved from St Pauls to Westminster Abbey, where still, after Mary's funeral, her 'hearse stands very fair'. That way, they could save the new queen a great deal of money. The obsequies for Charles V seemed splendid enough, but in part that was achieved by recycling furnishings from Mary's funeral, an unexpected contribution on her behalf to the memory of the man who had, for so many years, been her mainstay and adviser. If, as seems likely, Mary's funeral was as nearly impressive as it seems, and the reason was to placate the Spanish on whom the Elizabethan regime was still relying to treat with the French over Calais, there is a nice irony in the second use of Mary's hearse for her cousin the Emperor.

SO WHO *WAS* MARY TUDOR?

It is clear enough that the official attacks on all that Mary and her regime represented were well under way by the time she was buried. It is worth remembering, however, that if Mary had produced a Catholic heir, it is likely that she would have enjoyed a very different funeral – and ever since a different reputation. Such matters as her humanist values and her encouragement of talented musicians after the Edwardian assaults on church music would have been among the grounds for acclamation.

As it is, because of the rapid restoration of a church much closer to that of Edward's reign, historians have been slow to recognise the extent to which her regime, with her as an active participant, established a basis for a restored and renewed Catholic church, which survived in an almost subterranean form some three centuries of official hostility in Protestant England. After the religious confusions of the reign of Henry VIII, and the outright assaults on it of the Edwardian years, the Catholic Church had been in a weakened and demoralised state, with a number of its more prominent leaders apparently acquiescing in all that happened to it. With the leadership she encouraged, Mary promoted a renewed and revived form of Catholicism. After all, during her reign, the universities were renewed, and the return to Catholicism of them had proceeded to such an extent that Oxford, for one, lost or had expelled several times the number of men at the beginning of Elizabeth's reign compared with those who had departed at the beginning of Mary's reign.

Mary's own historical reputation is currently under renewed consideration. Although the story of Mary's public career as princess, illegitimate daughter, suspect heir and first queen regnant has often and variously been told, there is still less interest in exploring the more personal life of this queen. That enterprise still faces a fundamental problem in the shortage of first-hand accounts of Mary. One reason for that was the speed with which May's regime was declared to be religiously wrong, intolerably cruel and politically disastrous. Very few personal memoirs of her reign have survived, probably because those who lived into Elizabeth's reign had little interest in speaking well of her half-sister or recalling their time spent with her. It is significant that the best known of the few works which survive is that of Jane Dormer, who as Countess Feria moved to Spain after Mary's death, and recalled her early years long after.

For nearly 300 years after Mary's death, Catholics in England were denied both religious freedom and many civil rights. It is hardly surprising that the most hostile accounts of Mary's character, constructed by her religious opponents as part of a wider attack on Catholicism, may have varied in the details of their assessments of her personality but usually found her a most unsatisfactory queen. From the start, some assessments were so virulent as to be almost self-defeating. Mary was, wrote Bartholomew Traheron in 1558, 'spiteful, cruel, bloody, wilful, furious, guileful, stuffed with painted processes, with simulation and dissimulation, devoid of honesty, devoid of upright dealing, devoid of all seemly virtues'.[6] The virulence of that makes John Foxe's assessment, in his editions of 1563 and 1583, of her reign as 'the horrible and bloody time of Queen Mary' seem almost a model of moderation.

The power of that critical tradition, however, has been the harder to confront precisely because of the dearth of more sympathetic material. Contemporaries were always more diverse in their judgements. Giovanni Michiel, Venetian ambassador to her court from May 1554 for three years, is one observer who offered some useful information about her, and when a distinction is drawn between what he knew first-hand and information he was likely to have been fed, instructive details of his assessment of Mary remain.

Back in Venice, in May 1557, he wrote a detailed report of England for the Venetian Senate, which included an account of the appearance, accomplishments and attributes of the then 'mistress of the kingdom'. Like everybody else, Michiel was struck by how small and slightly built Mary was. He wrote that she no longer enjoyed the 'beauty exceeding mediocrity' of earlier days, but she had few wrinkles, and those 'caused by anxieties more than by age'. Her eyes were 'so piercing that they inspire, not only respect but also fear'. Actually she was significantly short-sighted, which may help explain the apparent intensity of her gaze. He also commented on the strength of her voice, an attribute which, it will be remembered, she deployed to great effect in her speeches to the gathered troops at Framlingham before she took the throne, and to the gathered worthies of London when Wyatt's troops were approaching the capital. Elsewhere, however, he commented, as did many others, on her 'gentle' manner of speaking.

Far from anticipating Elton's judgment that she was 'in a word, stupid', Michiel was particularly impressed by her mind, not just for her quickness of understanding, which he deemed quite masculine (for a woman, that was high praise indeed) but also for her grasp of languages: English, Latin, French Spanish and Italian, although when spoken to in Italian she preferred to answer in Latin. She was skilled in embroidery, that essential female accomplishment and still pursued the musical interests she had followed all her life. Although by then she seldom played the lute, on her clavichord (a variety of spinet) she could still astonish 'the best performers' by the speed of her hand and the style of her playing. He did not, however, comment on the important support she had given to leading musicians attracted back to England by the revival of church music in her reign. It is less surprising that he had nothing to say about her love of hunting, that most royal pastime, which she increasingly abandoned as queen, nor on her lifelong love of gaming, mainly at cards.

The ambassador found much in the queen to admire. Mary was:

> so courageous and resolute that neither in adversity or peril; did she ... commit any act of cowardice or pusillanimity, maintaining always ... a wonderful grandeur and dignity, knowing what became the dignity of a sovereign as well as any of the most consummate statesmen in her service.

This quality of regal inscrutability, which Mary had been trained into from infancy, was often noted with approval. It is just that capacity which gives rise to scepticism about those reports of Mary's deeply felt passion for Philip. Michiel himself wrote of her reported love for Philip, and added an important qualification: 'as far as could be known whilst they lived together'.

She was, he wrote, 'sudden and passionate' (which makes her sound, perhaps, like a true daughter of Henry VIII) and 'close and miserly' rather more than would become a 'bountiful and generous' queen. But that view was countered by Soranzo, the previous Venetian ambassador, who thought that she was very generous, 'but not to the extent of letting it appear that she rests her chief claim to commendation on that'.[7] Because he believed Mary was 'of a sex which cannot becomingly take more than a moderate part' in government, and because he had no way of knowing how many hours she spent with her documents, Michiel probably underestimated her administrative role. He again allowed his construction of 'female' to inform his judgment when he reported that

Mary was prone to deep melancholy, since she was a victim of 'suffocation of the womb', a common early modern explanation for female behaviour. Given his earlier insistence of her public composure and the very restricted access he had to the court, it is likely that his judgment of her moodiness and the diagnosis were both, at best, second hand. But his is a fascinating late report on Mary as a person.

Foxe tells a story which also reflects something of Mary's dignity and composure. It may also cast some doubt about the bigotry with which she has so often been charged. When she was at Hunsden in September 1552, Ridley, then Bishop of London, and to Mary a leading destroyer of true religion, visited her. She talked, Foxe reported, with Ridley 'very pleasantly', recalling details of a sermon which Ridley had preached for a court wedding in Henry's time. After dining with her officers Ridley, perhaps beguiled by her pleasant demeanour, offered to preach for her. She replied that, as bishop, he could of course choose to preach in the local church, but that neither she nor her household would hear him.

That exchange seems to have led to an alteration, at least in Ridley's behaviour. After some debate about how his understanding of 'God's word' had changed since Henry VIII's time, Ridley challenged Mary over her disobedience to the new laws. She repeated her standard response that she would obey them if they remained after Edward came of age. As Ridley withdrew, Mary thanked him pleasantly for calling on her. Out of her presence, it was Ridley who raged against himself for accepting any hospitality in a house where 'God's word' had been refused.[8] Mary, it would seem, remained composed throughout.

One feature of Mary's reign, which distinguishes her from the conventional view of Elizabeth, is the extent to which she maintained and made use of her female friends. It was not just the striking number of women in her retinue at her coronation, but also her friendship with many élite Tudor women. For Tudor men and women, advancing family interests through their networks of friends was an essential part of personal, family and political business. Mary had always made good use of her female contacts, including the wives of Edward's most powerful councillors, before her accession. After it, when so many positions of influence and authority were reversed, and Mary became the dispenser of patronage, the female networks were still worked hard, often to good effect.

Petitioners who were in a position to have access to Mary's friends Gertrude Courtenay, Marchioness of Exeter, and Susan Clarencius were well placed to have their requests carefully considered. Jane Dudley, Northumberland's wife, was forbidden to meet with Mary herself, but made a desperate plea to an intermediary to intercede for her sons and 'their father who was to me and to my mind the most best gentleman that ever living woman was matched with'.[9] This plea could not save the duke, but it may have contributed to the survival of his sons until Philip befriended them, and to the relatively benign treatment of Jane Dudley herself. There were many such pleas to Mary, often enabling her to reward those who had been kind to her in much more trying times.

She was never so swayed, however, that Gertrude Courtenay was able to save her increasingly unsatisfactory son from exile after his involvement in the Wyatt uprising. Nevertheless, particularly in the early months of her reign Mary was so responsive to those requests that her councillors despaired at so much clemency, not a quality often acknowledged in Mary's posthumous reputation. That clemency did gradually give way to more conventional ways of dealing with rebels, but it is difficult to identify any occasions when, by contemporary standards, she could reasonably be described as 'pitiless' let alone 'evil', not least because she was always careful to follow legal processes.

Mary was often described as a sweet and gentle person. In her childhood this was so much a preferred female quality that the comment might seem obligatory. But the quality apparently endured into adulthood. Once restored to his favour, Mary was constantly at her father's court, and she had excellent relations with three of his four later wives, the exception being Katherine Howard, with whom she had nothing in common. Until their differences of opinion in religious matters emerged, Edward had been very fond of his elder sister, although it is less clear just when or precisely why Mary and Elizabeth grew more distant.

Her pleasant personality may be indicated by the loyalty of those members of her household who were with her during the years she was out of favour with the Edwardian regime. The most striking example of such loyalty was Susan Clarencius. Wife and then widow to Thomas Tonge, Clarencieux king-of-arms, she was an important member of Mary's household from 1536 to Mary's death. In 1553 she was mistress of Mary's robes, and chief gentlewoman of her privy chamber, so much in Mary's confidence that she was sole witness to Mary's solemn (and very secret) early promise that she would indeed marry Philip.

More unexpectedly, Mary's Edwardian and later household included the scholarly Lady Anne Bacon. Given her reputation as a lifelong Protestant, Anne Bacon's presence provides one of several instances which counter the charge of bigotry that have often been made against Mary. As discussed elsewhere, soon after she was queen Mary declared her considerable esteem for William Cecil, whose Protestant sympathies were beyond doubt in Edward's reign, and who fell from favour only after a (secular) policy disagreement. What Mary required was what any Tudor required, an outward conformity to the laws. For Mary this included participating, at prescribed times, in the mass. If she could accommodate Protestants who formally conformed, as Bacon and Cecil did, the bigotry charge must refer to Mary's punishment of obdurate Protestants who would not conform to her laws, but no Tudor could have ignored such defiance – or did ignore it.

Jane Dormer was another of Mary's most trusted confidantes. Once a playmate for the young prince, sharing with him such pastimes as reading and playing cards, she joined Mary's household some time before 1552. When Mary became queen, Dormer frequently enjoyed marks of special confidence from the monarch. She shared religious devotions with her queen, and went with Mary when she occasionally visited her cousin Cardinal Pole at Croydon. There, Dormer reported, was where the queen went among the poor, ensuring the local people received proper payment from royal officials for the foodstuffs they perforce supplied for the royal entourage. She also explained why Mary made no extended progresses once she was queen; it was a time of such poor harvests that the queen was reluctant to make extra demands on the local inhabitants for those supplies necessary for the great numbers necessarily with her.[10]

Jane Dormer was wooed and won by Count Feria, who came to England in Philip's entourage, but was still unmarried at the time of Mary's death because both the king and her betrothed were fighting on the continent. So Jane was much with the queen in her dying days, which she later recalled in some detail, as we have seen. Her husband remained in England for a time as Philip's ambassador to Elizabeth, and when he left his company included not only his new wife, 12 monks and three lay brothers whom Elizabeth allowed him (after initial reluctance) to take out of the country, but also Susan Clarencius, who remained with Jane in their new country until her death. There they could both follow the religion they had always professed.

In Mary's time it was still usual for great households to have fools, or 'innocents'.[11] Jane, Mary's fool for 20 years, appears first in her expense accounts in 1537, leading to suggestions she may previously have been in Anne Boleyn's household. Jane shows up in Mary's accounts as provided with her own horse, and often with new clothes in sumptuous fabrics. Her presence around the court and in court festivities is reflected in several surviving sources, most unexpectedly when Henry commissioned a painting of his family, now called *The Family of Henry VIII*. It showed Henry with Jane Seymour and his three children. To one side of the painting is his own fool Will Somers and on the other Mary's Jane, presumably a mark of the affection with which they were both regarded. Mary had her carefully cared for when ill, and gave gifts to those who looked after her. She placed her last order of clothes for Jane on 31 October 1558, when she herself was already seriously ill. The care and apparent affection for and kindness to her fool over two decades suggest again that at least the 'private' Mary was a person far from being pitiless, evil or cruel.

MARY TUDOR, ENGLAND'S FIRST QUEEN REGNANT

Historians have conventionally paid more attention to defining Mary's rule by reference to her allegedly serious moral faults, less to her significant achievements as England's first effective queen regnant in a profoundly patriarchal society. This is the more surprising because her five years on the throne did much to pave the way for Elizabeth as England's more renowned queen regnant. The twelfth-century Matilda, England's first queen regnant, had never controlled the whole realm, nor did she reign long enough to be crowned.

Mary therefore, had no English precedents to guide her establishment of female monarchy in a society which assumed that political power was the natural prerogative of a small group of privileged men. What she did have, however, was some knowledge from her mother of the strategies her grandmother Isabella of Castile had practised when married to Ferdinand of Aragon. There, each had been co-ruler in their partner's realms, and monarch in their own. Mary's practice, however much her own subjects had difficulty in understanding it, was similar in intention to that of her Spanish grandparents. One expression of that ideal outside England is to be found in Gouda. In 1557, Philip and Mary donated a stained glass window to Sint Janskerk in Gouda, as thanksgiving for the victory at St Quentin. The donors can be seen near the base of the window, Philip more prominent and Mary less so, fittingly enough since the church was in his domains rather than hers, but Mary is shown in the full regalia of an English monarch. That was an expression of the kind of mutual reciprocity of status Mary's marriage treaty had envisaged.

Mary's most problematic decision was always to marry Philip of Spain. Given that Elizabeth, religiously and morally suspect in Mary's eyes, was also legally her heir, the only way for Mary to overturn that was by producing an heir of her own. But marriage produced its own problems. Philip may have been (was) outraged when he first saw the marriage treaty which made it clear that she was head of her realm, and he a leading councillor. That a woman should claim precedence before her husband apparently challenged the Pauline prescription that wives should be obedient to their husbands. The other early modern tenet basic to Mary's position – that office took precedence over gender – was much less familiar, although not without numerous English precedents among the élite.

Mary took precedence in most other ways, but the titles were what people heard most commonly. Philip's titles coming first on all acts, proclamations and documents reinforced the general understanding that husbands took precedence over their wives. The act passed in 1554, before Mary's marriage, had reiterated that, as she was then England's 'sole and only' queen, so she would remain sole possessor of the crown and sovereignty of England after her marriage. That may have been widely proclaimed, but it seems not to have been so widely comprehended.

Mary's disaffected subjects saw little in that ideal of a royal marriage relationship to accept, let alone admire. As the propaganda for several attempted rebellions demonstrated – most notably those of Wyatt and Dudley – the prevailing patriarchal assumptions, and the associated expectation of the subordination of a wife, made it easy for Englishmen to argue that Mary's husband was about to take over her realm. That Philip was male, a husband and named king were all seen as indicators that he was, or should be, pre-eminent, whatever steps he took to be seen as adviser, not ruler – or so the disaffected could plausibly, and did, argue. Even his prolonged absences from England could not silence those critics.

Historians have also found Mary's status and attitudes after her marriage ambiguous, diplomatically as well as politically. Much, for example, has been made of Mary withdrawing her representative from Venice after her marriage She argued that it was unnecessary to have separate representatives for both husband and wife. Yet she made repeated protests that she and her realm had been snubbed when Venice attached a representative to Philip, then almost permanently on the continent, leaving no representative in England. She accepted that practice might be acceptable if both monarchs were at the same court, but she and Philip were not. The struggle to maintain the separate identity she believed she retained as queen of England quite independently of Philip was difficult in those patriarchal times.

At the beginning of her reign, in July 1553, her being female was almost irrelevant for Mary, less because she was Henry's next heir by statute than because there were no plausible male candidates to challenge her claim. History demonstrated that a male claimant, even with a weaker claim, usually prevailed. At that point Henry VIII's destruction of possible Yorkist contenders probably greatly eased his daughter's path to the throne. Therefore, once Mary had been accepted as queen, the first practical problems arising from her being female were issues of how a female monarch might embody magnificence and how far the ceremonial rites and very language of monarchy needed some adaptation.

Magnificence itself, which Sydney Anglo has summarised as 'those splendid appearances which served as the external sign of intrinsic power', had long been recognised as an indispensable component of royal authority.[12] The iconic pyramidal shape which Holbein employed when painting his king made – and still makes – Henry VIII immediately recognisable as idealised monarchy. Holbein augmented the spectacular richness of the king's clothing with an authoritative image of physical power. The same stance was imitated in some portraits of the young Edward, both when he was prince and after he became king. Lacking the impressive physique of his father, the stance – with arms slightly akimbo and straddled legs – nevertheless echoed a masculine image, emphasised by the relation of the right hand to the codpiece. In his father's case, that gesture celebrated his continuation of the dynastic line with Jane Seymour. In Edward's case it conveyed implicit assurance that the line would be continued. To provide an heir was, after all, a primary responsibility of any monarch.

Manifestly, such an aggressively masculine stance was quite unsuitable for representing any sixteenth-century female, let alone a queen. A primary function of her representation was to reassure the onlooker that, although powerful, she was still the embodiment of modesty and chastity. That was important because of the age-old tradition that if a woman were too powerful she was likely to become sexually predatory. Mary's impeccable reputation and consistently virtuous comportment were undisputed, and remained so. But the first queen regnant needed to do more than display herself as impeccably virtuous; she also needed to display herself as royally magnificent. This she pursued through the use of spectacularly rich fabrics and extensive jewellery, including many rings. The painting on the cover of this book, made soon after her marriage, shows her in a suitably demure stance, her elbows slightly angled to show to advantage the great sweep of sable stole, the most sumptuous fur of all. Her heavily embroidered fabrics, her ornate jewellery, and her several rings were all more powerfully part of the strategy for representing a monarch than was the cloth of estate behind her.

One consequence of such sumptuous dressing is that Mary has often been charged by more recent historians with bad or garish taste. Such accusations were fed by the repeated preference for men from other countries to see her dressed in the styles familiar to them, partly by more modern failure to understand the importance of female power-dressing for a sixteenth-century queen. In a uniquely serious study of Mary's dress, Alison Carter has confirmed that she did indeed prefer very expensive fabrics, and furs particularly, as her portraits demonstrate. Carter also revisited the question of Mary's dress sense and taste. After her careful exploration of the dress codes of the times, she concludes that Mary dressed indeed with the 'utmost sumptuosity and yet propriety'.[13] Indeed, Mary's dress styles – though to a lesser degree their sumptuousness – were copied by her ladies-in-waiting. Such imitation was intended as complimentary. Changing fashion could also reflect the changing political alignment; modes of dress shifted between 1554 and 1557 from predominately Italian to Spanish patterns. On occasion, however, when Mary wished to flatter a particular ambassador, she would dress in the fashion of his country.

Despite her preoccupation with rich clothes, Mary was not extravagant by the standards of the Tudor court. At the end of Henry's reign, the annual costs of the Great Wardrobe were £8,000 a year. During the reign of the young Edward the costs were, unsurprisingly enough, cut to £4,000. They soared during Mary's first years with the costs of both a coronation and a wedding to £18,000 but thereafter dropped back to £6,000, a level close to which they remained when Elizabeth assumed the throne.

She was, in theory, a king in everything except her ability to lead an army to war – but both underage and aged male monarchs had the same 'defect'. Yet she did, at least twice, demonstrate her ability to rally her supporters to arms by her public oratory. So, as discussed in previous chapters, Mary established markers for the extent to which a queen regnant was indeed a female king, with the most sacred capacities of that office. England's first queen regnant was prepared to fight her way to the throne. But above all, Mary, who had come to the throne at a mature age, as the daughter of a widely respected mother, and with an impeccable reputation, had normalised the idea of a female monarch to such an extent that Elizabeth succeeded her without challenge within England. That smooth transition was Mary's final gift – albeit a reluctant one – to Elizabeth. Given the differences between them, Elizabeth could never afford to acknowledge that debt, but it may well be time for more historians to reconsider the implications of that achievement.

NOTES

INTRODUCTION

1 Mark Goldie, 'Ideology', in T. Ball, J. Farr, J. and R. L.Hanson, eds, *Political Innovation and Conceptual Change* (Cambridge, 1989), p. 278.

2 Papal Bull: 'Regnans in Excelsis', 1570. *The Tudor Constitution*, ed. G. R. Elton (Cambridge, 1968), pp. 414–18.

3 David Hume, *The History of England ... to the Revolution of 1688*, 1754–61 (London, 1864), 5 vols, Vol. III, p. 19.

4 George Eliot, *The Mill on the Floss* (Harmondsworth, 1979), p. 379.

5 W. C. Sellars and R. J. Yeatman, *1066 and All That* (London, 1930).

6 John A. Wagner, *Bosworth Field to Bloody Mary* (Westport, 2003).

7 G. R. Elton, *Reform and Reformation: England, 1509–1558* (London, 1977), p. 376. D. M. Loades, *Mary Tudor: A Life* (Oxford, 1989), p. 8; John Guy, *Tudor England* (Oxford, 1990), p. 227; Susan Brigden, *New Worlds, Lost Worlds: The Rule of the Tudors 1485–1603* (Harmondsworth, 2000), p. 199. A. N. McLaren *Political Culture in the Reign of Elizabeth 1: Queen and Commonwealth, 1558–1585* (Cambridge, 1999), p. 16; see also pp. 90–103.

1 ESTABLISHING THE TUDOR REGIME

1 There are several accounts of the death of Owen Tudor. See Glanmor Williams, *Recovery Reorientation and Reformation Wales c. 1415–1642* (Oxford, 1987), pp. 188–9.

2 Act for the Confirmation of Henry VII (1485). *The Tudor Constitution*, ed. G. R. Elton (Cambridge, 1968), p. 4.

3 TRP, 'Summarising Papal Bull Recognizing Henry VII', Vol. I, No. 5, p. 6.

4 Sir John Fortescue, *The Governance of England*, ed. Charles Plummer (London, 1885), pp. 119, 125.

5 Sydney Anglo, *Spectacle, Pageantry and Early Tudor Policy* (Oxford, 1969), discusses this in some detail.

6   'Flamank's Information', *Letters and Papers Illustrative of the reigns of Richard III and Henry VII*, ed. J. G. Gairdner (1861–3), 2 vols, Vol. I, pp. 231–40.

7   C. J. Harrison, 'The Petition of Edmund Dudley', *English Historical Review*, No. 87, January 1972, pp. 86, 85.

2   THE EARLY YEARS OF MARY TUDOR

1   L&P II, 4340.

2   Peter Martyr gave this report, but other humanists soon picked it up and passed it on, perhaps an indicator of the esteem in which they held Katherine.

3   CSPV II, No. 1010, p. 433.

4   Ibid, Nos 1085, 1088, pp. 462–7. For more details, see also L&P II, 4468, 4481.

5   L&P III, 873.

6   L&P III, 1150.

7   G. Williams, *Recovery, Reorientation and Reformation Wales c. 1415–1642*, (Oxford), p. 249.

8   J. J. Scarisbrick, *Henry VIII* (Harmondsworth, 1971), p. 184.

3   THE EDUCATION OF A PRINCESS: LEARNING LIFE AND POLITICS, 1525–1536

1   *The Lay Folks Mass Book or the Manner of Hearing Mass*, ed. T. F. Simmons (London, 1879), p. 158.

2   John Standish, *A Discourse Wherin Is Debated Whether the Scripture Would Be in English* (1554), sig Kviii.

3   H. Ellis, *Original Letters Illustrative of English History* (First series) (London, 1824), 3 vols, Vol. II, p. 20.

4   J. L. McIntosh, *Sovereign Princesses: Mary and Elizabeth Tudor as Heads of Princely Households and the Accomplishment of the Female Succession in Tudor England, 1516–1558* (PhD, Johns Hopkins University, 2002), esp. pp 78–86.

5   Loades, *Mary Tudor*, pp. 46–7.

6   CSPV IV, May 1527, No. 101, p. 56.

7   CSPV IV, August 1531 No. 682, esp. p. 288.

8   CSPV IV, December 1530, No. 643, p. 271.

9   CPSV IV, April 1531, No. 664, p. 279.

10 John Sadler, *The Sicke Womans Private Looking-Glasse* (London, 1636), 'Introduction'. 'Hysteria', from the Greek for womb, was still a popular nineteenth-century explanation of female disorders when these texts were translated.

11 Charles Wriothesley, *A Chronicle of England during the Reign of the Tudors*, ed. W. D. Hamilton (London, Camden Society, 1875), 2 vols, Vol. I. pp. 17–18, 32–3.

12 1536: 28 Henry VIII, c. 10.

13 The letter and some discussion is published in Garret Mattingly, *Catherine of Aragon* (London, 1950), pp. 292–3. For Loades' discussion, see *Mary Tudor*, pp 77–8.

14 CSPSp IV, February 1535, No. 263, p. 100.

15 Gunton, Symon, *The History of the Church of Peterburgh* (1686), p. 57.

16 B. L. Cotton: Titus C VIII f179 is a copy of Mary's submission to her father in a later hand.

4 THE RESTORATION OF LADY MARY, 1536–1547

1 Wriothesley, *A Chronicle of England*, Vol. I, pp. 51, 53.

2 L&P XI, 132.

3 Brigden, *New Worlds, Lost Worlds*, p. 80.

4 Wriothesley, *A Chronicle of England*, Vol. I, p. 109.

5 Jennifer Loach, *Edward VI* (New Haven, 1999), p. 7.

6 Scarisbrick, *Henry VIII*, p. 626.

7 BL: Cotton MS Appendix XXIX, f 63.

8 Wriothesley. *A Chronicle of England*, Vol. I, pp. 119–20.

9 Susan James, *Kateryn Parr: The Making of a Queen* (Aldershot, 1999), p. 90.

10 *Letters of Royal and Illustrious Ladies of Great Britain*, ed. M. E A. Wood (London, 1846–8), 3 vols, Vol. III, pp. 176–7.

11 Gardiner to Paget, November 1545, L&P XXII, 725.

12 L&P XXI, 355; L&P XX, 899.

13 *Letters of Royal and Illustrious Ladies* ..., ed. M. E. A. Wood (1846), Vol. III, pp. 180–1. For the original letter, with elaborate ornamentations, in Latin and scribed by Elizabeth, see BL: Cotton Vesp. F 3, f 37.

14 *The Paraphrases of Erasmus upon the New Testament*, ed. Nicholas Udall (London, 1548), Vol. III, f.ii.

15 L&P XVII, 317.

16 Loach, *Edward VI*, p. 16.

5 MARY IN THE REIGN OF EDWARD VI, 1547–1553

1 McIntosh, *Sovereign Princesses*, pp. 206ff, pp. 106–7.

2 David M. Head, *The Ebbs and Flows of Fortune: The life of Thomas Howard, Third Duke of Norfolk* (Athens, 1995), p. 84.

3 P. F. Tytler, *England under the Reigns of Edward VI and Mary* (1839), Vol. I, pp. 51–2.

4 CSP.Edward VI, 185 (January? 1549).

5 For Mary's letter to Seymour, see *Original Letters Illustrative of English History*, ed. H. Ellis, First Series, 4 vols (1824–46), Vol. II, pp. 150–1.For Elizabeth's reply to Mary, see Green, *Letters of Royal Ladies*, Vol. III, pp. 193–4.

6 Quoted in James, *Kateryn Parr*, p. 330.

7 'The Archbishop's Speech at the Coronation of Edward VI', *Miscellaneous Writings and Letters of Thomas Cranmer*, ed. J. E. Cox (Cambridge, 1846), p. 126.

8 *The Paraphrases of Erasmus upon the New Testament*, Vol. III, f.ii.

9 *Letters of Stephen Gardiner*, ed. J. A. Mueller (Cambridge, 1933), letter 28 February 1527, p. 266; letter 14 October 1547, p. 382.

10 Quoted in Diarmaid MacCulloch, *Tudor Church Militant* (London, 1999), p. 20.

11 Loach, *Edward VI*, p. 70.

12 MacCulloch, *Tudor Church Militant*, pp. 81, 62.

13 John Bossy, 'The Mass as a Social Institution', *Past & Present*, No. 100 (August 1983), p. 33.

14 G. Burnett, *The History of the Reformation of the Church of England*, ed. Nicholas Pocock (Oxford, 1865), Vol. II, p. 91.

15 BL MS Lansd. 1236 f. 28. Draft in Mary's hand.

16 CSPSp IX, pp. 360–1.

17 APC II, pp. 291–2.

18 Burnet, *The History of the Reformation*, Vol. II p. 87.

19 'The Chronicle of Edward VI', *The Chronicle and Political Papers of King Edward VI*, ed. W. K. Jordan (London, 1966), p. 44.

20 Tytler, *England under the Reigns*, Vol. I, pp. 346–7.

21 Loades, *Mary Tudor*, p. 159.

22 CSPSp X, pp. 209–12.

23 *The Diary of Henry Machyn*, ed. J. G. Nichols (London, 1848), pp. 4–5.

24 'The Chronicle of Edward VI', p. 55.

6 EDWARD AND MARY: THE FINAL STRUGGLES

1 Edward, *Chronicle*, dated 29 August 1551, p. 78.

2 Queen Dowager to Scheyfve, 14 October 1551, CSPSp X, p. 383.

3 Machyn, *Diary*, pp. 30–1.

4 John Guy, *Tudor England* (Oxford, 1990), p. 212.

5 Loades, *John Dudley*, p. 233.

6 Loach, *Edward VI*, p. 162.

7 Copies of the will, including all the alterations, and of the Letters Patent setting out Edward's reasons more fully, are printed in *The Chronicle of Queen Jane and of Two Years of Queen Mary*, ed. J. G. Nichols (London, 1850), pp. 89–100.

8 For a detailed discussion of these changes, see Stephen Alford, *Kingship and Politics in the Reign of Edward VI* (Cambridge, 2002), pp. 171–3.

9 Machyn, p. 35.

10 Wriothesley, *Chronicle*, Vol. II, p. 88.

11 This letter, dated 9 July 1553, is reproduced in Robert Tittler, *The Reign of Queen Mary I* (London, 1991), pp. 81–2.

12 Dale Hoak, 'Two Revolutions in Government: The Formation and Organization of Mary I's Privy Council', *Revolution Reassessed: Revisions in the History of Tudor Government and Administration*, ed. Christopher Coleman and David Starkey (Oxford, 1984), pp. 87–115, esp. p. 95.

13 'The *Vitae Mariae Angliae Reginae* of Robert Wingfield of Brantham', ed. and trans. Diarmaid MacCulloch, *Camden Miscellany, XXVIII* (London, 1984), p. 252.

14 Robert Tittler, and Susan Battley, 'The Local Community and the Crown in 1553: The Accession of Mary Tudor revisited', *Bulletin of the Institute of Historical Research*, Vol. 57, No. 136, November 1984, pp. 131–9.

15 *The Accession of Queen Mary: Being the Contemporary Narrative of Antonio de Guares, A Spanish Merchant Resident in London*, trans Richard Garnett (London, 1892), p. 92.

16 *Chronicle of the Grey Friars of London*, ed. J. G. Nichols (London, 1852), p. 79.

7 ESTABLISHING ENGLAND'S FIRST FEMALE MONARCH

1 For a splendid example of this, see the slightly later *Field Book of Walsham-le-willows 1577*, ed. K. M. Dodd (Ipswich, 1977).

2   Paul Slack, 'Social Policy and the Constraints of Government, 1547–58', in *The Mid-Tudor Polity c. 1540–1560*, ed. Jennifer Loach and Robert Tittler (London, 1980), p. 96.

3   David Loades, *The Reign of Mary Tudor*, 2nd edition (London, 1991), p. 129.

4   'A Sermon Made at the Burial of Queen Mary', B. L. Cott Vesp D XVIII x fo 104.

5   For further discussion, see my 'Gender Difference and Tudor Monarchy: The significance of Queen Mary', *Parergon*, Vol. 21, No. 2 (2004), pp. 27–46.

6   BL: MS Lansd 3, art. 26.

7   Wriothesley, *Chronicle*, Vol. II, pp. 93–4.

8   CSPSp XI, p. 151.

9   Susan Brigden, *London and the Reformation* (Oxford, 1989), p. 529.

10   Diarmaid MacCulloch, *Thomas Cranmer: A Life* (New Haven, 1996), p. 547.

11   CSPSp XI, pp. 259–60.

12   Judith M. Richards, 'Mary Tudor as "Sole Quene"?: Gendering Tudor Monarchy', *The Historical Journal*, Vol. 40, No. 4 (1997), pp. 895–924, esp. pp. 900–2.

13   J. Mychel, *A Breviat Cronicle* (1554), sig. Oii.

14   *The Chronicle of Queen Jane*, pp. 31–2.

15   Jennifer Loach, *Parliament and the Crown in the Reign of Mary Tudor* (Oxford, 1986), p. 76.

8   PROBLEMS FOR A MARRYING QUEEN REGNANT

1   CSPSp XI, p. 282, Emperor to Renard, 10 October 1553.

2   See Genesis 3, v. 16 (King James Version).

3   CSPSp XI, p. 288, Renard to the Emperor, 12 October 1553.

4   Cited in Tytler, *England under the Reigns*, Vol. II, p. 267.

5   *Calendar of State papers, Foreign Series 1553–1558* (London, 1861), Council to Dr Wotton, 7 December 1553, p. 35.

6   CSPSp XI p. 364, Renard to the Emperor, 17 November 1553. Renard was summarising Mary's account to him.

7   Wriothesley, *Chronicle*, Vol. II, p. 106.

8   Quoted in D. M. Loades, *Two Tudor Conspiracies* (Cambridge, 1965), p. 56.

9   John Proctor, *The Historie of Wyates Rebellion* (London, 1554).

10   John Foxe, *Actes and Monumentes* (1563), pp. 1746–7.

11   John Proctor, *The Historie of Wyates Rebellion* (London, 1554), f 76v.

12   CSP.Mary, 108, SP 11/4/3.

13   Henry Kamen, *Philip of Spain* (New Haven and London, 1997), p. 59.

14 CSPSp XIII p. 6 (29 July) de Silova to de Eraso.

15 For a fuller discussion of the complexities of that occasion, see my 'Mary Tudor as "Sole Queen"?', esp. pp. 911–14.

16 John Elder, *A Copie of a Letter Sent unto Scotlande* (1555), sig A vi (v). This is reprinted in full in *The Chronicle of Queen Jane*.

17 CSPSp XII, p. 269 (7 June 1554).

9 THE PROSPEROUS YEAR OF PHILIP AND MARY, JULY 1554 TO AUGUST 1555?

1   CSPV V, No. 934, p. 532, 18 August 1554.

2   'The Narrative of Edward Underhill', in *The Chronicle of Queen Jane*, ed. J. G. Gough (London, 1850), p. 170.

3   CSPSp XIII, p. 1, de Courrieres and Renard to Emperor, 26 July 1554.

4   TPR II, No. 415, 15 September 1554.

5   Kamen, *Philip II*, p. 58.

6   Wriothesley, *Chronicle*, Vol. II, p. 122.

7   *The Chronicle of Queen Jane*, p. 80.

8   Ibid. p. 81.

9   CSPSp XIII, 81, 13 Nov 1554.

10 Foxe, 'The Tenoure of Cardinall Pooles Oration', *Actes* (1563), p. 1009.

11 Loach, *Parliament and the Crown*, p. 126.

12 James Owen Drife, 'Phantom Pregnancy', *British Medical Journal*, No. 291 (1985).

13 Sir John Mason to the King and Queen, quoted in Tytler, *England under ... Edward and Mary*, p. 455.

14 'A Devout Praier, for the Prosperous State of our Sovereign Lords and Lady', Foxe, *Actes* (1563), p. 1016.

15 Bodl. MS Gough Misc Antiq, 3, fo. 114.

16 A helpful discussion of the full process of negotiating Philip's hypothetical powers and status as regent is to be found in Loach, *Parliament*, pp. 116–23.

17 Lady Lilse's 'pregnancy' and responses to it is fully discussed in Catherine Mann, '*My Lord Lysles Man*': Household and Identity in Sixteenth-Century Letters, PhD, University of Melbourne (2002), pp. 147–67.

10   RELIGIOUS TRIALS AND OTHER TRIBULATIONS

1   Sir Thomas Smith, *De Republica Anglorum A Discourse of the Commonwealth of England*, ed. L. Alston (Cambridge, 1906), p. 62.

2   Kamen, *Philip of Spain* p. 62. For a different view see Glyn Redworth, '"Matters Impertinent to Women": Male and Female Monarchy under Philip and Mary', *English Historical Review*, Vol. 112, No. 447 (1997), pp. 593–613.

3   CSP.Mary, 240, SP 11/6/28.

4   Slack, 'Social Policy', in Loach and Tittler, p. 112.

5   D. MacCulloch, *Tudor Church Militant*, p. 108.

6   A. G. R. Smith, ed., *The Anonymous Life of William Cecil, Lord Burghley* (Lampeter, 1990), p. 52.

7   Robert Tittler, *Nicholas Bacon: The Making of a Tudor Statesman* (London, 1976), p. 53.

8   Glyn Redworth, *In Defence of the Church Catholic* (Cambridge, Mass., 1990), p. 293.

9   SP14/90 ff 133–133v, CSP.Mary, 140; this is a seventeenth-century copy of the 1554 original.

10 William Wizeman, *The Theology and Spirituality of Mary Tudor's Church* (Aldershot, 2006), p. 232.

11 For a more detailed discussion of these women, see Tom Freeman, 'The Ladies were for Burning: The Marian Persecution and the Women Martyrs', in *Women Martyrs in the Crucible of Confessional Conflict*, ed. Elizabeth Evenden (Ashgate, forthcoming). All details of numbers of victims listed here, I owe to Tom Freeman, to whom I am grateful for his many discussions on the Marian burnings.

12 Brad S. Gregory, *Salvation at Stake: Christian Martyrdom in Early Modern Europe* (Cambridge, Mass., 1999), pp. 1, 7.

13 Kamen, *Philip of Spain*, p. 75.

14 Gina Alexander, 'Bonner and the Marian Persecutions', *History*, Vol. 60, No. 200, October 1975, pp. 374–91.

15 Quoted in Petegree, *Marian Protestants* p. 92.

16 David Loades, 'The English Church during the Reign of Mary', in *Reforming Catholicism in the England of Mary Tudor*, ed. J. Edwards and R. Truman (Burlington, Vt., 2005), pp. 33–48, esp. pp 34–9.

17 *CSP Mary I*, No. 140, ed. C. S. Knighton, SP 14/190, December 1554.

18 John Foxe, *Actes and Monumentes* (1583), p. 1529; Henry Kamen, *Crisis and Change in Early Modern Spain* (Brookfield, Vt., 1993), VI, p. 13.

19 CSPSp, XIII, No. 229, 2 August 1555.

20   Gregory, quoting Gachard, *Correspondence de Philippe II sur les affaires des Pays-Bas*,
      Vol. 1 (Brussels, Muqardt, 1848), 12 August 1566, No. 448, p. 446.

21   Eamon Duffy, 'Cardinal Pole Preaching: St Andrew's Day, 1557', in Eamon Duffy
      and David Loades, *The Church of Mary Tudor* (Aldershot, 2006), pp. 196–7.

22   MacCulloch, *Thomas Cranmer*.

11   THE ROAD TO WAR AND THE LOSS OF CALAIS

1   See E. H. Harbison, *Rival Ambassadors at the Court of Queen Mary* (Princeton,
      1940), pp. 50–3 for a discussion of the evidence and probabilities of this.

2   TPR II, No. 398, 'Announcing Articles of Marriage with Philip of Spain'.

3   Quoted in Frederic J Baumgartner, *Henry II King of France 1547–1559* (Durham,
      1988), p. 133.

4   Harbison, p. 242.

5   CSP.Mary, 445, SP 11/8 70.

6   For details of this plot, see Loades, *Two Tudor Conspiracies*, pp. 190–1.

7   CSPSp, XIII, 23 November 1554.

8   See Loach, *Parliament and the Crown* pp. 194–6. The misreading is made clear by
      the text of CSP.Mary, 413, SP 11/8//43.

9   Russell, Elizabeth, 'Mary Tudor and Mr Jorkins', *Historical Research*, Vol. 63 (1990),
      p. 264.

10   Loades, *Mary Tudor*, pp. 277–8.

11   Ibid. p. 291.

12   APC 1554–6, p. 180.

13   Quoted in C. S. L. Davies 'England and the French War', in *The mid-Tudor Polity*,
      ed. R. Loach and J. Tittler (London, 1980), p. 162.

14   CSP.Mary, 697. SP11/12/20.

15   Foxe, *Actes and Monumentes*, p. 2297.

12   THE END OF THE REGIME OF MARY TUDOR

1   'The Count of Feria's Dispatch to Philip II of 14 November 1558', ed. M. J. Rodriguez-
      Salgado and Simon Adams, *Camden Miscellany 28* (London, 1984), p. 328.

2   Philip to the Princess Dowager of Portugal, Regent of Spain, dated 4 December
      1558. CSPSp XIII,p. 40.

3   TRP II, No. 448,17 November 1558.

4   Sydney Anglo, *Images of Tudor Kingship* (London, 1992), p. 106.

5   Peter Sherlock, 'The Monuments of Elizabeth Tudor and Mary Stuart: King James and the Manipulation of Memory', *Journal of British Studies*, Vol. 46, No. 2, April 2007, pp. 263–89, p. 267. Emphasis added.

6   Bartholomew Traheron, *A Warning to England to Repente, and to Turn to God from Idolatrie and Poperie* (1558).

7   CSPV V No. 934, p. 533, report dated 18 August 1554.

8   John Foxe, *Actes and Monumentes* (1570), pp. 1565–6.

9   'A Letter of Jane, Duchess of Northumberland, in 1553', ed. S. J. Gunn, *English Historical Review*, Vol. 114, No. 459, November 1999, pp. 1267–71.

10   Henry Clifford, *The Life of Jane Dormer, Duchess of Feria*, ed. J. Stevenson (London, 1887), passim.

11   John Southworth, *Fools and Jesters at the English Court* (Stroud, 1998), p. 5 ff.

12   Anglo, *Images of Tudor Kingship*, p. 6.

13   Alison J. Carter, *Mary Tudor's Wardrobe of Robes*, M.A., Courtauld Institute of Art (1982), p. 24 and passim. The following paragraphs draw extensively from this thesis.

FURTHER READING BY CHAPTER

Generally, less manuscript material has survived from Mary's reign than for other Tudors, and most of what has survived is held in the British Library and the Public Record Office. There is, however, an abundance of printed versions (and often translations) of contemporary documents, many of which add important information (and misinformation) about the period.

Letters and Papers, Foreign and Domestic, of the Reign of Henry VIII, 1509–1547, J. S. Brewer, J. Gairdner and R. H. Brodie, eds, 21 Vols (London, 1862). This is a unique compilation from many sources, but should be treated carefully since it includes many summaries and extracts. Each volume has an index, an indispensable guide through the documents.

Many ambassadorial reports have also survived, but should be treated cautiously. Ambassadors were seldom near the centre of English politics, and their reports always served many different purposes. The two most important series are available in translation:

Calendar of State Papers, Spanish (London, from 1862)
Calendar of State Papers, Venetian (London, from 1864).

The French ambassadors' reports are printed as

Vertot, l'abbe de, *Ambassades de Messieurs de Noailles en Angleterre*, 5 vols (Paris, 1763).

Other useful printed sources include:

Acts of the Privy Council of England: Queen Mary, Vols IV–VI, 1552–8 (London, 1892)
Calendar of State Papers, Domestic Edward VI 1547–1553. ed. C. S. Knighton (London, 1992)

Calendar of State Papers, Domestic Mary I 1553–1558, ed. C. S. Knighton (London, 1998)

Chronicle of Queen Jane and of Two Years of Queen Mary, ed. J. G. Nichols (London, 1850)

Chronicle of the Grey Friars of London, ed. J. G. Nichols (London, 1852)

England Under the Reigns of Edward VI and Mary, ed. P. F. Tytler, 2 Vols (London, 1839)

Letters of Royal and Illustrious Ladies of Great Britain, ed. Mary Anne Everett Wood, 3 Vols (London, 1846–8)

F. E. Madden, *The Privy Purse Expenses of the Princess Mary* (London, 1831)

Original Letters Illustrative of English History, ed. H. Ellis (London, 1824–46) – in three series

The Diary of Henry Machyn, Citizen and Merchant of London, ed. J. G. Nichols (London, 1848)

The Tudor Constitution Documents and Commentary, ed. G. R. Elton (Cambridge, 1968)

Tudor Royal Proclamations, ed. Paul L Hughes and James F. Larkin, 3 Vols (New Haven, 1964–69)

Charles Wriothesley, Windsor Herald, *A Chronicle of England during the Reign of the Tudors from AD 1485 to 1559*, 2 Vols, ed. W. D. Hamilton (London, 1875, 1877).

For a guide to the complex genealogies of probable and possible claimants to the Tudor throne, see:

Mortimer Levine, *Tudor Dynastic Problems 1460–1571* (London, 1973).

For the importance of the public face of Tudor monarchs, see:

Sydney Anglo, *Images of Tudor Kingship* (London, 1992).

Standard Tudor biographies include:

David M. Head, *The Ebbs and Flows of Fortune The life of Thomas Howard, Third Duke of Norfolk* (Athens, Ga., 1995)

Henry Kamen, *Philip of Spain* (New Haven, Conn., 1997)

Jennifer Loach, *Edward VI* (New Haven, Conn., 1999)

David Loades, *Mary Tudor: A Life* (London, 1989)

David Loades, *John Dudley Duke of Northumberland 1504–1553* (Oxford, 1996)

Diarmaid MacCulloch, *Thomas Cranmer: A Life* (New Haven, Conn., 1996)

Garrett Mattingly, *Catherine of Aragon* (London, 1942)

Glyn Redworth, *In defence of the Church Catholic: The Life of Stephen Gardiner* (Oxford, 1990)

J. J. Scarisbrick, *Henry VIII* (Harmondsworth, 1971).

A useful source for recent biographies of many other personalities involved in Mary's life is the *Oxford Dictionary of National Biography* (Oxford, 2004–7).

Important unpublished theses include:

Elizabeth Ann Drey, *The portraits of Mary I, Queen of England* (M.A., Courtauld Institute of Art, 1990)

Alison J. Carter, *Mary Tudor's Wardrobe of Robes* (M.A., Courtauld Institute, 1982)

G. A. Lemasters, *The Privy Council in the Reign of Mary I* (PhD., Cambridge, 1971)

J. L. McIntosh, *Sovereign Princesses: Mary and Elizabeth Tudor as Heads of Princely Households and the Accomplishment of the Female Succession in Tudor England, 1516–1558* (PhD., Johns Hopkins, 2002)

D. B. Page, *Uniform and Catholic Church Music in the Reign of Mary Tudor 1553–1558* (PhD., Brandeis, 1996).

FURTHER READING FOR EACH CHAPTER

CHAPTER 1: ESTABLISHING THE TUDOR REGIME

Michael Bennett, *The Battle of Bosworth* (Gloucester, 1985)

S. B. Chrimes, *Henry VII* (London, 1972)

Sean Cunningham, *Henry VII* (London, 2007)

Barbara J. Harris, 'Property, power and personal relations: elite mothers and sons in Yorkist and early Tudor England', *Signs*, Vol. 15 No. 31, (1990) pp. 606–32

Michael K. Jones and Malcolm G. Underwood, *The King's Mother Lady Margaret Beaufort, Countess of Richmond and Derby* (Cambridge, 1992).

James Gairdner, ed., *Letters and Papers Illustrative of the reigns of Richard III and Henry VII*, 2 Vols (Rolls Series, London, 1861–3)

Gordon Kipling, ed., *The Receyt of the Ladie Kateryne* (Oxford, 1990).

CHAPTER 2: THE EARLY YEARS OF MARY TUDOR

Carlos G. Noreña, *Juan Luis Vives* (The Hague, 1970).

John E. Paul, *Catherine of Aragon and her Friends* (London, 1966)

Maria Dowling, *Humanism in the Age of Henry VIII* (Wolfeboro, N.H., 1986).

CHAPTER 3: THE EDUCATION OF A PRINCESS

For an introduction to the politics of Henry's first divorce, see *The Divorce Tracts of Henry VIII*, ed. E. Surtz and Virginia Murphy (Angers, Moreana, 1988).

One recent study of Henry VIII's break with the Church of Rome is G. W. Bernard, *The King's Reformation: Henry VIII and the Remaking of the English Church* (New Haven, 2005).

Eric Ives, *The Life and Death of Anne Boleyn: 'The Most Happy'* (Malden, Mass., 2004)

Maria Dowling, 'A woman's place? Learning and the wives of Henry VIII', *History Today*, Vol. 41, No. 6 (June, 1991), pp. 38–42

Maria Dowling, 'Humanist support for Katherine of Aragon', *Bulletin of the Institute of Historical Research*, Vol. 57, No. 135 (May, 1984), pp.46–55

Richard Rex, *Henry VIII and the English Reformation* (Basingstoke, 1993).

CHAPTER 4: THE RESTORATION OF LADY MARY, 1536–1548

R. McEntegart, 'Fatal matrimony: Henry VIII and the marriage of Anne of Cleves', in D. Starkey, ed. *Henry VIII: A European Court* (London, 1991)

Retha M. Warnicke, *The Marrying of Anne of Cleves: Royal Protocol in Early Modern England* (New York, 2000)

L. B. Smith, *A Tudor Tragedy: The Life and Times of Catherine Howard* (New York, 1961)

Susan E. James, *Kateryn Parr: The Making of a Queen* (Aldershot, 1991).

CHAPTER 5: MARY IN THE REIGN OF EDWARD VI, 1547–1553

W. K. Jordan, ed. *The Chronicle and Political Papers of King Edward VI* (London, 1966)

Diarmaid MacCulloch, *Tudor Church Militant: Edward VI and the Protestant Reformation* (London, 1999)

Jennifer Loach, George Bernard and Penry Williams eds. *Edward VI* (New Haven, Conn., 1999).

CHAPTER 6: EDWARD AND MARY: THE FINAL STRUGGLES

Reading as above and

J. D. Alsop, 'A regime at sea: the navy and the 1553 succession crisis', *Albion*, Vol. 24, No. 4 (Winter, 1992), pp. 577–90

Diarmaid MacCulloch, trans. and ed. 'The *Vitae Mariae Angliae Reginae* of Robert Wingfield of Brantham', Camden Miscellany XXVIII (London, 1984)

J. G. Nichols, ed. *The Chronicle of Queen Jane and of Two Years of Queen Mary* (London, 1850)

D. M. Loades, *John Dudley Duke of Northumberland 1504–1553* (Oxford, 1996).

CHAPTER 7: ESTABLISHING ENGLAND'S FIRST FEMALE MONARCH

Dale Hoak, 'Two revolutions in Tudor government: the formation and organisation of Mary I's Privy Council', in Christopher Coleman and David Starkey, eds, *Revolution Reassessed: Revisions in the History of Tudor Government and Administration* (Oxford, 1986) pp. 87–115

Judith M. Richards, '"To promote a woman to beare rule": talking of queens in mid-Tudor England', *Sixteenth Century Journal*, Vol. 28, No. 1 (Spring, 1997), pp. 101–21

Diarmaid MacCulloch, trans. and ed. 'The *Vitae Mariae Angliae Reginae* of Robert Wingfield of Brantham', Camden Miscellany XXVIII (London, 1984)

J. G. Nichols, ed. *The Chronicle of Queen Jane and of Two Years of Queen Mary* (London, 1850)

D. M. Loades, *John Dudley Duke of Northumberland 1504–1553* (Oxford, 1996).

CHAPTER 8: PROBLEMS FOR A MARRYING QUEEN REGNANT

J. G. Nichols, ed. *The Chronicle of Queen Jane and of Two Years of Queen Mary* (London, 1850)

John Elder, *A Copie of a Letter Sent into Scotland*

Jennifer Loach, *Parliament and the Crown in the Reign of Mary Tudor* (Oxford, 1986)

D. M. Loades, *Two Tudor Conspiracies* (Cambridge, 1965)

Alexander Samson, 'Changing places: the marriage and royal entry of Philip, Prince of Austria, and Mary Tudor, July–August 1554', *The Sixteenth Century Journal*, Vol. 36, No. 3 (Fall, 2005), pp. 761–84.

CHAPTER 9: THE PROSPEROUS YEAR OF PHILIP AND MARY?

David Loades, 'Philip II and the government of England', in Claire Cross, D. M. Loades and J. J. Scarisbrick, eds, *Law and Government under the Tudors: Essays Presented to Sir Geoffrey Elton on his Retirement* (Cambridge, 1980)

Glyn Redworth, '"Matters impertinent to women": male and female monarchy under Philip and Mary', *English Historical Review*, Vol. 112, No. 447, 1997 pp. 593–613

Elizabeth Russell, 'Mary Tudor and Mr. Jorkins', *Historical Research*, Vol. 63, No. 152, 1990 pp. 263–76.

CHAPTER 10: RELIGIOUS TRIALS AND OTHER TRIBULATIONS

Eamon Duffy, 'Mary', in Peter Marshall, ed. *The Impact of the English Reformations 1500–1640* (London, 1997), pp. 192–229

Eamon Duffy and David Loades, ed. *The Church of Mary Tudor* (Aldershot, 2006)

John Edwards and Ronald Truman, *Reforming Catholicism in the England of Mary Tudor* (Aldershot, 2005)

Andrew Petegree, 'Nicodemism and the English Reformation', in his *Marian Protestantism* (Aldershot, 1996), pp. 86–117

Susan Wabuda, 'Equivocation and recantation during the English Reformation: the "subtle shadows" of Dr Edward Crome', *Journal of Ecclesiastical History*, Vol. 44, No. 2, 1993 pp. 224–42

William Wizeman, *The Theology and Spirituality of Mary Tudor's Church* (Aldershot, 2006).

CHAPTER 11: THE ROAD TO WAR AND THE LOSS OF CALAIS

Frederic J. Baumgartner, *Henry II King of France 1547–1559* (Durham, N.C., 1988)

Henry Kamen, *Philip of Spain* (New Haven, Conn., 1997)

C. S. L. Davies, 'England and the French War', in Jennifer Loach and Robert Tittler, eds, *The mid-Tudor Polity c. 1540–1560* (London, 1980), 159–96

D. M. Loades, *Two Tudor Conspiracies* (Cambridge, 1965).

INDEX

Anne Boleyn, Henry VIII's second
    queen, 36, 50, 51, 52, 53–4, 55,
    56, 58, 60, 61, 65, 143, 154
Anne of Cleves, Henry VIII's fourth
    queen, 74–5, 76, 78, 87, 136, 138
Arthur, Prince of Wales, 21, 23, 24,
    47, 50, 161

Bacon, Lady Anne, 80, 182, 189, 237
Beaufort, Margaret, Countess of
    Richmond and Derby, 15, 16,
    18–9, 23, 24, 28–9, 123, 124,
    182
Bonner, Edmund, Bishop, 61, 96, 132,
Brandon, Charles, Duke of Suffolk, 32,
    36, 68
Browne, Sir Anthony 61, 83
Browne, Sir Anthony (son of the above),
    129

Calais, 39, 204, 220–1 221–2, 226
Carew, Sir Peter, 150, 218
Catherine Howard, Henry VIII's fifth
    queen, 56, 74–5, 76–7

Cecil, William, 188, 189, 237
Chapuys, Eustache, Imperial
    Ambassador, 52, 58–9, 62, 69,
    70, 76, 79
Charles of Spain, later Emperor
    Charles V, 36, 37, 40–1, 48,
    50, 53, 55, 59, 67–8, 69, 74, 79,
    84, 89, 93, 94, 97, 98, 107, 113,
    115, 143, 145, 148, 159, 161,
    166, 170, 174, 180, 205, 226,
    231
chivalric values, 27–8, 164, 165, 177
Clarencius, Susan, 64, 177, 235, 236,
    237
Courtenay, Edward, Earl of Devon, 72,
    129, 135, 144, 147–8, 149, 150,
    152, 153, 154, 155, 180, 236
Courtenay, Gertrude, Marchioness of
    Exeter 72, 137, 144, 235–6
Courtenay, Henry, Marquis of Exeter,
    71–2
Cranmer, Thomas Archbishop of
    Canterbury, 53–4, 60, 68, 76, 91,
    102, 111, 112, 115, 131, 132,

134, 173, 190, 193, 194, 200, 201

Cromwell, Thomas, 57, 61, 63, 67, 72

de la Pole, Edmund, 25
de la Pole, Richard, 43, 44
Dormer, Jane, 135, 185, 226, 227, 232, 237
Douglas, Margaret, Lady, 45, 55–6, 57, 64–5, 78, 154, 224
Dudley, Edmund, 26
Dudley, Sir Henry, 207–9, 210
Dudley, John later Duke of Northumberland, 77, 80, 83, 95–6, 102, 105, 109, 112, 115, 117, 118, 119, 127, 132–3, 134, 204, 219
Dudley, Robert, 118, 164–5, 218

economic and social problems: 67, 95, 105, 121–2, 201–2, 213, 219
Edward IV, 14, 15, 18
Edward VI, 3, 12, 46, 68–9, 87, 89–90, 91, 95, 97, 98, 99–101, 102, 103,104, 106, 107–10, 112, 113, 132, 144, 153, 176, 206
Edward Plantagenet, Earl of Warwick, 21, 25
Elizabeth of York, 18, 23, 24, 123, 231
Elizabeth I,
  accession, 4, 218, 227
  birth and infancy, 36, 55–6, 57–8, 64
  education, 46, 79, 80
  relations with Henry, 78–9, 84
  relations with Mary, 65, 88,127–8, 135, 136, 153–6, 224, 226, 231
  and Thomas Seymour, 86–8
  reputation, 2, 3, 10, 11
  also mentioned 138, 143, 149, 195, 207

Erasmus, Desiderius, 29, 46, 47, 65, 80, 90, 206

female rule, problems of and adjustments for, 44, 111–2, 122–4, 127, 129, 136–7, 138–9, 140–1, 142–3, 148, 160, 175–6 215–6, 230, 240–1, 242
Fitzalan, Henry, twelfth Earl of Arundel, 119, 136, 147
Fitzroy, Henry, Duke of Richmond, 32, 44, 47–8, 64, 85

Gardiner, Stephen, Bishop, 61, 83, 90, 129, 130, 131, 133, 137–8, 140, 144, 147, 150, 155, 159, 171, 190, 194
Grey, Henry, Duke of Suffolk, 68, 118, 119, 127, 150, 153
Grey, Lady Jane, 10, 88, 108, 109, 110, 111, 113, 114, 115, 118, 119, 120, 122, 125, 133, 134, 143, 149, 150, 153, 156, 187, 205

Henry VI, 15, 19, 20
Henry VII, 12, 16–25, 27, 28, 90, 190
Henry VIII,
  accession and first marriage, 25–6, 27–31
  attitude to Mary, 31–2, 34, 35, 37, 38, 41, 43–4, 45–6, 49, 52–3, 56, 57, 58, 59, 60–2, 64, 70, 77–8, 79, 84
  first 'divorce' and remarriage, 49–50, 53–5
  second remarriage, 60, 68–9
  third remarriage, 74–5
  fourth remarriage, 75–7
  final remarriage, 78–9

death and will, 82–5, 86, 88,
    100–101
diplomacy involving Mary, 37, 39,
    40, 41, 42, 50–1, 70, 73–4, 81,
    143
also mentioned 12, 32, 33, 34, 35,
    37, 39, 41, 63, 65, 66, 67, 72, 87,
    90, 91, 93, 95, 119, 121, 124,
    139, 140, 144, 195, 229, 232
Henry II of France, 145, 194, 204, 205,
    206, 207, 209, 213, 215–6
'heretics', punishment of, 3, 4, 5, 73,
    94, 192–7
Howard, Thomas, second Duke of
    Norfolk, 32
Howard, Thomas, third Duke of
    Norfolk, 56, 61, 67, 68, 69, 83,
    85, 129, 133, 136, 147, 150–1

infant mortality and pregnancy
    problems, 12–3, 31, 68–9, 88,
    176

Jane Seymour, Henry VIII's third
    queen, 45, 60, 63, 64, 68, 69, 73

Katherine Parr, Henry VIII's sixth
    queen, 77–9, 80–1, 82, 86–8
Katherine of Aragon, Henry VIII's first
    queen, 4, 13, 21–4, 27–31, 36,
    38, 45–6, 48, 49, 52–4, 55, 57–8,
    59–60, 67, 73, 75, 145, 161

Lancaster, house of, ix, 14–5, 20
Loach, Jennifer, 2, 10, 68, 110, 191,
Loades, David, 2, 9, 58, 99, 110, 197,
    199, 214, 217

Mary I,
    birth and christening, 31–4

declared illegitimate, 54, 113, 119,
    and legitimate, 140
descriptions of, 51, 158, 162, 208,
    233–5
diplomatic value, 34–6, 37–40,
    40–1, 41, 50–1, 73–4,
education and scholarly pursuits, 46,
    47–8, 51, 75, 79–80, 182, 191
health, 51–2, 58–9, 77, 80, 89, 99,
    104, 106, 224–6
heir to Henry?, 38, 44, 45, 54, 64,
    67, 69–70, 79, 84, 107, 109 112,
    113, 114, 115–6, 117, 124–5
household, 35, 47–8, 51, 55–6, 57,
    64, 84–6, 103–5, 106
Guildhall speech, 151–2
marriage, 140–1, 142–6, 147–9,
    158–9, 162–3, 167–9, 179–80,
    183–4, 238–40
musical accomplishments and
    interests, 40, 45–6, 183
putative pregnancy, 173–5, 178–9,
    233
religious views and practice, 47,
    61–2, 65–6, 92–3, 97, 99–100,
    101, 102–3, 104–5, 106, 198–9,
    217
reputation, 1–11, 79–80, 85, 129,
    182, 192, 197–9, 221, 232, 233
Mary of Hungary, Regent of the
    Netherlands, 84, 89, 98, 105, 226
Mary Tudor, sister to Henry VIII,
    Queen of France, 33, 36, 37, 109
Mary Stuart, Queen of Scots, 1, 65, 95,
    119
Matilda/Maud, Queen, 13–4, 123, 238

Noailles, Antoine de, French
    Ambassador, 78, 112, 140, 204,
    205, 206–7, 208, 209, 211

Paget, William, 119, 126, 147, 148, 214

Paulet, William, Marquis of Winchester, 60, 108, 165, 228, 229, 231

Philip II of Spain,
  as heir to Charles V, 146, 176–7, 179, 195, 205, 212–3, 217, 220, 226–7
  as Queen Mary's prospective husband, 145–6, 147, 148, 156, 157–8
  as royal husband, 159–61, 162–4, 165–9, 175–7, 179–80, 183–4, 199–200, 205, 207, 213, 215, 218–9, 221, 224, 225, 229
  wishes for and rumours of his coronation, 167–8, 184, 208, 210–1
  also mentioned: 4, 41, 98, 182, 198

Plantagenet line, x, 14, 16, 17, 18, 21, 22, 25, 44, 72

Pole, Margaret, Countess of Salisbury, 22, 33, 35, 43–4, 48–9, 55–7, 59, 71, 72

Pole, Reginald, Cardinal, 71, 74, 78, 140, 169, 170–2, 174, 179, 194, 200, 216–7, 221, 223–4, 227

'popery', polemical uses of, 3–4, 5, 6, 90, 185

Popes: Innocent VIII, 18; Clement VII, 54, 55; Paul III, 70; Julius III, 216; Paul IV, 204, 209, 212, 216–8

Radcliffe, Henry, second Earl of Sussex, 116–7, 126

Religious policy:under Henry VIII, 53–5, 61–2, 65, 66–7, 69–72, 74, 82–3, 232

under Edward VI, 89–92, 94, 96–8, 101, 103, 105, 110–1, 232

under Mary I, 130–1, 132, 133, 140, 149, 169–73, 187, 188–92, 232

Renard, Simon, Imperial Ambassador, 126, 127, 132, 134, 145, 155, 160, 200, 210

Richard III, 12, 14, 15–6, 17

Ridley, Nicholas, Bishop, 96, 113, 129, 201, 235

Rochester, Robert, 103, 125

Scheyfve, Jehan, Imperial Ambassador, 100, 103, 108

Seymour, Edward, Duke of Somerset, 83, 86, 92, 95, 96, 105, 107, 134, 219

Seymour, Thomas, Lord Seymour of Sudeley, 83, 86–7, 88, 144

Stafford, Henry, second Duke of Buckingham, 16

Stafford, Edward, third Duke of Buckingham, 25, 33, 42–3

Stafford, Thomas, 213–5

Tunstall, Cuthbert, Bishop, 61, 78, 96–7, 132

Tudor, house of, ix, 14–9, 20, 34

Van der Veldt, Francis, Imperial ambassador, 83, 89, 95, 97–8

Vives, Juan Luis, 29, 46, 48

Waldegrave, Edward, 103, 125

Wolsey, Thomas, Cardinal, 32, 38, 42, 48, 50, 67, 85

Wyatt, Sir Thomas, rebellion by 149–53, 154–5, 156, 205

York, house of, x, 14–6, 18, 25, 33–4, 71

Renaissance World

John Jeffries Martin

With an interdisciplinary approach that encompasses the history of ideas, political history, cultural history and art history, this volume, in the successful *Routledge Worlds* series, offers a sweeping survey of Europe in the Renaissance, from the late thirteenth to early seventeenth centuries, and shows how the Renaissance laid key foundations for many aspects of the modern world.

Collating thirty-four essays from the field's leading scholars, John Jeffries Martin shows that this period of rapid and complex change resulted from a convergence of a new set of social, economic and technological forces alongside a cluster of interrelated practices including painting, sculpture, humanism and science, in which the elites engaged.

Unique in its balance of emphasis on elite and popular culture, on humanism and society, and on women as well as men, *The Renaissance World* grapples with issues as diverse as Renaissance patronage and the development of the slave trade.

Beginning with a section on the antecedents of the Renaissance world, and ending with its lasting influence, this book is an invaluable read, which students and scholars of history and the Renaissance will dip into again and again.

ISBN10: 0-415-33259-1 (hbk)
ISBN10: 0-415-45511-1 (pbk)

ISBN13: 978-0-415-33259-0 (hbk)
ISBN13: 978-0-415-45511-4 (pbk)

England under the Tudors

Third Edition

G. R. Elton

'The best full-length introductory history of the Tudor period ...
Written with great verve, it will delight both the scholar and the
general reader.' *The Spectator* 'Students of history owe Elton major
debts. He has shown that political history is still worth investigation, that it offers the possibility of exciting discovery and genuine
debate. He has demonstrated that scholarly work can be presented
in prose that is witty, muscular, clear and above everything, readable.' *The Times Education Supplement*

First published in 1955 and never out of print, this wonderfully
written text by one of the great historians of the twentieth century
has guided generations of students through the turbulent history
of Tudor England.

Now in its third edition, *England Under the Tudors* charts a historical period that saw some monumental changes in religion,
monarchy, government and the arts. Elton's classic and highly
readable introduction to the Tudor period offers an essential source
of information from the start of Henry VII's reign to the death of
Elizabeth I.

ISBN10: 0-415-06533-X (pbk)
ISBN13: 978-0-415-06533-7 (pbk)

Available at all good bookshops
For ordering and further information please visit:
www.routledge.com

A Political History of Tudor and Stuart England: A Sourcebook

Victor Slater

A Political History of Tudor and Stuart England draws together a fascinating selection of sources to illuminate this turbulent era of English history. From the bloody overthrow of Richard III in 1485, to the creation of a worldwide imperial state under Queen Anne, these sources illustrate England's difficult transition from the medieval to the modern.

Covering a period characterised by conflict and division, this wide-ranging single-volume collection presents the accounts of Yorkists and Lancastrians, Protestants and Catholics, and Roundheads and Cavaliers side by side. *A Political History of Tudor and Stuart England* provides a crucial opportunity for students to examine the institutions and events that moulded English history in the early modern era at first-hand.

ISBN10: 415-20743-6 (hbk)
ISBN10: 415-20744-4 (pbk)

ISBN13: 978-0-415-20743-0 (hbk)
ISBN13: 978-0-415-20744-7 (pbk)

Available at all good bookshops
For ordering and further information please visit:
www.routledge.com